Pro Python 3

Features and Tools for
Professional Development

Third Edition

J. Burton Browning
Marty Alchin

Apress®

Pro Python 3: Features and Tools for Professional Development

J. Burton Browning
Oak Island, NC, USA

Marty Alchin
Agoura Hills, CA, USA

ISBN-13 (pbk): 978-1-4842-4384-8
https://doi.org/10.1007/978-1-4842-4385-5

ISBN-13 (electronic): 978-1-4842-4385-5

Library of Congress Control Number: 2019936454

Managing Director, Apress Media LLC: Welmoed Spahr
Acquisitions Editor: Todd Green
Development Editor: James Markham
Coordinating Editor: Jill Balzano

Cover designed by eStudioCalamar

Cover image designed by Freepik (www.freepik.com)

Distributed to the book trade worldwide by Springer Science+Business Media New York, 233 Spring Street, 6th Floor, New York, NY 10013. Phone 1-800-SPRINGER, fax (201) 348-4505, e-mail orders-ny@springer-sbm.com, or visit www.springeronline.com. Apress Media, LLC is a California LLC and the sole member (owner) is Springer Science + Business Media Finance Inc (SSBM Finance Inc). SSBM Finance Inc is a **Delaware** corporation.

For information on translations, please e-mail rights@apress.com, or visit http://www.apress.com/rights-permissions.

Apress titles may be purchased in bulk for academic, corporate, or promotional use. eBook versions and licenses are also available for most titles. For more information, reference our Print and eBook Bulk Sales web page at http://www.apress.com/bulk-sales.

Any source code or other supplementary material referenced by the author in this book is available to readers on GitHub via the book's product page, located at www.apress.com/9781484243848. For more detailed information, please visit http://www.apress.com/source-code.

Printed on acid-free paper

This edition is dedicated to Champion Suyaki Mamma Mia of Misibo and her sister Champion Sienna of Olympia of Misibo, two of the best Siamese cats who ever owned me.

Table of Contents

About the Authors

Dr. J. Burton Browning earned his doctorate from North Carolina State University. He has conducted research in areas including distance learning, programming, and instructional technology. As a lifelong learner and someone who has interests in topics such as programming, photography, robotics, car restoration, woodworking, hunting, reading, fishing, and archery, he is never at a loss for something to do. The art and joy of serving as a professor suits his inquisitive nature. Dr. Browning's previous publications include works on Cross-Functional Learning Teams (CFLT), the Utopian School (teacher-led school model), computer programming (several languages), open-source software, healthcare statistics and data mining, CNC plasma cutter operation, educational technology, biography, mobile learning, online teaching, and more.

By day, **Marty Alchin** works as a senior software engineer at Heroku, and after that, he writes and codes for fun and community. His blog can be found at `http://martyalchin.com` and he has profiles on many other services under the name Gulopine. In particular, his code can be found on GitHub and his random thoughts are on Twitter. He also accepts tips for his open source work at `https://gittip.com/gulopine`.

About the Technical Reviewer

 Michael Thomas has worked in software development for over 20 years as an individual contributor, team lead, program manager, and vice president of engineering. Michael has over 10 years of experience working with mobile devices. His current focus is in the medical sector, using mobile devices to accelerate information transfer between patients and healthcare providers.

Acknowledgments

This third edition covers some exciting library features available in the Python 3 language. Try the samples and expand on your own projects with what you learn. Do not be afraid to experiment and have fun!

J. Burton Browning

I wouldn't have even started this project if not for the endless encouragement from my lovely wife, Angel. She's been my sounding board, my task manager, my copyeditor, and my own personal cheerleader. There's no way I could do anything like this without her help and support.

I'd also like to thank my technical reviewer, George, for everything he's done to help me out. He's gone above and beyond the limits of his role, helping with everything from code to grammar and even a good bit of style. After enjoying his help on *Pro Django*, I wouldn't have even signed on for another book without him by my side.

Lastly, I never would've considered a book like this if not for the wonderful community around Python. The willingness of Python programmers to open their minds and their code is, I believe, unrivaled among our peers. It's this spirit of openness that encourages me every day, leading me to discover new things and push myself beyond the limits of what I knew yesterday.

We learn by doing and by seeing what others have done. I hope that you'll take the contents of this book and do more with it than what I've done. There's no better reward for all this hard work than to see better programmers writing better code.

Marty Alchin

Introduction

This third edition expands on Marty's original work. Found in each chapter of this third edition are useful libraries that any Python programmer will find of value. Use what you learn for your own projects and enjoyment!

J. Burton Browning

When I wrote my first book, *Pro Django*, I didn't have much of an idea what my readers would find interesting. I had gained a lot of information I thought would be useful for others to learn, but I didn't really know what would be the most valuable thing they'd take away. As it turned out, in nearly 300 pages, the most popular chapter in the book barely mentioned Django at all. It was about Python.

The response was overwhelming. There was clearly a desire to learn more about how to go from a simple Python application to a detailed framework like Django. It's all Python code, but it can be hard to understand based on even a reasonably thorough understanding of the language. The tools and techniques involved require some extra knowledge that you might not run into in general use.

This gave me a new goal with *Pro Python*: to take you from proficient to professional. Being a true professional requires more experience than you can get from a book, but I want to at least give you the tools you'll need. Combined with the rich philosophy of the Python community, you'll find plenty of information to take your code to the next level.

Marty Alchin

Who This Book Is For

The goal is to bring intermediate programmers to a more advanced level; we wrote this book with the expectation that you'll already be familiar with Python on some basic level. You should be comfortable using the interactive interpreter, writing control structures, and [using] a basic object-oriented approach.

That's not a very difficult prerequisite. If you've tried your hand at writing a Python application—even if you haven't released it into the wild, or even finished it—you likely have all the necessary knowledge to get started. The rest of the information you'll need is contained in these pages.

CHAPTER 1

Principles and Philosophy

Over 350 years ago, the famous Japanese swordsman Miyamoto Musashi wrote *The Book of Five Rings* about what he learned from fighting and winning over 60 duels between the ages of 13 and 29. His book might be related to a Zen Buddhist martial arts instruction book for sword fighting. In the text, which originally was a five-part letter written to the students at the martial arts school he founded, Musashi outlines general thoughts, ideals, and philosophical principles to lead his students to success.

If it seems strange to begin a programming book with a chapter about philosophy, that's actually why this chapter is so important. Similar to Musashi's method, Python was created to embody and encourage a certain set of ideals that have helped guide the decisions of its maintainers and its community for nearly 20 years. Understanding these concepts will help you to make the most out of what the language and its community have to offer.

Of course, we're not talking about Plato or Nietzsche here. Python deals with programming problems, and its philosophies are designed to help build reliable, maintainable solutions. Some of these philosophies are officially branded into the Python landscape, whereas others are guidelines commonly accepted by Python programmers, but all of them will help you to write code that is powerful, easy to maintain, and understandable to other programmers.

The philosophies laid out in this chapter can be read from start to finish, but don't expect to commit them all to memory in one pass. The rest of this book will refer back to this chapter by illustrating which concepts come into play in various situations. After all, the real value of philosophy is in understanding how to apply it when it matters most.

As for practical convention, throughout the book you will see icons for a command prompt, a script, and scissors. When you see a command prompt icon, the code is shown as if you were going to try it (and you should) from a command prompt. If you see a script icon, try the code as a Python script instead. Finally, scissors show only a code snippet that would need additional snippets to run. The only other conventions are that you have Python 3.x installed and have at least some computer programming background.

© J. Burton Browning and Marty Alchin 2019
J. B. Browning and M. Alchin, *Pro Python 3*, https://doi.org/10.1007/978-1-4842-4385-5_1

The Zen of Python

Perhaps the best-known collection of Python philosophy was written by Tim Peters, longtime contributor to the language and its newsgroup, `comp.lang.python`.[1] This Zen of Python condenses some of the most common philosophical concerns into a brief list that has been recorded as both its own Python Enhancement Proposal (PEP) and within Python itself. Something of an Easter egg, Python includes a module called `this`.

```
>>> import this
The Zen of Python, by Tim Peters

Beautiful is better than ugly.
Explicit is better than implicit.
Simple is better than complex.
Complex is better than complicated.
Flat is better than nested.
Sparse is better than dense.
Readability counts.
Special cases aren't special enough to break the rules.
Although practicality beats purity.
Errors should never pass silently.
Unless explicitly silenced.
In the face of ambiguity, refuse the temptation to guess.
There should be one -- and preferably only one -- obvious way to do it.
Although that way may not be obvious at first unless you're Dutch.
Now is better than never.
Although never is often better than *right* now.
If the implementation is hard to explain, it's a bad idea.
If the implementation is easy to explain, it may be a good idea.
Namespaces are one honking great idea -- let's do more of those!
```

---

[1]See the newsgroup at `http://propython.com/comp-lang-python`.

CHAPTER 1   PRINCIPLES AND PHILOSOPHY

This list was primarily intended as a humorous accounting of Python philosophy, but over the years, numerous Python applications have used these guidelines to greatly improve the quality, readability, and maintainability of their code. Just listing the Zen of Python is of little value, however, so the following sections will explain each idiom in more detail.

Beautiful Is Better Than Ugly

Perhaps it's fitting that this first notion is arguably the most subjective of the whole bunch. After all, beauty is in the eye of the beholder, a fact that has been discussed for centuries. It serves as a blatant reminder that philosophy is far from absolute. Still, having something like this in writing provides a goal to strive for, which is the ultimate purpose of all these ideals.

One obvious application of this philosophy is in Python's own language structure, which minimizes the use of punctuation, instead preferring English words where appropriate. Another advantage is Python's focus on keyword arguments, which help clarify function calls that would otherwise be difficult to understand. Consider the following two possible ways of writing the same code, and consider which one looks more beautiful:

```
is_valid = form != null && form.is_valid(true)
is_valid = form is not None and form.is_valid(include_hidden_fields=True)
```

The second example reads a bit more like natural English, and explicitly including the name of the argument gives greater insight into its purpose. In addition to language concerns, coding style can be influenced by similar notions of beauty. The name is_valid, for example, asks a simple question, which the method can then be expected to answer with its return value. A name such as validate would have been ambiguous because it would be an accurate name even if no value were returned at all.

It's dangerous, however, to rely too heavily on beauty as a criterion for a design decision. If other ideals have been considered and you're still left with two workable options, certainly consider factoring beauty into the equation, but do make sure that other facets are taken into account first. You'll likely find a good choice using some of the other criteria long before reaching this point.

Explicit Is Better Than Implicit

Although this notion may seem easier to interpret, it's actually one of the trickier guidelines to follow. On the surface, it seems simple enough: don't do anything the programmer didn't explicitly command. Beyond just Python itself, frameworks and libraries have a similar responsibility because their code will be accessed by other programmers, whose goals will not always be known in advance.

Unfortunately, truly explicit code must account for every nuance of a program's execution, from memory management to display routines. Some programming languages do expect that level of detail from their programmers, but Python doesn't. In order to make the programmer's job easier and allow you to focus on the problem at hand, there need to be some trade-offs.

In general, Python asks you to declare your intentions explicitly rather than issue every command necessary to make that intention a reality. For example, when assigning a value to a variable, you don't need to worry about setting aside the necessary memory, assigning a pointer to the value, and cleaning up the memory once it's no longer in use. Memory management is a necessary part of variable assignment, so Python takes care of it behind the scenes. Assigning the value is enough of an explicit declaration of intent to justify the implicit behavior.

By contrast, regular expressions in the Perl programming language automatically assign values to special variables any time a match is found. Someone unfamiliar with the way Perl handles that situation wouldn't understand a code snippet that relies on it because variables would seem to come from thin air, with no assignments related to them. Python programmers try to avoid this type of implicit behavior in favor of more readable code.

Because different applications will have different ways of declaring intentions, no single generic explanation will apply to all cases. Instead, this guideline will come up quite frequently throughout the book, clarifying how it would be applied to various situations.

```
tax = .07  #make a variable named tax that is floating point
print (id(tax))  #shows identity number of tax
print("Tax now changing value and identity number")
```

```
tax = .08  #create a new variable, in a different location in memory
            # and mask the first one we created
print (id(tax))  # shows identity of tax
print("Now we switch tax back...")
tax = .07  #change tax back to .07 (mask the second one and reuse first
print (id(tax))  #now we see the original identity of tax
```

Simple Is Better Than Complex

This is a considerably more concrete guideline, with implications primarily in the design of interfaces to frameworks and libraries. The goal here is to keep the interface as straightforward as possible, leveraging a programmer's knowledge of existing interfaces as much as possible. For example, a caching framework could use the same interface as standard dictionaries rather than inventing a whole new set of method calls.

Of course, there are many other applications of this rule, such as taking advantage of the fact that most expressions can evaluate to true or false without explicit tests. For example, the following two lines of code are functionally identical for strings, but notice the difference in complexity between them:

```
if value is not None and value != ":
if value:
```

As you can see, the second option is much simpler to read and understand. All of the situations covered in the first example will evaluate to false anyway, so the simpler test is just as effective. It also has two other benefits: it runs faster, having fewer tests to perform, and it also works in more cases, because individual objects can define their own method of determining whether they should evaluate to true or false.

It may seem like this is something of a convoluted example, but it's just the type of thing that comes up quite frequently. By relying on simpler interfaces, you can often take advantage of optimizations and increased flexibility while producing more readable code.

5

Complex Is Better Than Complicated

Sometimes, however, a certain level of complexity is required in order to get the job done. Database adapters, for example, don't have the luxury of using a simple dictionary-style interface but instead require an extensive set of objects and methods to cover all of their features. The important thing to remember in those situations is that complexity doesn't necessarily require it to be complicated.

The tricky bit with this one, obviously, is distinguishing between the two. Dictionary definitions of each term often reference the other, considerably blurring the line between the two. For the sake of this guideline, most situations tend to take the following view of the two terms:

- *Complex*: Made up of many interconnected parts

- *Complicated*: So complex as to be difficult to understand

So in the face of an interface that requires a large number of things to keep track of, it's even more important to retain as much simplicity as possible. This can take the form of consolidating methods onto a smaller number of objects, perhaps grouping objects into more logical arrangements or even simply making sure to use names that make sense without having to dig into the code to understand them.

Flat Is Better Than Nested

This guideline might not seem to make sense at first, but it's about how structures are laid out. The structures in question could be objects and their attributes, packages and their included modules, or even code blocks within a function. The goal is to keep things as relationships of peers as much possible, rather than parents and children. For example, take the following code snippet:

```
if x > 0:
    if y > 100:
        raise ValueError("Value for y is too large.")
    else:
        return y
```

```
else:
    if x == 0:
        return False
    else:
        raise ValueError("Value for x cannot be negative.")
```

In this example, it's fairly difficult to follow what's really going on because the nested nature of the code blocks requires you to keep track of multiple levels of conditions. Consider the following alternative approach to writing the same code, flattening it out:

```
x=1
y=399   # change to 39 and run a second time

def checker(x,y):
    if x > 0 and y > 100:
        raise ValueError("Value for y is too large.")
    elif x > 0:
        return y
    elif x == 0:
        return False
    else:
        raise ValueError("Value for x cannot be negative.")

print(checker(x,y))
```

Put in a function, and flattened out, you can see how much easier it is to follow the logic in the second example because all of the conditions are at the same level. It even saves two lines of code by avoiding the extraneous else blocks along the way. While this idea is common to programming in general, this is actually the main reason for the existence of the elif keyword; Python's use of indentation means that complex if blocks can otherwise quickly get out of hand. With the elif keyword, there is no *switch* or *select case* structure in Python as in C++ or VB.NET. To handle the issue of needing a multiple selection structure, Python uses a series of if, elif, elif, else as the situation requires. There have been PEPs suggesting the inclusion of a switch-type structure; however, none have been successful.

Caution   What might not be as obvious is that the refactoring of this example ends up testing x > 0 twice, where it was only performed once previously. If that test had been an expensive operation, such as a database query, refactoring it in this way would reduce the performance of the program, so it wouldn't be worth it. This is covered in detail in a later guideline, "Practicality Beats Purity."

In the case of package layouts, flat structures can often allow a single import to make the entire package available under a single namespace. Otherwise, the programmer would need to know the full structure in order to find the particular class or function required. Some packages are so complex that a nested structure will help reduce clutter on each individual namespace, but it's best to start flat and nest only when problems arise.

Sparse Is Better Than Dense

This principle largely pertains to the visual appearance of Python source code, favoring the use of whitespace to differentiate among blocks of code. The goal is to keep highly related snippets together while separating them from subsequent or unrelated code, rather than simply having everything run together in an effort to save a few bytes on disk. Those familiar with JAVA, C++, and other languages that use { } to denote statement blocks also know that as long as statement blocks lie within the braces, whitespace or indentation has only readability value and has no effect on code execution.

In the real world, there are plenty of specific concerns to address, such as how to separate module-level classes or deal with one-line if blocks. Although no single set of rules will be appropriate for all projects, PEP 8[2] does specify many aspects of source code layout that help you adhere to this principle. It provides a number of hints on how to format import statements, classes, functions, and even many types of expressions.

It's interesting to note that PEP 8 includes a number of rules about expressions in particular, which specifically encourage avoiding extra spaces. Take the following examples, which are straight from PEP 8:

---

[2]See "PEP 8—Style Guide for Python Code," http://propython.com/pep-8.

```
Yes: spam(ham[1], {eggs: 2})
No:  spam( ham[ 1 ], { eggs: 2 } )

Yes: if x == 4: print x, y; x, y = y, x
No:  if x == 4 : print x , y ; x , y = y , x

Yes: spam(1)
No:  spam (1)

Yes: dict['key'] = list[index]
No:  dict ['key'] = list [index]
```

The key to this apparent discrepancy is that whitespace is a valuable resource and should be distributed responsibly. After all, if everything tries to stand out in any one particular way, nothing really does stand out at all. If you use whitespace to separate even highly related bits of code like the preceding expressions, truly unrelated code isn't any different from the rest.

That's perhaps the most important part of this principle and the key to applying it to other aspects of code design. When writing libraries or frameworks, it's generally better to define a small set of unique types of objects and interfaces that can be reused across the application, maintaining similarity where appropriate and differentiating the rest.

Readability Counts

Finally, we have a principle everybody in the Python world can get behind, but that's mostly because it's one of the most vague in the entire collection. In a way, it sums up the whole of Python philosophy in one deft stroke, but it also leaves so much undefined that it's worth examining it a bit further.

Readability covers a wide range of issues, such as the names of modules, classes, functions, and variables. It includes the style of individual blocks of code and the whitespace between them. It can even pertain to the separation of responsibilities among multiple functions or classes if that separation is done so that it's more readable to the human eye.

That's the real point here: code gets read not only by computers, but also by humans who have to maintain it. Those humans have to read existing code far more often than they have to write new code, and it's often code that was written by someone else. Readability is all about actively promoting human understanding of code.

Development is much easier in the long run when everyone involved can simply open up a file and easily understand what's going on in it. This seems like a given in organizations with high turnover, where new programmers must regularly read the code of their predecessors, but it's true even for those who have to read their own code weeks, months, or even years after it was written. Once we lose our original train of thought, all we have to remind us is the code itself, so it's valuable to take the extra time to make it easy to read. Another good practice is to add comments and notes in the code. It doesn't hurt and certainly can help even the original programmer when sufficient time has passed such that you can't remember what you tried or what your intent was.

The best part is how little extra time it often takes. It can be as simple as adding a blank line between two functions or naming variables with nouns and functions with verbs. It's really more of a frame of mind than a set of rules, however. A focus on readability requires you to always look at your code as a human being would, rather than only as a computer would. Remember the Golden Rule: do for others what you'd like them to do for you. Readability is random acts of kindness sprinkled throughout your code.

Special Cases Aren't Special Enough to Break the Rules

Just as "readability counts" is a banner phrase for how we should approach our code at all times, this principle is about the conviction with which we must pursue it. It's all well and good to get it right most of the time, but all it takes is one ugly chunk of code to undermine all that hard work.

What's perhaps most interesting about this rule, though, is that it doesn't pertain just to readability or any other single aspect of code. It's really just about the conviction to stand behind the decisions you've made, regardless of what those are. If you're committed to backward compatibility, internationalization, readability, or anything else, don't break those promises just because a new feature comes along and makes some things a bit easier.

Practicality Beats Purity

And here's where things get tricky. The previous principle encourages you to always do the right thing, regardless of how exceptional one situation might be, where this one seems to allow exceptions whenever the right thing gets difficult. The reality is a bit more complicated, however, and merits some discussion.

Up to this point, it seemed simple enough at a glance: the fastest, most efficient code might not always be the most readable, so you may have to accept subpar performance to gain code that's easier to maintain. This is certainly true in many cases, and much of Python's standard library is less than ideal in terms of raw performance, instead opting for pure Python implementations that are more readable and more portable to other environments, such as Jython or IronPython. On a larger scale, however, the problem goes deeper than that.

When designing a system at any level, it's easy to get into a head-down mode, where you focus exclusively on the problem at hand and how best to solve it. This might involve algorithms, optimizations, interface schemes, or even refactorings, but it typically boils down to working on one thing so hard that you don't look at the bigger picture for a while. In that mode, programmers commonly do what seems best within the current context, but when backing out a bit for a better look, those decisions don't match up with the rest of the application.

It's not always easy to know which way to go at this point. Do you try to optimize the rest of the application to match that perfect routine you just wrote? Do you rewrite the otherwise perfect function in hopes of gaining a more cohesive whole? Or do you just leave the inconsistency alone, hoping it doesn't trip anybody up? The answer, as usual, depends on the situation, but one of those options will often seem more practical in context than the others.

Typically, it's preferable to maintain greater overall consistency at the expense of a few small areas that may be less than ideal. Again, most of Python's standard library uses this approach, but there are exceptions. Packages that require a lot of computational power or get used in applications that need to avoid bottlenecks will often be written in C to improve performance, at the cost of maintainability. These packages then need to be ported over to other environments and tested more rigorously on different systems, but the speed gained serves a more practical purpose than a purer Python implementation would allow.

Errors Should Never Pass Silently

Python supports a robust error-handling system, with dozens of built-in exceptions provided out of the box, but there's often doubt about when those exceptions should be used and when new ones are necessary. The guidance provided by this line of the Zen of Python is quite simple, but as with so many others, there's much more beneath the surface.

The first task is to clarify the definitions of errors and exceptions. Even though these words, like so many others in the world of computing, are often overloaded with additional meaning, there's definite value in looking at them as they're used in general language. Consider the following definitions, as found in the *Merriam-Webster Dictionary*:

- An act or condition of ignorant or imprudent deviation from a code of behavior

- A case to which a rule does not apply

The terms have been left out here to help illustrate just how similar the two definitions can be. In real life, the biggest observed difference between the two terms is the severity of the problems caused by deviations from the norm. Exceptions are typically considered less disruptive and thus more acceptable, but both exceptions and errors amount to the same thing: a violation of some kind of expectation. For the purposes of this discussion, the term "exception" will be used to refer to any such departure from the norm.

Note   One important thing to realize is that not all exceptions are errors. Some are used to enhance code flow options, such as using `StopIteration`, which is documented in Chapter 5. In code flow usage, exceptions provide a way to indicate what happened inside a function, even though that indication has no relationship to its return value.

This interpretation makes it impossible to describe exceptions on their own; they must be placed in the context of an expectation that can be violated. Every time we write a piece of code, we make a promise that it will work in a specific way. Exceptions break that promise, so we need to understand what types of promises we make and how they can be broken. Take the following simple Python function and look for any promises that can be broken:

```
def validate(data):
    if data['username'].startswith('_'):
        raise ValueError("Username must not begin with an underscore.")
```

The obvious promise here is that of the validate() method: if the incoming data is valid, the function will return silently. Violations of that rule, such as a username beginning with an underscore, are explicitly treated as an exception, neatly illustrating this practice of not allowing errors to pass silently. Raising an exception draws attention to the situation and provides enough information for the code that called this function to understand what happened.

The tricky bit here is to see the other exceptions that may get raised. For example, if the data dictionary doesn't contain a username key, as the function expects, Python will raise a KeyError. If that key does exist, but its value isn't a string, Python will raise an AttributeError when trying to access the startswith() method. If data isn't a dictionary at all, Python would raise a TypeError.

Most of those assumptions are true requirements for proper operation, but they don't all have to be. Let's assume this validation function could be called from a number of contexts, some of which may not have even asked for a username. In those cases, a missing username isn't actually an exception at all but just another flow that needs to be accounted for.

With that new requirement in mind, validate() can be slightly altered to no longer rely on the presence of a username key to work properly. All the other assumptions should stay intact, however, and should raise their respective exceptions when violated. Here's how it might look after this change.

```
def validate(data):
    if 'username' in data and data['username'].startswith('_'):
        raise ValueError("Username must not begin with an underscore.")
```

And just like that, one assumption has been removed and the function can now run just fine without a username supplied in the data dictionary. Alternately, you could now check for a missing username explicitly and raise a more specific exception, if truly required. How the remaining exceptions are handled depends on the needs of the code that calls validate(), and there's a complementary principle to deal with that situation.

Unless Explicitly Silenced

Like any other language that supports exceptions, Python allows the code that triggers exceptions to trap them and handle them in different ways. In the preceding validation example, it's likely that the validation errors should be shown to the user in a nicer way than a full traceback. Consider a small command-line program that accepts a username as an argument and validates it against the rules defined previously:

```
import sys
def validate(data):
    if 'username' in data and data['username'].startswith('_'):
        raise ValueError("Username must not begin with an underscore.")
if __name__ == '__main__':
    username = sys.argv[1]
    try:
        validate({'username': username})
    except (TypeError, ValueError) as e:
        print (e)
        #out of range since username is empty and there is no
        #second [1] position
```

The syntax used to catch the exception and store it as the variable e in this example was first made available in Python 3.0. In this example, all those exceptions that might be raised will simply get caught by this code, and the message alone will be displayed to the user, not the full traceback. This form of error handling allows for complex code to use exceptions to indicate violated expectations without taking down the whole program.

EXPLICIT IS BETTER THAN IMPLICIT

In a nutshell, this error-handling system is a simple example of the previous rule favoring explicit declarations over implicit behavior. The default behavior is as obvious as possible, given that exceptions always propagate upward to higher levels of code, but can be overridden using an explicit syntax.

In the Face of Ambiguity, Refuse the Temptation to Guess

Sometimes, when using or implementing interfaces between pieces of code written by different people, certain aspects may not always be clear. For example, one common practice is to pass around byte strings without any information about what encoding they rely on. This means that if any code needs to convert those strings to Unicode or ensure that they use a specific encoding, there's not enough information available to do so.

It's tempting to play the odds in this situation, blindly picking what seems to be the most common encoding. Surely it would handle most cases, and that should be enough for any real-world application. Alas, no. Encoding problems raise exceptions in Python, so those could either take down the application or they could be caught and ignored, which could inadvertently cause other parts of the application to think strings were properly converted when they actually weren't.

Worse yet, your application now relies on a guess. It's an educated guess, of course, perhaps with the odds on your side, but real life has a nasty habit of flying in the face of probability. You might well find that what you assumed to be most common is in fact less likely when given real data from real people. Not only could incorrect encodings cause problems with your application, those problems could occur far more frequently than you realize.

A better approach would be to only accept Unicode strings, which can then be written to byte strings using whatever encoding your application chooses. That removes all ambiguity, so your code doesn't have to guess anymore. Of course, if your application doesn't need to deal with Unicode and can simply pass byte strings through unconverted, it should accept byte strings only, rather than you having to guess an encoding to use in order to produce byte strings.

There Should Be One—and Preferably Only One—Obvious Way to Do It

Although similar to the previous principle, this one is generally applied only to development of libraries and frameworks. When designing a module, class, or function, it may be tempting to implement a number of entry points, each accounting for a slightly different scenario. In the byte string example from the previous section, for example, you might consider having one function to handle byte strings and another to handle Unicode strings.

The problem with that approach is that every interface adds a burden on developers who have to use it. Not only are there more things to remember; it may not always be clear which function to use even when all the options are known. Choosing the right option often comes down to little more than naming, which can sometimes be a guess.

In the previous example the simple solution is to accept only Unicode strings, which neatly avoids other problems, but for this principle, the recommendation is broader. Stick to simpler, more common interfaces where you can, such as the protocols illustrated in Chapter 5, adding on only when you have a truly different task to perform.

You might have noticed that Python seems to violate this rule sometimes, most notably in its dictionary implementation. The preferred way to access a value is to use the bracket syntax, `my_dict['key']`, but dictionaries also have a `get()` method, which seems to do the exact same thing. Conflicts like this come up fairly frequently when dealing with such an extensive set of principles, but there are often good reasons if you're willing to consider them.

In the dictionary case, it comes back to the notion of raising an exception when a rule is violated. When thinking about violations of a rule, we have to examine the rules implied by these two available access methods. The bracket syntax follows a very basic rule: return the value referenced by the key provided. It's really that simple. Anything that gets in the way of that, such as an invalid key, a missing value, or some additional behavior provided by an overridden protocol, results in an exception being raised.

The `get()` method, by contrast, follows a more complicated set of rules. It checks to see whether the provided key is present in the dictionary; if it is, the associated value is returned. If the key isn't in the dictionary, an alternate value is returned instead. By default the alternate value is `None`, but that can be overridden by providing a second argument.

By laying out the rules each technique follows, it becomes clearer why there are two different options. Bracket syntax is the common use case, failing loudly in all but the most optimistic situations, while `get()` offers more flexibility for those situations that need it. One refuses to allow errors to pass silently, while the other explicitly silences them. Essentially, providing two options allows dictionaries to satisfy both principles.

More to the point, though, is that the philosophy states there should only be one *obvious* way to do it. Even in the dictionary example, which has two ways to get values, only one—the bracket syntax—is obvious. The `get()` method is available, but it isn't very well known, and it certainly isn't promoted as the primary interface for working with dictionaries. It's okay to provide multiple ways to do something as long as they're for sufficiently different use cases, and the most common use case is presented as the obvious choice.

Although That Way May Not Be Obvious at First, Unless You're Dutch

This is a nod to the homeland of Python's creator and "Benevolent Dictator for Life," as he is known, Guido van Rossum. More importantly, however, it's an acknowledgment that not everyone sees things the same way. What seems obvious to one person might seem completely foreign to somebody else, and though there are any number of reasons for those types of differences, none of them are wrong. Different people are different, and that's all there is to it.

The easiest way to overcome these differences is to properly document your work so that even if the code isn't obvious, your documentation can point the way. You might still need to answer questions beyond the documentation, so it's often useful to have a more direct line of communication with users, such as a mailing list. The ultimate goal is to give users an easy way to know how you intend them to use your code. Use the # sign for single line comments or """" """" triple quotes for block comments to the advantage of you and your users.

```python
print('Block comments')
"""
This
is
a'
block
comment """
print('Single line comments too!')
# bye for now!
```

Now Is Better Than Never

We've all heard the saying "Don't put off 'til tomorrow what you can do today." That's a valid lesson for all of us, but it happens to be especially true in programming. By the time we get around to something we've set aside, we might have long since forgotten the information we need to do it right. The best time to do it is when it's on our mind.

Okay, so that part was obvious, but as Python programmers, this antiprocrastination clause has special meaning for us. Python as a language is designed in large part to help you spend your time solving real problems rather than fighting with the language just to get the program to work.

This focus lends itself well to iterative development, allowing you to quickly rough out a basic implementation and then refine it over time. In essence, it's another application of this principle because it allows you to get working quickly rather than trying to plan everything out in advance, possibly never actually writing any code.

Although Never Is Often Better Than *Right* Now

Even iterative development takes time. It's valuable to get started quickly, but it can be very dangerous to try to finish immediately. Taking the time to refine and clarify an idea is essential to getting it right, and failing to do so usually produces code that could be described as—at best—mediocre. Users and other developers will generally be better off not having your work at all than having something substandard.

We have no way of knowing how many otherwise useful projects never see the light of day because of this notion. Whether in that case or in the case of a poorly made release, the result is essentially the same: people looking for a solution to the same problem you tried to tackle won't have a viable option to use. The only way to really help anyone is to take the time required to get it right.

If the Implementation Is Hard to Explain, It's a Bad Idea

This is something of a combination of two other rules already mentioned: simple is better than complex, and complex is better than complicated. The interesting thing about the combination here is that it provides a way to identify when you've crossed the line from simple to complex or from complex to complicated. When in doubt, run it by someone else and see how much effort it takes to get them on board with your implementation.

This also reinforces the importance of communication to good development. In open source development, like that of Python, communication is an obvious part of the process, but it's not limited to publicly contributed projects. Any development team can provide greater value if its members talk to each other, bounce ideas around, and help refine implementations. Single-person development teams can sometimes prosper, but they're missing out on crucial editing that can only be provided by others.

If the Implementation Is Easy to Explain, It May Be a Good Idea

At a glance, this seems to be just an obvious extension of the previous principle, simply swapping "hard" and "bad" for "easy" and "good." Closer examination reveals that adjectives aren't the only things that changed. A verb changes its form as well: "is" became "may be." That may seem like a subtle, inconsequential change, but it's actually quite important.

Although Python highly values simplicity, many very bad ideas are easy to explain. Being able to communicate your ideas to your peers is valuable, but only as a first step that leads to real discussion. The best thing about peer review is the ability for different points of view to clarify and refine ideas, turning something good into something great.

Of course, that's not to discount the abilities of individual programmers. One person can do amazing things all alone, there's no doubt about it. But most useful projects involve other people at some point or another, even if only your users. Once those other people are in the know, even if they don't have access to your code, be prepared to accept their feedback and criticism. Even though you may think your ideas are great, other perspectives often bring new insight into old problems, which only serves to make it a better product overall.

Namespaces Are One Honking Great Idea: Let's Do More of Those!

In Python, namespaces are used in a variety of ways—from package and module hierarchies to object attributes—to allow programmers to choose the names of functions and variables without fear of conflicting with the choices of others. Namespaces avoid collisions without requiring every name to include some kind of unique prefix, which would otherwise be necessary.

For the most part, you can take advantage of Python's namespace handling without really doing anything special. If you add attributes or methods to an object, Python will take care of the namespace for that. If you add functions or classes to a module, or a module to a package, Python takes care of it. But there are a few decisions you can make to explicitly take advantage of better namespaces.

One common example is wrapping module-level functions into classes. This creates a bit of a hierarchy, allowing similarly named functions to coexist peacefully. It also has the benefit of allowing those classes to be customized using arguments, which can then affect the behavior of the individual methods. Otherwise, your code might have to rely on module-level settings that are modified by module-level functions, restricting how flexible it can be.

Not all sets of functions need to be wrapped up into classes, however. Remember that flat is better than nested, so as long as there are no conflicts or confusion, it's usually best to leave those at the module level. Similarly, if you don't have a number of modules with similar functionality and overlapping names, there's little point in splitting them up into a package.

Don't Repeat Yourself

Designing frameworks can be a very complicated process; programmers are often expected to specify a variety of different types of information. Sometimes, however, the same information might need to be supplied to multiple different parts of the framework. How often this happens depends on the nature of the framework involved, but having to provide the same information multiple times is always a burden and should be avoided wherever possible.

Essentially, the goal is to ask your users to provide configurations and other information just once and then use Python's introspection tools, described in detail in later chapters, to extract that information and reuse it in the other areas that need it. Once that information has been provided, the programmer's intentions are explicitly clear, so there's still no guesswork involved at all.

It's also important to note that this isn't limited to your own application. If your code relies on the Django web framework, for instance, you have access to all the configuration information required to work with Django, which is often quite extensive. You might only need to ask your users to point out which part of their code to use and access its structure to get anything else you need.

In addition to configuration details, code can be copied from one function to another if they share some common behaviors. In accordance with this principle, it's often better to move that common code out into a separate utility function. Then, each function that needs that code can defer to the utility function, paving the way for future functions that need that same behavior.

This type of code factoring showcases some of the more pragmatic reasons to avoid repetition. The obvious advantage to reusable code is that it reduces the number of places where bugs can occur. Better yet, when you find a bug you can fix it in one place, rather than worry about finding all the places that same bug might crop up. Perhaps best of all, having the code isolated in a separate function makes it much easier to test programmatically, to help reduce the likelihood of bugs occurring in the first place. Testing is covered in detail in Chapter 9.

Don't Repeat Yourself (DRY) is also one of the most commonly abbreviated principles, given that its initials spell a word so clearly. Interestingly, though, it can actually be used in a few different ways, depending on context.

- *An adjective*: "Wow, this feels very DRY!"

- *A noun*: "This code violates DRY."

- *A verb*: "Let's DRY this up a bit, shall we?"

Loose Coupling

Larger libraries and frameworks often have to split their code into separate subsystems with different responsibilities. This is typically advantageous from a maintenance perspective, with each section containing a substantially different aspect of the code. The concern here is about how much each section has to know about the others, because it can negatively affect the maintainability of the code.

It's not about having each subsystem completely ignorant of the others, nor is it to avoid them ever interacting at all. Any application written to be *that* separated wouldn't be able to actually do anything of interest. Code that doesn't talk to other code just can't be useful. Instead, it's more about how much each subsystem relies on how the other subsystems work.

In a way, you can look at each subsystem as its own complete system, with its own interface to implement. Each subsystem can then call into the other ones, supplying only the information pertinent to the function being called and getting the result, all without relying on what the other subsystem does inside that function.

There are a few good reasons for this behavior, the most obvious being that it helps make the code easier to maintain. If each subsystem only needs to know how its own functions work, changes to those functions should be localized enough to not cause problems with other subsystems that access them. You're able to maintain a finite collection of publicly reliable interfaces while allowing everything else to change as necessary over time.

Another potential advantage of loose coupling is how much easier it is to split off a subsystem into its own full application, which can then be included in other applications later on. Better yet, applications created like this can often be released to the development community at large, allowing others to utilize your work or even expand on it if you choose to accept patches from outside sources.

The Samurai Principle

As I stated in the opening to this chapter, the samurai warriors of ancient Japan were known for following the code of Bushido, which governed most of their actions in wartime. One particularly well-known aspect of Bushido was that warriors should return from battle victorious or not at all. The parallel in programming, as may be indicated by the keyword *return,* is the behavior of functions in the event that any exceptions are encountered along the way.

It's not a unique concept among those listed in this chapter, but rather an extension of the notion that errors should never pass silently and should avoid ambiguity. If something goes wrong while executing a function that ordinarily returns a value, any return value could be misconstrued as a successful call, rather than identifying that an error occurred. The exact nature of what occurred is very ambiguous and may produce errors down the road, in code that's unrelated to what really went wrong.

Of course, functions that don't return anything interesting don't have a problem with ambiguity because nothing is relying on the return value. Rather than allowing those functions to return without raising exceptions, they're actually the ones that are most in need of exceptions. After all, if there's no code that can validate the return value, there's no way of knowing that anything went wrong.

The Pareto Principle

In 1906, Italian economist Vilfredo Pareto noted that 80 percent of the wealth in Italy was held by just 20 percent of its citizens. Since then this idea has been put to the test in a number of fields beyond economics, and similar patterns have been found. The exact percentages may vary, but the general observation has emerged over time: the vast majority of effects in many systems are a result of just a small number of the causes.

In programming, this principle can manifest itself in a number of different ways. One of the more common is with regard to early optimization. Donald Knuth, the noted computer scientist, once said that premature optimization is the root of all evil, and many people take that to mean that optimization should be avoided until all other aspects of the code have been finished.

Knuth was referring to a focus solely on performance too early in the process. It's useless to try to tweak every ounce of speed out of a program until you've verified that it even does what it's supposed to. The Pareto principle teaches us that a little bit of work at the outset can have a large impact on performance.

Striking that balance can be difficult, but there are a few easy things that can be done while designing a program, which can handle the bulk of the performance problems with little effort. Some such techniques are listed throughout the remainder of this book, under sidebars labeled Optimization.

Another application of the Pareto principle involves prioritization of features in a complex application or framework. Rather than trying to build everything all at once, it's often better to start with the minority of features that will provide the most benefit to your users. Doing so allows you to get started on the core focus of the application and get it out to the people who need to use it, while you can refine additional features based on feedback.

The Robustness Principle

During early development of the Internet, it was evident that many of the protocols being designed would have to be implemented by countless different programs and that they'd all have to work together in order to be productive. Getting the specifications right was important, but getting people to implement them interoperably was even more important.

In 1980, the Transmission Control Protocol (TCP) was updated with RFC 761,[3] which included what has become one of the most significant guidelines in protocol design: be conservative in what you do; be liberal in what you accept from others. It was called "a general principle of robustness," but it's also been referred to as Postel's law, after its author, Jon Postel.

---

[3]See "title," http://propython.com/rfc-761.

It's easy to see how this principle would be useful when guiding the implementations of protocols designed for the Internet. Essentially, programs that follow this principle will be able to work much more reliably with programs that don't. By sticking to the rules when generating output, that output is more likely to be understood by software that doesn't necessarily follow the specification completely. Likewise, if you allow for some variations in the incoming data, incorrect implementations can still send you data you can understand.

Moving beyond protocol design, an obvious application of this principle is in functions. If you can be a bit liberal in what values you accept as arguments, you can accommodate usage alongside other code that provides different types of values. A common example is a function that accepts floating point numbers, which can work just as well when given an integer or a decimal because they can both be converted to floats.

The return value is also important to the integration of a function with the code that calls it. One common way this comes into play is when a function can't do what it's supposed to and thus can't produce a useful return value. Some programmers will opt to return None in these cases, but then it's up to the code that called the function to identify that and handle it separately. The samurai principle recommends that in these cases, the code should raise an exception rather than return an unusable value. Because Python returns None by default, if no other value was returned, it's important to consider the return value explicitly.

It's always useful, though, to try to find some return value that would still satisfy requirements. For example, for a function that's designed to find all instances of a particular word within a passage of text, what happens when the given word can't be found at all? One option is to return None; another is to raise some WordNotFound exception.

If the function is supposed to return *all* instances, however, it should already be returning a list or an iterator, so finding no words presents an easy solution: return an empty list or an iterator that produces nothing. The key here is that the calling code can always expect a certain type of value, and as long as the function follows the robustness principle, everything will work just fine.

If you're unsure which approach would be best, you can provide two different methods, each with a different set of intentions. In Chapter 5, I will explain how dictionaries can support both get() and __getitem__() methods, each reacting differently when a specified key doesn't exist.

In addition to code interaction, robustness also applies when dealing with the people who use the software. If you're writing a program that accepts input from human beings, whether it is text- or mouse-based, it's always helpful to be lenient with what you're given. You can allow command-line arguments to be specified out of order, make buttons bigger, allow incoming files to be slightly malformed, or anything else that helps people use the software without sacrificing being explicit.

Backward Compatibility

Programming is iterative in nature, and nowhere is that more noticeable than when you distribute your code for other people to use in their own projects. Each new version not only comes with new features but also the risk that existing features will change in some way that will break code that relies on its behavior. By committing yourself to backward compatibility, you can minimize that risk for your users, giving them more confidence in your code.

Unfortunately, backward compatibility is something of a double-edged sword when it comes to designing your application. On the one hand, you should always try to make your code the best it can be, and sometimes that involves changes to repair decisions that were made early on in the process. On the other hand, once you make major decisions, you need to commit to maintaining those decisions in the long run. The two sides run contrary to each other, so it's quite a balancing act.

Perhaps the biggest advantage you can give yourself is to make a distinction between public and private interfaces. Then, you can commit to long-term support of the public interfaces, while leaving the private interfaces for more rigorous refinement and change. Once the private interfaces are more finalized, they can then be promoted to the public API and documented for users.

Documentation is one of the main differentiators between public and private interfaces, but naming can also play an important role. Functions and attributes that begin with an underscore are generally understood to be private in nature, even without documentation. Adhering to this will help your users look at the source and decide which interfaces they'd like to use, taking on the risk themselves if they choose to use the private ones.

Sometimes, however, even the publicly safe interfaces might need to change in order to accommodate new features. It's usually best to wait until a major version number change, though, and warn users in advance of the incompatible changes that will occur. Then, going forward, you can commit to the long-term compatibility of the new interfaces. That's the approach Python took while working toward its long-awaited 3.0 release.

Taking It With You

The principles and philosophies presented in this chapter represent many of the ideals that are highly valued by the Python community at large, but they're of value only when applied to actual design decisions in real code. The rest of this book will frequently refer to this chapter, explaining how these decisions went into the code described. In the next chapter, I'll examine some of the more fundamental techniques that you can build on to put these principles to work in your code.

CHAPTER 2

Advanced Basics

Like any other book on programming, the remainder of this book relies on quite a few features that may or may not be considered commonplace by readers. You, the reader, are expected to know a good deal about Python and programming in general, but there are a variety of lesser-used features that are extremely useful in the operations of many techniques shown throughout the book.

Therefore, as unusual as it may seem, this chapter focuses on a concept of advanced basics. The tools and techniques in this chapter aren't necessarily common knowledge, but they form a solid foundation for more advanced implementations to follow. Let's start off with some of the general concepts that tend to come up often in Python development.

General Concepts

Before getting into more concrete details, it's important to get a feel for the concepts that lurk behind the specifics covered later in this chapter. These are different from the principles and philosophies discussed in Chapter 1 in that they are concerned more with actual programming techniques, whereas those discussed previously are more generic design goals.

Think of Chapter 1 as a design guide, whereas the concepts presented in this chapter are more of an implementation guide. Of course, there's only so specific a description like this can get without getting bogged down in too many details, so this section will defer to chapters throughout the rest of the book for more detailed information.

Iteration

Although there is a nearly infinite number of different types of sequences that might come up in Python code—more on that later in this chapter and in Chapter 5—most code that uses them can be placed in one of two categories: those that actually use the sequence as a whole and those that just need the items within it. Most functions use

© J. Burton Browning and Marty Alchin 2019
J. B. Browning and M. Alchin, *Pro Python 3*, https://doi.org/10.1007/978-1-4842-4385-5_2

both approaches in various ways, but the distinction is important in order to understand what tools Python makes available and how they should be used.

Looking at things from a purely object-oriented perspective, as opposed to a functional programming perspective, it's easy to understand how to work with sequences that your code actually needs to use. You'll have a concrete item such as a list, set, or dictionary, which not only has data associated with it but also has methods that allow for accessing and modifying that data. You may need to iterate over it multiple times, access individual items out of order, or return it from other methods for other code to use, all of which works well with more traditional object usage.

Then again, you may not actually need to work with the entire sequence as a whole; you may be interested solely in each item within it. This is often the case when looping over a range of numbers, for instance, because what's important is having each number available within the loop, not having the whole list of numbers available.

The difference between the two approaches is primarily about intention, but there are technological implications as well. Not all sequences need to be loaded into memory, and many don't even need to have a finite upper limit at all, such as a network stream. This category includes the set of positive odd numbers, squares of integers, and the Fibonacci sequence, all of which are infinite in length and easily computable. Therefore, they're best suited for pure iteration, without the need to populate a list in advance, which also saves a bit of memory.

The main benefit to this is memory allocation. A program designed to print out the entire range of the Fibonacci sequence only needs to keep a few variables in memory at any given time, because each value in the sequence can be calculated from the two previous values. Populating a list of the values, even with a limited length, requires loading all the included values into memory before iterating over them. If the full list will never be acted on as a whole, it's far more efficient to simply generate each item as it's necessary and discard it once it's no longer required in order to produce new items.

Python as a language offers a few different ways of implementation to iterate over a sequence without pushing all its values into memory at once. In its standard library, Python uses those techniques in many of its provided features, which may sometimes lead to confusion. Python allows you to write a for loop without a problem, but many sequences won't have the methods and attributes you might expect to see on a list. To see two types of looping in action, try the following:

```
last_name='Smith'
count=0
for letter in last_name:
    print(letter,' ' ,count) # note a space between ' '
    count += 1

print('---and the second loop----')
count = 0
while (count<5):
    print(last_name[count], ' ', count)
    count += 1
```

The section on iteration later in this chapter covers some of the more common ways to create iterable sequences and also a simple way to convert those sequences to lists when you truly do need to operate on the sequence as a whole. Sometimes, however, it's useful to have an object that can function in both respects, which requires the use of caching.

Caching

Outside of computing, a cache is a hidden collection, typically of items either too dangerous or too valuable to be made directly accessible. The definition in computing is related, with caches storing data in a way that doesn't impact a public-facing interface. Perhaps the most common real-world example is a Web browser, which downloads a document from the Web when it's first requested but keeps a copy of that document. When the user requests that same document again (if the document has not changed) at a later time, the browser loads the private copy and displays it to the user instead of hitting the remote server again.

In the browser example, the public interface could be the address bar, an entry in the user's favorites or a link from another web site, where the user never has to indicate whether the document should be retrieved remotely or accessed from a local cache. Instead, the software uses the cache to reduce the number of remote requests that need to be made, as long as the document doesn't change quickly. The details of Web document caching are beyond the scope of this book, but it's a good example of how caching works in general:

```
import webbrowser
webbrowser.open_new('http://www.python.org/')
#more info at:  https://docs.python.org/3.4/library/webbrowser.html
```

More specifically, a cache should be looked at as a time-saving or performance-boosting utility that doesn't explicitly need to exist in order for a feature to work properly. If the cache gets deleted or is otherwise unavailable the function that utilizes it should continue to work properly, perhaps with a dip in performance because it needs to refetch the items that were lost. That also means that code utilizing a cache must always accept enough information to generate a valid result without the use of the cache.

The nature of caching also means that you need to be careful about ensuring that the cache is as up-to-date as your needs demand. In the Web browser example, servers can specify how long a browser should hold on to a cached copy of a document before requesting a fresh one from the server. In simple mathematical examples, the result can be cached theoretically forever, because the result should always be the same, given the same input. Chapter 3 covers a technique called *memoization* that does exactly that.

A useful compromise is to cache a value indefinitely but update it immediately when the value is updated. This isn't always an option, particularly if values are retrieved from an external source, but when the value is updated within your application, updating the cache is an easy step to include, which saves the trouble of having to invalidate the cache and retrieve the value from scratch later on. Doing so can incur a performance penalty, however, so you'll have to weigh the merits of live updates against the time you might lose by doing so.

Transparency

Whether describing building materials, image formats, or government actions, transparency refers to the ability to see through or inside of something, and its use in programming is no different. For our purposes, transparency refers to the ability of your code to see—and, in many cases, even edit—nearly everything that the computer has access to.

Python doesn't support the notion of private variables typical in many other programming languages, so all attributes are accessible to any requester. Some languages consider that type of openness to be a risk to maintainability, instead allowing the code that implements an object to be solely responsible for that object's data. Although that does prevent some occasional misuses of internal data structures, Python doesn't take any measures to restrict access to that data.

Although the most obvious use of transparent access is in class instance attributes—which is where many other languages allow more privacy—Python allows you to inspect a wide range of aspects of objects and the code that implements them. In fact, you can even get access to the compiled bytecode that Python uses to execute functions. Here are just a few examples of information available at runtime:

- Attributes of an object

- The names of attributes available for an object

- The type of an object

- The module in which a class or function was defined

- The location (typically a filename) in which a module was loaded

- The bytecode of a function object

Most of this information is only used internally, but it's available because there are potential uses that can't be accounted for when code is first written. Accessing or examining that information at runtime is called *introspection* and is a common tactic in systems that implement principles such as DRY (Don't Repeat Yourself). The definition by Hunt and Thomas for DRY is that "Every piece of knowledge must have a single, unambiguous, authoritative representation within a system" (*The Pragmatic Programmer*, 2000, by A. Hunt and D. Thomas).

The rest of this book contains many different introspection techniques in the sections where such information is available. For those rare occasions where data should indeed be protected, Chapters 3 and 4 show how data can show the intent of privacy or be hidden entirely.

Control Flow

Generally speaking, the control flow of a program is the path the program takes during execution. The more common examples of control flow, including of course the *sequence* structure, are the `if`, `for,` and `while` blocks, which are used to manage the most fundamental branches your code could need. Those blocks are also some of the first things a Python programmer will learn, so this section will instead focus on some of the lesser-used and underutilized control flow mechanisms.

Catching Exceptions

Chapter 1 explained how Python philosophy encourages the use of exceptions wherever an expectation is violated, but expectations often vary between different uses. This is especially common when one application or module relies on another, but it's also quite common within a single application. Essentially, any time one function calls another, it can add its own expectations on top of the exceptions the called function already handles.

Exceptions are raised with a simple syntax using the `raise` keyword, but catching them is slightly more complicated because it uses a combination of keywords. The `try` keyword begins a block where you feel exceptions are likely to occur, while the `except` keyword marks a block to execute when an exception is raised. The first part is easy, as `try` doesn't have anything to go along with it, and the simplest form of `except` also doesn't require any additional information:

```python
def count_lines(filename):
    """
    Count the number of lines in a file. If the file can't be
    opened, it should be treated the same as if it was empty.
    """
    try:
        return len(open(filename, 'r').readlines())
    except:
        print('exception error reading the file or calculating lines!')
```

```
        # Something went wrong reading the file
        # or calculating the number of lines.
        return 0
myfile=input('Enter a file to open:  ')
print(count_lines(myfile))
```

Any time an exception is raised inside the try block, the code in the except block will be executed. As it stands, this doesn't make any distinction among the many various exceptions that could be raised; no matter what happens, the function will always return a number. It's actually fairly rare that you'd want to do that, however, because many exceptions should in fact propagate up to the caller—errors should never pass silently. Some notable examples are SystemExit and KeyboardInterrupt, both of which should usually cause the program to stop running.

In order to account for those and other exceptions that your code shouldn't interfere with, the except keyword can accept one or more exception types that should be caught explicitly. Any others will simply be raised as if you didn't have a try block at all. This focuses the except block on just those situations that should definitely be handled, so your code only has to deal with what it's supposed to manage. Make the minor changes to what you just tried, as shown here, to see this in action:

```
def count_lines(file_name):
    """

    Count the number of lines in a file. If the file can't be
    opened, it should be treated the same as if it was empty.
    """

    try:
        return len(open(file_name, 'r').readlines())
    except IOError:
        # Something went wrong reading the file.
        return 0
my_file=input('Enter a file to open:  ')
print(count_lines(my_file))
```

By changing the code to accept IOError explicitly, the except block will only execute if there was a problem accessing the file from the filesystem. Any other errors, such as a filename that's not even a string, will be raised outside of this function, to be handled by some other piece of code in the call stack.

If you need to catch multiple exception types, there are two approaches. The first and easiest is to simply catch some base class that all the necessary exceptions derive from. Because exception handling matches against the specified class and all its subclasses, this approach works quite well when all the types you need to catch do have a common base class. In the line counting example, you could encounter either IOError or OSError, both of which are descendants of EnvironmentError:

```
def count_lines(file_name):
    """
    Count the number of lines in a file. If the file can't be
    opened, it should be treated the same as if it was empty.
    """
    try:
        return len(open(file_name, 'r').readlines())
    except EnvironmentError:
        # Something went wrong reading the file.
        return 0
```

Note   Even though we're only interested in IOError and OSError, all subclasses of EnvironmentError will get caught as well. In this case, that's fine because those are the only subclasses of EnvironmentError, but in general you'll want to make sure you're not catching too many exceptions.

Other times, you may want to catch multiple exception types that don't share a common base class or perhaps limit it to a smaller list of types. In these cases, you need to specify each type individually, separated by commas. In the case of count_lines(), there's also the possibility of a TypeError that could be raised if the filename passed in isn't a valid string:

```python
def count_lines(file_name):
    """
    Count the number of lines in a file. If the file can't be
    opened, it should be treated the same as if it was empty.
    """
    try:
        return len(open(file_name, 'r').readlines())
    except (EnvironmentError, TypeError):
        # Something went wrong reading the file.
        return 0
```

If you need to access the exception object itself, perhaps to log the message for later, you can do so by adding an *as* clause with a name (*as e* in the next example), which will be bound to the exception object:

```python
import logging

def count_lines(file_name):
    """
    Count the number of lines in a file. If the file can't be
    opened, it should be treated the same as if it was empty.
    """
    try:
        return len(open(file_name, 'r').readlines())
    except (EnvironmentError, TypeError) as e:
        # Something went wrong reading the file.
        logging.error(e)
        return 0
```

COMPATIBILITY: PRIOR TO 3.0

In Python 3.0, the syntax for catching exceptions changed to be more explicit, alleviating some common errors. In older versions, a comma separated the exception types from the variable used to store the exception object. In order to catch more than one exception type, you'd need to explicitly wrap the types in parentheses to form a tuple.

It was very easy, therefore, when trying to catch two exception types but not store the value anywhere, to accidentally forget the parentheses. It wouldn't be a syntax error but would instead catch only the first type of exception, storing its value under the name of the second type of exception. Using `except TypeError, ValueError` actually stored a `TypeError` object under the name `ValueError`!

To resolve the situation, the `as` keyword was added and became the only way to store an exception object. Even though this removes the ambiguity, multiple exceptions must still be wrapped in a tuple for clarity.

Multiple `except` clauses can be used, allowing you to handle different exception types in different ways. For example, `EnvironmentError` OSError's constructor optionally takes two arguments, an error code and an error message, that combine to form its complete string representation. In order to log just the error message in that case, but still correctly handle the `TypeError` case, two `except` clauses could be used:

```python
import logging

def count_lines(file_name):
    """
    Count the number of lines in a file. If the file can't be
    opened, it should be treated the same as if it was empty.
    """
    try:
        return len(open(file_name, 'r').readlines())
    except TypeError as e:
        # The filename wasn't valid for use with the filesystem.
        logging.error(e)
```

```
            return 0
    except EnvironmentError as e:
        # Something went wrong reading the file.
        logging.error(e.args[1])
        return 0
```

Exception Chains

Sometimes, while handling one exception, another exception might get raised along the way. This can happen either explicitly with a `raise` keyword or implicitly through some other code that gets executed as part of the handling. Either way, this situation brings up the question of which exception is important enough to present itself to the rest of the application. Exactly how that question is answered depends on how the code is laid out, so let's take a look at a simple example, where the exception handling code opens and writes to a log file:

```
def get_value(dictionary, name):
    try:
        return dictionary[name]
    except Exception as e:
        print("exception hit..writing to file")
        log = open('logfile.txt', 'w')
        log.write('%s\n' % e)
        log.close()
names={"Jack":113, "Jill":32,"Yoda":395}
print(get_value(names,"Jackz"))#change to Jack and it runs fine
```

If anything should go wrong when writing to the log, a separate exception will be raised. Even though this new exception is important, there was already an exception in play that shouldn't be forgotten. To retain the original information, the file exception gains a new attribute, called __context__, which holds the original exception object. Each exception can possibly reference one other, forming a chain that represents everything that went wrong, in order. Consider what happens when get_value() fails, but logfile.txt is a read-only file:

```
 get_value({}, 'test')
Traceback (most recent call last):

KeyError: 'test'

During handling of the above exception, another exception occurred:

Traceback (most recent call last):

IOError: [Errno 13] Permission denied: 'logfile.txt'
```

This is an implicit chain, because the exceptions are linked only by how they're encountered during execution. Sometimes you'll be generating an exception yourself, and you may need to include an exception that was generated elsewhere. One common example of this is validating values using a function that was passed in. Validation functions, as described in Chapters 3 and 4, generally raise a ValueError, regardless of what was wrong.

This is a great opportunity to form an explicit chain, so we can raise a ValueError directly, while retaining the actual exception behind the scenes. Python allows this by including the from keyword at the end of the raise statement:

```
 def validate(value, validator):
     try:
         return validator(value)
     except Exception as e:
         raise ValueError('Invalid value: %s' % value) from e

 def validator(value):
     if len(value) > 10:
         raise ValueError("Value can't exceed 10 characters")

 validate('test', validator)
 validate(False, validator)
Traceback (most recent call last):
```

```
TypeError: object of type 'bool' has no len()
```

```
The above exception was the direct cause of the following exception:
```

```
Traceback (most recent call last):
  ValueError: invalid value: False
```

Because this wraps multiple exceptions into a single object, it may seem ambiguous as to which exception is really being passed around. A simple rule to remember is that the most recent exception is the one being raised, with any others available by way of the __context__ attribute. This is easy to test by wrapping one of these functions in a new try block and checking the type of the exception:

```
try:
    validate(False, validator)
except Exception as e:
    print(type(e))
```

```
<class 'ValueError'>
```

When Everything Goes Right

On the other end of the spectrum, you may find that you have a complex block of code where you need to catch exceptions that may crop up from part of it, but code after that part should proceed without any error handling. The obvious approach is to simply add that code outside of the try/except blocks. Here's how we might adjust the count_lines() function to contain the error-generating code inside the try block, while the line counting takes place after the exceptions have been handled:

```
import logging
```

```
def count_lines(file_name):
    """
```

```
Count the number of lines in a file. If the file can't be
opened, it should be treated the same as if it was empty.
"""
try:
    file = open(file_name, 'r')
except TypeError as e:
    # The filename wasn't valid for use with the filesystem.
    logging.error(e)
    return 0
except EnvironmentError as e:
    # Something went wrong reading the file.
    logging.error(e.args[1])
    return 0
return len(file.readlines())
```

In this particular case, the function will work as expected, so all seems fine. Unfortunately, it's misleading because of the nature of this specific case. Because each of the except blocks explicitly returns a value from the function, the code after the error handling will only be reached if no exceptions were raised.

Note   We could place the file reading code directly after the file is opened, but then if any exceptions are raised there, they'd get caught using the same error handling as the file opening. Separating them is a way to better control how exceptions are handled overall. You may also notice that the file isn't closed anywhere here. That will be handled in later sections, as this function continues expanding.

If, however, the except blocks simply logged the error and moved on, Python would try to count the lines in the file, even though no file was ever opened. Instead, we need a way to specify a block of code should be run only if no exceptions were raised at all, so it doesn't matter how your except blocks execute. Python provides this feature by way of the else keyword, which defines a separate block:

```
import logging

def count_lines(filename):
    """

    Count the number of lines in a file. If the file can't be
    opened, it should be treated the same as if it was empty.
    """

    try:
        file = open(filename, 'r')
    except TypeError as e:
        # The filename wasn't valid for use with the filesystem.
        logging.error(e)
        return 0
    except EnvironmentError as e:
        # Something went wrong reading the file.
        logging.error(e.args[1])
        return 0
    else:
        return len(file.readlines())
```

Caution   Raising an exception isn't the only thing that tells Python to avoid the
`else` block. If the function returns a value at any time inside the `try` block, Python
will simply return the value as instructed, skipping the `else` block altogether.

Proceeding Regardless of Exceptions

Many functions perform some kind of setup or resource allocation that must be cleaned
up before returning control to external code. In the face of exceptions the cleanup code
might not always be executed, which can leave files or sockets open or perhaps leave
large objects in memory when they're no longer needed.

To facilitate this, Python also allows the use of a `finally` block, which gets executed every time the associated `try`, `except`, and `else` blocks finish. Because `count_lines()` opens a file, best practice would suggest that it also explicitly close the file, rather than waiting for garbage collection to deal with it later. Using `finally` provides a way to make sure the file always gets closed.

There is still one thing to consider. So far, `count_lines()` only anticipates exceptions that could occur while trying to open the file, even though there's a common one that comes up when reading the file: `UnicodeDecodeError`. Chapter 7 covers a bit of Unicode and how Python deals with it, but for now, just know that it comes up fairly often. In order to catch this new exception, it's necessary to move the `readlines ()` call back into the `try` block, but we can still leave the line counting in the `else` block:

```python
import logging

def count_lines(file_name):
    """
    Count the number of lines in a file. If the file can't be
    opened, it should be treated the same as if it was empty.
    """
    file = None  # file must always have a value
    try:
        file = open(file_name, 'r')
        lines = file.readlines()
    except TypeError as e:
        # The filename wasn't valid for use with the filesystem.
        logging.error(e)
        return 0
    except EnvironmentError as e:
        # Something went wrong reading the file.
        logging.error(e.args[1])
        return 0
    except UnicodeDecodeError as e:
        # The contents of the file were in an unknown encoding.
        logging.error(e)
```

```
        return 0
    else:
        return len(lines)
    finally:
        if file:
            file.close()
```

Of course, it's not very likely that you'd have this much error handling in a simple line counting function. After all, it really only exists because we wanted to return 0 in the event of any errors. In the real world, you're much more likely to just let the exceptions run their course outside of count_lines(), letting other code be responsible for how to handle it.

Tip   Some of this handling can be made a bit simpler using a `with` block, described later in this chapter.

Optimizing Loops

Because loops of some kind or another are very common in most types of code, it's important to make sure that they can run as efficiently as possible. The iteration section later in this chapter covers a variety of ways to optimize the design of any loops, whereas Chapter 5 explains how you can control the behavior of `for` loops. Instead, this section focuses on the optimization of the `while` loop.

Typically, `while` is used to check a condition that may change during the course of the loop, so that the loop can finish executing once the condition evaluates to false. When that condition is too complicated to distill into a single expression or when the loop is expected to break due to an exception, it makes more sense to keep the `while` expression always true and end the loop using a `break` statement where appropriate.

Although any expression that evaluates to true will induce the intended functionality, there is one specific value you can use to make it even better. Python knows that `True` will always evaluate to true, so it makes some additional optimizations behind the scenes to speed up the loop. Essentially, it doesn't even bother checking the condition each time; it just runs the code inside the loop indefinitely, until it encounters an exception, a `break` statement, or a `return` statement:

```python
def echo():
    """Returns everything you type until you press Ctrl-C"""

    while True:
        try:
            print(input'Type Something or CTRL C to exit: ')
        except KeyboardInterrupt:
            print()  # Make sure the prompt appears on a new line.
            print('bye for now...:')
            break
echo()
```

The *with* Statement

The `finally` block covered in the exception handling section earlier in this chapter is
a convenient way to clean up after a function, but sometimes that's the only reason to
use a `try` block in the first place. Sometimes you don't want to silence any exceptions,
but you still want to make sure the cleanup code executes, regardless of what happens.
Working solely with exception handling, a simpler version of `count_lines()` might look
something like this:

```python
def count_lines(file_name):
    """Count the number of lines in a file."""

    file = open(file_name, 'r')
    try:
        return len(file.readlines())
    finally:
        file.close()
```

If the file fails to open, it will raise an exception before even entering the `try` block, while everything else that could go wrong would do so inside the try block, which will cause the `finally` block to clean up the file. Unfortunately, it's something of a waste to use the power of the exception handling system just for that. Instead, Python provides another option that has some other advantages over exception handling as well.

The `with` keyword can be used to start a new block of code, much like `try`, but with a very different purpose in mind. By using a `with` block, you're defining a specific context in which the contents of the block should execute. The beauty of it, however, is that the object you provide in the `with` statement gets to determine what that context means.

For example, you can use `open()` in a `with` statement to run some code in the context of that file. In this case, `with` also provides an `as` clause, which allows an object to be returned for use while executing in the current context. Here's how to rewrite the new version of `count_lines()` to take advantage of all of this:

```
def count_lines(file_name):
    """Count the number of lines in a file."""

    with open(file_name, 'r') as file:
        return len(file.readlines())
```

That's really all that's left of `count_lines()` after switching to use the `with` statement. The exception handling gets done by the code that manages the `with` statement, whereas the file closing behavior is actually provided by the file itself, by way of a context manager. Context managers are special objects that know about the `with` statement and can define exactly what it means to have code executed in their context.

In a nutshell, the context manager gets a chance to run its own code before the `with` block executes; then it gets to run some more cleanup code after it's finished. Exactly what happens at each of those stages will vary. In the case of `open()`, it opens the file and closes it automatically when the block finishes executing.

With files, the context obviously always revolves an open file object, which is made available to the block using the name given in the `as` clause. Sometimes, however, the context is entirely environmental, so there is no such object to use during execution. To support those cases, the `as` clause is optional.

In fact, you can even leave off the as clause in the case of open() without causing any errors. Of course, you also won't have the file available to your code, so it'd be of little use, but there's nothing in Python that prevents you from doing so. If you include an as clause when using a context manager that doesn't provide an object, the variable you define will simply be populated with None instead, because all functions return None if no other value is specified.

There are several context managers available in Python, some of which will be detailed throughout the rest of this book. In addition, Chapter 5 shows how you can write your own context managers so that you can customize the contextual behavior to match the needs of your own code.

Conditional Expressions

Fairly often, you may find yourself needing to access one of two values, and which one you use depends on evaluating an expression. For instance, it's quite common to display one string to a user if the value exceeds a particular value and a different one otherwise. Typically, this would be done using an if/else combination, as here:

```
def test_value(value):
    if value < 100:
        return 'The value is just right.'
    else:
        return 'The value is too big!'
print(test_value(55))
```

Rather than writing this out into four separate lines, it's possible to condense it into a single line using a conditional expression. By converting the if and else blocks into clauses in an expression, Python does the same effect much more concisely:

```
def test_value(value):
    return 'The value is ' + ('just right.' if value < 100 else 'too big!')
print(test_value(55))
```

READABILITY COUNTS

If you're used to this behavior from other programming languages, Python's ordering may seem unusual at first. Other languages, such as C++, implement something of the form `expression ? value_1 : value_2`. That is, the expression to test comes first, followed by the value to use if the expression is true, then the value to use if the expression is false.

Instead, Python attempts to use a form that more explicitly describes what's really going on. The expectation is that the expression will be true most of the time, so the associated value comes first, followed by the expression, then the value to use if the expression is false. This takes the entire statement into account by putting the more common value in the place it would be if there were no expression at all. For example, you end up with things like `return value ...` and `x = value ...`.

Because the expression is then tacked on afterward, it highlights the notion that the expression is just a qualification of the first value. "Use this value whenever this expression is true; otherwise, use the other one." It may seem a little odd if you're used to another language, but it makes sense when thinking about the equivalent in plain English.

There's another approach that is sometimes used to simulate the behavior of the conditional expression described in this section. This was often used in older Python installations where the `if`/`else` expression wasn't yet available. In its place, many programmers relied on the behavior of the and and or operators, which could be made to do something very similar. Here's how the previous example could be rewritten using only these operators:

```python
def test_value(value):
    return 'The value is ' + (value < 100 and 'just right.' or 'too big!')
```

This puts the order of components more in line with the form used in other programming languages. That fact may make it more comfortable for programmers used to working with those languages, and it certainly maintains compatibility with even older versions of Python. Unfortunately, it comes with a hidden danger that is often left unknown until it breaks an otherwise working program with little explanation. To understand why, let's examine what's going on.

The and operator works like the && operator in many languages, checking to see if the value to the left of the operator evaluates to true. If it doesn't, and returns the value to its left; otherwise, the value to the left is evaluated and returned. So if a value of 50 was passed into test_value(), the left side evaluates to true, and the and clause evaluates to the string, 'just right.' Factoring in that process, here's how the code would look:

```
return 'The value is ' + ('just right.' or 'too big!')
```

From here, the or operator works similarly to and, checking the value to its left to see if it evaluates to true. The difference is that if the value is true, that value is returned, without even evaluating the right-hand side of the operator at all. Looking at the condensed code here, it's clear that or would then return the string, 'just right.'

By contrast, if the value passed into the test_value() function was 150, the behavior is changed. Because 150 < 100 evaluates to false, the and operator returns that value, without evaluating the right-hand side. In that case, here's the resulting expression:

```
return 'The value is ' + (False or 'too big!')
```

Because False is obviously false, the or operator returns the value to its right instead, 'too big!' This behavior has led many people to rely on the and/or combination for conditional expressions. But have you noticed the problem? One of the assumptions being made here causes the whole thing to break down in many situations.

The problem is in the or clause when the left side of the and clause is true. In that case, the behavior of the or clause depends entirely on the value to the left of the operator. In the case shown here, it's a nonempty string, which will always evaluate to true, but what happens if you supply it an empty string, the number 0 or, worst of all, a variable that could contain a value you can't be sure of until the code executes?

What essentially happens is that the left side of the and clause evaluates to true, but the right side evaluates to false, so the end result of that clause is a false value. Then, when the or clause evaluates, its left side is false, so it returns the value to its right. In the end, the expression will always return the item to the right of the or operator, *regardless of the value at the beginning of the expression.*

Because no exceptions are raised, it doesn't look like anything is actually broken in the code. Instead, it simply looks like the first value in the expression was false, because it's returning the value that you would expect in that case. This may lead you to try to debug whatever code defines *that* value, rather than looking at the real problem, which is the value between the two operators.

Ultimately, what makes it so hard to pin down is that you have to distrust your own code, removing any assumptions you may have had about how it should work. You have to really look at it the way Python sees it, rather than how a human would see it.

Iteration

There are generally two ways of looking at sequences: as a collection of items, or as a way to access a single item at a time. These two aren't mutually exclusive, but it's useful to separate them in order to understand the different features available in each case. Working on the collection as a whole requires that all the items be in memory at once, but accessing them one at a time can often be done much more efficiently.

Iteration refers to this more efficient form of traversing a collection, working with just one item at a time before moving on to the next. Iteration is an option for any type of sequence, but the real advantage comes in special types of objects that don't need to load everything in memory all at once. The canonical example of this is Python's built-in range() function, which appears to iterate over the integers that fall within a given range:

```
>>>for x in range(5):
    print(x)
0
1
2
3
4
```

At a glance, it may appear like range() returns a list containing the appropriate values, but it doesn't. This shows if you examine its return value on its own, without iterating over it:

```
>>>range(5)
>>>range(0, 5)
>>>list(range(5))
[0, 1, 2, 3, 4]
```

The range object itself doesn't contain any of the values in the sequence. Instead, it generates them one at a time, on demand, during iteration. If you truly want a list that you can add or remove items from, you can convert one by passing the range object into a new list object. This internally iterates just like a for loop, so the generated list uses the same values that are available when iterating over the range itself.

Chapter 5 shows how you can write your own iterable objects that work similarly to range(). In addition to providing iterable objects, there are a number of ways to iterate over these objects in different situations, for different purposes. The for loop is the most obvious technique, but Python offers other forms of syntax as well, which are outlined in this section.

Sequence Unpacking

Generally, you would assign one value to one variable at a time, so when you have a sequence, you would assign the entire sequence to a single variable. When the sequences are small and you know how many items are in the sequence and what each item will be, this is fairly limiting, because you'll often end up just accessing each item individually, rather than dealing with them as a sequence.

This is particularly common when working with tuples, where the sequence often has a fixed length and each item in the sequence has a predetermined meaning. Tuples of this type are also the preferred way to return multiple values from a function, which makes it all the more annoying to have to bother with them as a sequence. Ideally, you should be able to retrieve them as individual items directly when getting the function's return value.

To allow for this, Python supports a special syntax called sequence unpacking. Rather than specifying a single name to assign a value, you can specify a number of names as a tuple on the left side of the = operator. This will cause Python to unpack the sequence on the right side of the operator, assigning each value to the related name on the left side:

```
>>> 'propython.com'.split('.')
['propython', 'com']
>>> components = 'propython.com'.split('.')
>>> components
['propython', 'com']
>>> domain, tld = 'propython.com'.split('.')
>>> domain
'propython'
>>> tld
'com'
>>> domain, tld = 'www.propython.com'.split('.')
Traceback (most recent call last):
  ...
ValueError: too many values to unpack
```

The error shown at the end of this example illustrates the only significant limitation of this approach: the number of variables to assign must match the number of items in the sequence. If they don't match, Python can't properly assign the values. If you look at the tuple as being similar to an argument list, however, there's another option available.

If you add an asterisk before the final name in the variable list, Python will keep a list of any values that couldn't be put into one of the other variables. The resulting list is stored in the final variable, so you can still assign a sequence that contains more items than you have explicit variables to hold them. This only works if you have more items in the sequence than you have variables to assign to. If the reverse is true, you'll still run into the TypeError shown previously:

```
>>> domain, *path = 'propython.com/example/url'.split('/')
>>> domain
'propython.com'
>>> path
['example', 'url']
```

51

Note   Chapter 3 shows how a similar syntax applies to function arguments as well.

List Comprehensions

When you have a sequence with more items than you really need, it's often useful to generate a new list and add just those items that meet a certain criteria. There are a few ways to do that, the most obvious being to use a simple `for` loop, adding each item in turn:

```
>>> output = []
>>> for value in range(10):
...     if value > 5:
...         output.append(str(value))
...
>>> output
['6', '7', '8', '9']
```

Unfortunately, that adds four lines and two levels of indentation to your code, even though it's an extremely common pattern to use. Instead, Python offers a more concise syntax for this case, which allows you to express the three main aspects of that code into a single line:

- A sequence to retrieve values from
- An expression that's used to determine whether a value should be included
- An expression that's used to provide a value to the new list

These are all combined into a syntax called list comprehensions. Here's how the preceding example would look, when rewritten to use this construct. The three basic segments of this form have been highlighted for clarity:

```
>>> output = [str(value) for value in range(10) if value > 5]
>>> output
['6', '7', '8', '9']
```

As you can see, the three portions of the overall form have been rearranged slightly, with the expression for the final value coming first, followed by the iteration and ending with the condition for deciding which items are included. You may also consider the variable that contains the new list to be its own fourth portion of the form, but because the comprehension is really just an expression, it doesn't have to be assigned to a name. It could just as easily be used to feed a list into a function:

```
>>> min([value for value in range(10) if value > 5])
6
```

Of course, this seems to violate the whole point of iteration that was pointed out earlier. After all, the comprehension returns a full list, only to have it thrown away when min() processes the values. For these situations, Python provides a different option: generator expressions.

Generator Expressions

Instead of creating an entire list based on certain criteria, it's often more useful to leverage the power of iteration for this process as well. Instead of surrounding the compression in brackets, which would indicate the creation of a proper list, you can instead surround it in parentheses, which will create a generator. Here's how it looks in action:

```
>>> gen = (value for value in range(10) if value > 5)
>>> gen
<generator object <genexpr> at 0x...>
```

```
>>> min(gen)
6
>>> min(gen)
Traceback (most recent call last):
  ...
ValueError: min() arg is an empty sequence
>>> min(value for value in range(10) if value > 5)
6
```

There are a few things going on here, but it's easier to understand once you've seen the output so that you have a frame of reference. First off, a generator is really just an iterable object that you don't have to create using the explicit interface. Chapter 5 shows how you can create iterators manually and even how to create generators with more flexibility, but the generator expression is the simplest way to deal with them.

When you create a generator—whether a generator expression or some other form—you don't immediately have access to the sequence. The generator object doesn't yet know what values it'll need to iterate over; it won't know that until it actually starts generating them. So if you view or inspect a generator without iterating over it, you won't have access to the full range of values.

In order to retrieve those values, all you need to do is iterate over the generator like you ordinarily would and it'll happily spit out values as needed. This step is implicitly performed inside many built-in functions, such as min(). If those functions are able to operate without building a complete list, you can use generators to dramatically improve performance over the use of other options. If they do have to create a new list, you're not losing anything by delaying until the function really needs to create it.

But notice what happens if you iterate over the generator twice. The second time through, you get an error that you tried to pass in an empty sequence. Remember, a generator doesn't contain all the values; it just iterates over them when asked to do so. Once the iteration is complete and there are no more values left to iterate; the generator doesn't restart. Instead, it simply returns an empty list each time it's called thereafter.

There are two main reasons behind this behavior. First, it's not always obvious how it should restart the sequence. Some iterables, such as range(), do have an obvious way to restart themselves, so those restart when iterated multiple times. Unfortunately, because there is any number of ways to create generators—and iterators in general—it's up to the iterable itself to determine when and how the sequence is reset. Chapter 5 explains this behavior, and how you can customize it for your own needs, in more detail.

Second, not all sequences should be reset once they complete. For example, you might implement an interface for cycling through a collection of active users, which may change over time. Once your code finishes iterating over the available users, it shouldn't simply reset to the same sequence over and over again. The nature of that ever-changing set of users means that Python itself can't possibly guess at how to control it. Instead, that behavior is controlled by more complex iterators.

One final thing to point out about generator expressions: even though they must always be surrounded by parentheses, those parentheses don't always need to be unique to the expression. The last expression in this section's example simply uses the parentheses from the function call to enclose the generator expression, which also works just fine.

This form may seem a little odd at first, but in this simple case, it saves you from having an extra set of parentheses hanging around. However, if the generator expression is just one of multiple arguments or if it's part of a more complex expression, you still need to include explicit parentheses around the generator expression itself, to make sure that Python knows your intent.

Set Comprehensions

Sets—described in more detail in their own section under "Collections"—are very similar to lists in their construction, so you can build a set using a comprehension in basically the same way as lists. The only significant difference between the two is the use of curly braces instead of brackets surrounding the expression:

```
>>> {str(value) for value in range(10) if value > 5}
{'6', '7', '8', '9'}
```

Note Unlike sequences, sets are unordered, so different platforms may display the items in a different order. The only guarantee is that the same items will be present in the set, regardless of the platform.

Dictionary Comprehensions

There's certainly a theme developing with the construction of comprehensions for different types, and it's limited solely to one-dimensional sequences. Dictionaries can also be a form of sequence, but each item is really a pair of a key and its value. This is reflected in the literal form, by separating each key from its value by the use of a colon.

Because that colon is the factor that distinguishes the syntax for dictionaries from that of sets, the same colon is what separates dictionary comprehensions from set comprehensions. Where you would ordinarily include a single value, simply supply a key/value pair, separated by a colon. The rest of the comprehension follows the same rules as the other types:

```
>>> {value: str(value) for value in range(10) if value > 5}
{8: '8', 9: '9', 6: '6', 7: '7'}
```

Note   Remember, dictionaries are unordered, so their keys work a lot like sets. If you need a dictionary with keys that can be reliably ordered, see the "Ordered Dictionaries" section later in this chapter.

Chaining Iterables Together

Working with one iterable is useful enough in most situations, but sometimes you'll need to access one right after another, performing the same operation on each. The simple approach would be to just use two separate loops, duplicating the code block for each loop. The logical next step would be to refactor the code into a function, but now you have an extra function call in the mix for something that really only needs to be done inside the loop.

Instead, Python provides the chain() function, as part of its itertools module. The itertools module includes a number of different utilities, some of which are described in the following sections. The chain() function, in particular, accepts any number of iterables and returns a new generator that will iterate over each one in turn:

```
>>> import itertools
>>> list(itertools.chain(range(3), range(4), range(5)))
[0, 1, 2, 0, 1, 2, 3, 0, 1, 2, 3, 4]
```

Zipping Iterables Together

Another common operation involving multiple iterables is to merge them together, side by side. The first items from each iterable would come together to form a single tuple as the first value returned by a new generator. All of the second items become part of the second tuple in the generator, and so on. The built-in `zip()` function provides this functionality when needed:

```
>>> list(zip(range(3), reversed(range(5))))
[(0, 4), (1, 3), (2, 2)]
```

Notice here that even though the second iterable has five values, the resulting sequence only contains three values. When given iterators of varying lengths, `zip()` goes with the least common denominator, so to speak. Essentially, `zip()` makes sure that each tuple in the resulting sequence has exactly as many values as there are iterators to join together. Once the smallest sequence has been exhausted, `zip()` simply stops looking through the others.

This functionality is particularly useful in creating dictionaries, because one sequence can be used to supply the keys, while another supplies the values. Using `zip()` can join these together into the proper pairings, which can then be passed directly into a new `dict()`. In the next example, 97 in the ASCII table is lowercase "a" and 98 is "b," up to, but not including, the last number specified (102), so 101 is "e." The `map()` function iterates over a group of values; this is then paired with zip to an index value from `values` to build the dictionary:

```
>>> keys = map(chr, range(97, 102))
>>> values = range(1, 6)
>>> dict(zip(keys, values))
{'a': 1, 'c': 3, 'b': 2, 'e': 5, 'd': 4}
```

Collections

There are a number of well-known objects that come standard with the Python distribution, both as built-ins available to all modules and as part of the standard package library. Objects such as integers, strings, lists, tuples, and dictionaries are in common use among nearly all Python programs, but others, including sets named tuples and some special types of dictionaries, are used less often and may be unfamiliar to those who haven't already needed to discover them.

Some of these are built-in types that are always available to every module, whereas others are part of the standard library included with every Python installation. There are still more that are provided by third-party applications, some of which have become fairly commonly installed, but this section will only cover those included with Python itself.

Sets

Typically, collections of objects are represented in Python by tuples and lists, but sets provide another way to work with the same data. Essentially a set works much like a list, but without allowing any duplicates, making it useful for identifying the unique objects in a collection. For example, here's how a simple function might use a set to determine which letters are used in a given string:

```
>>> def unique_letters(word):
...     return set(word.lower())
...
```

```
>>> unique_letters('spam')
{'a', 'p', 's', 'm'}
>>> unique_letters('eggs')
{'s', 'e', 'g'}
```

Note the following:

- First, the built-in set type takes a sequence as its argument, which populates the set with all the unique elements found in that sequence. This is valid for any sequence, such as a string as shown in the example as well as lists, tuples, dictionary keys, or custom iterable objects.

- Second, the items in the set aren't ordered the same way they appeared in the original string. Sets are concerned solely with membership. They keep track of items that are in the set, without any notion of ordering. That seems like a limitation, but if you need ordering, you probably want a list anyway. Sets are very efficient when you only need to know if an item is a member of a collection, without regard to where it is in the collection or how many times it has otherwise appeared.

- Third, the representation showed when displaying the set in the interactive shell. As these representations are intended to be formatted in the same way as you can type into your source file, this indicates a syntax for declaring sets as literals in your code. It looks very similar to a dictionary but without any values associated with the keys. That's actually a fairly accurate analogy, because a set works very much like the collection of keys in a dictionary.

Because sets are designed for a different purpose than sequences and dictionaries, the available operations and methods are a bit different than you might be used to. To start, however, let's look at the way that sets behave in relation to other types. Perhaps the most common use of sets is to determine membership, a task often asked of both lists and dictionaries. In the spirit of matching expectations, this uses the in keyword, familiar from other types:

```
>>> example = {1, 2, 3, 4, 5}
>>> 4 in  example
True
>>> 6 in  example
False
```

In addition, items can be added to or removed from the set later on. The list's append() method isn't suitable for sets, because to append an item is to add it at the end, which then implies that the order of items in the collection is important. Because sets aren't at all concerned with ordering, they instead use the add() method, which just makes sure that the specified item ends up in the set. If it was already there, add() does nothing; otherwise, it adds the item to the set, so there are never any duplicates:

```
>>> example.add(6)
>>> example
{1, 2, 3, 4, 5, 6}
>>>
>>> example
{1, 2, 3, 4, 5, 6}
```

Dictionaries have the useful update() method, which adds the contents of a new dictionary to one that already exists. Sets have an update() method as well, performing the same task:

```
>>> example.update({6, 7, 8, 9})
>>> example
{1, 2, 3, 4, 5, 6, 7, 8, 9}
```

Removing items from the set can be done in a few different ways, each serving a different need. The most direct complement to add() is the remove() method, which removes a specific item from the set. If that item wasn't in the set in the first place, it raises a KeyError:

```
>>> example.remove(9)
>>> example.remove(9)
Traceback (most recent call last):
  ...
KeyError: 9
>>> example
{1, 2, 3, 4, 5, 6, 7, 8}
```

Many times, however, it doesn't matter whether the item was already in the set or not; you may only care that it's not in the set when you're done with it. For this purpose sets also have a discard() method, which works just like remove() but without raising an exception if the specified item wasn't in the set:

```
>>> example.discard(8)
>>> example.discard(8)
>>> example
{1, 2, 3, 4, 5, 6, 7}
```

Of course, remove() and discard() both assume that you already know what object you want to remove from the set. To simply remove any item from a set, use the pop() method, which again is borrowed from the list API but differs slightly. Because sets aren't explicitly ordered, there's no real end of the set for an item to be popped off. Instead, the set's pop() method picks one, unpredictably returning it for use outside the set:

```
>>> example.pop()
1
>>> example
{2, 3, 4, 5, 6, 7}
```

Finally, sets also provide a way to remove all items in one shot, resetting it to an empty state. The clear() method is used for this purpose:

```
>>> example.clear()
>>> example
set()
```

Note   The representation of an empty set is set(), rather than {}, because Python needs to maintain a distinction between sets and dictionaries. In order to preserve compatibility with older code written before the introduction of set literals, empty curly braces remain dedicated to dictionaries, so sets use their name instead.

In addition to methods for modifying the contents in place, sets also provide operations in which two sets combine in some way to return a new set. The most common of these is a union, in which the contents of two sets are joined together so the resulting new set contains all items that were in both of the original sets. It's essentially the same as using the update() method, except that none of the original sets is altered.

The union of two sets is a lot like a bit-wise OR operation, so Python represents it with the pipe character (|), which is the same as is used for bit-wise OR (where each byte is compared). In addition, sets offer the same functionality using the union() method, which can be called from either set involved:

```
>>> {1, 2, 3} | {4, 5, 6}
{1, 2, 3, 4, 5, 6}
>>> {1, 2, 3}.union({4, 5, 6})
{1, 2, 3, 4, 5, 6}
```

The logical complement to that operation is the intersection, where the result is the set of all items common to the original sets. Again, this is analogous to a bit-wise operation, but this time it's the bit-wise AND, and again, Python uses the ampersand (&) to represent the operation as it pertains to sets. Sets also have an intersection() method, which performs the same task:

```
>>> {1, 2, 3, 4, 5} & {4, 5, 6, 7, 8}
{4, 5}
>>> {1, 2, 3, 4, 5}.intersection({4, 5, 6, 7, 8})
{4, 5}
```

You can also determine the difference between two sets, resulting in a set of all the items that exist in one of the sets but not the other. By removing the contents of one set from another, it works a lot like subtraction, so Python uses the subtraction operator (–) to perform this operation, along with the difference() method:

```
>>> {1, 2, 3, 4, 5} - {2, 4, 6}
{1, 3, 5}
>>> {1, 2, 3, 4, 5}.difference({2, 4, 6})
{1, 3, 5}
```

In addition to that basic difference, Python sets offer a variation called a *symmetric difference*, using the `symmetric_difference()` method. Using this method, the resulting set contains *all items that were in either set, but not in both*. This is equivalent to the bit-wise exclusive OR operation, commonly referred to as XOR. Because Python uses the caret (^) to represent the XOR operation elsewhere, sets use the same operator as well as the method:

```
>>> {1, 2, 3, 4, 5} ^ {4, 5, 6}
{1, 2, 3, 6}
>>> {1, 2, 3, 4, 5}.symmetric_difference({4, 5, 6})
{1, 2, 3, 6}
```

Finally, it's possible to determine whether all the items in one set also exist in another. If one set contains all the items of another, the first is considered to be a superset of the other, even if the first set contains additional items not present in the second. The inverse, where all the items in first are contained in the second, even if the second has more items, means the first set is a subset of the second.

Testing to see if one set is a subset or a superset of another is performed by two methods, `issubset()` and `issuperset()`, respectively. The same test can be performed manually by subtracting one set from the other and checking to see if any items remain. If no items are left the set evaluates to `False`, and the first is definitely a subset of the second, and testing for a superset is as simple as swapping the two sets in the operation. Using these methods avoids creating a new set just to have it reduce to a Boolean anyway:

```
>>> {1, 2, 3}.issubset({1, 2, 3, 4, 5})
True
>>> {1, 2, 3, 4, 5}.issubset({1, 2, 3})
False
>>> {1, 2, 3}.issuperset({1, 2, 3, 4, 5})
False
```

```
>>> {1, 2, 3, 4, 5}.issuperset({1, 2, 3})
True
>>> not ({1, 2, 3} - {1, 2, 3, 4, 5})
True
>>> not ({1, 2, 3, 4, 5} - {1, 2, 3})
False
```

Note   Looking at how subsets and supersets can be determined using subtraction, you might notice that two identical sets will always subtract to an empty set, and the order of the two sets is irrelevant. This is correct, and because {1, 2, 3} - {1, 2, 3} is always empty, each set is both a subset and a superset of the other.

Named Tuples

Dictionaries are extremely useful, but sometimes you may have a fixed set of possible keys available, so you don't need that much flexibility. Instead, Python uses named tuples, which provide some of the same functionality, but they're much more efficient because the instances don't need to contain any of the keys, only the values associated with them.

Named tuples are created using a factory function from the collections module, called namedtuple(). Rather than returning an individual object, namedtuple() returns a new class, which is customized for a given set of names. The first argument is the name of the tuple class itself, but the second is, unfortunately, less straightforward. It takes a string of attribute names, which are separated by either a space or a comma:

```
>>> from collections import namedtuple
>>> Point = namedtuple('Point', 'x y')
>>> point = Point(13, 25)
>>> point
Point(x=13, y=25)
>>> point.x, point.y
```

```
(13, 25)
>>> point[0], point[1]
(13, 25)
```

As an efficient trade-off between tuples and dictionaries, many functions that need to return multiple values can do so using named tuples to be as useful as possible. There's no need to populate a full dictionary, but values can still be referenced by useful names rather than integer indexes.

Ordered Dictionaries

If you've ever iterated over the keys of a dictionary or printed its contents to the interactive prompt, as has been done previously in this chapter, you'll notice that its keys don't always follow a predictable order. Sometimes they may look like they're sorted numerically or alphabetically, but other times it seems completely random.

Dictionary keys, like sets, are considered to be unordered. Even though there may occasionally appear to be patterns, these are merely the by-product of the implementation and aren't formally defined. Not only is the ordering inconsistent from one dictionary to another, variations are even more significant when using a different Python implementation, such as Jython or IronPython.

Most of the time, what you're really looking for from a dictionary is a way to map specific keys to associated values, so the ordering of the keys is irrelevant. Sometimes, though, it's also useful to be able to iterate over those keys in a reliable manner. To offer the best of both worlds, Python offers the OrderedDict class by way of its collections module. This provides all the features of a dictionary but with reliable ordering of keys:

```
>>> from collections import OrderedDict
>>> d = OrderedDict((value, str(value)) for value in range(10) if value > 5)
>>> d
OrderedDict([(6, '6'), (7, '7'), (8, '8'), (9, '9')])
>>> d[10] = '10'
>>> d
```

```
OrderedDict([(6, '6'), (7, '7'), (8, '8'), (9, '9'), (10, '10')])
>>> del d[7]
>>> d
OrderedDict([(6, '6'), (8, '8'), (9, '9'), (10, '10')])
```

As you can see, the same construction used previously now results in a properly ordered dictionary that does the right thing even as you add and remove items.

Caution   In the example given here, notice that the values for the dictionary are provided using a generator expression. If you supply a standard dictionary, that means your supplied values are unordered prior to going into the ordered database, which will then assume that order was intentional and preserve it. This also occurs if you supply values as keyword arguments, because those are passed as a regular dictionary internally. The only reliable way to supply ordering to OrderedDict() is to use a standard sequence, such as a list or a generator expression.

Dictionaries with Defaults

Another common pattern using dictionaries is to always assume some default value in the event that a key can't be found in the mapping. This behavior can be achieved either by explicitly catching the KeyError raised when accessing the key or by using the available get() method, which can return a suitable default if the key wasn't found. One such example of this pattern is using a dictionary to track how many times each word appears in some text:

```
def count_words(text):
    count = {}
    for word in text.split(' '):
        current = count.get(word, 0) # Make sure we always have a number
        count[word] = current + 1
    return count
```

Instead of having to deal with that extra `get()` call, the `collections` module provides a `defaultdict` class that can handle that step for you. When you create it, you can pass in a callable as the single argument, which will be used to create a new value when a requested key doesn't exist. In most cases you can just supply one of the built-in types, which will provide a useful basic value to work with. In the case of `count_words()`, we can use `int`:

```python
from collections import defaultdict

def count_words(text):
    count = defaultdict(int)
    for word in text.split(' '):
        count[word] += 1
    return count
```

Essentially any callable can be used, but the built-in types tend to provide optimal default values for whatever you need to work with. Using `list` will give you an empty list, `str` returns an empty string, `int` returns 0, and `dict` returns an empty dictionary. If you have more specialized needs, any callable that can be used without any arguments will work. Chapter 3 introduces lambda functions, which are convenient for cases like this.

Importing Code

Complex Python applications are typically made up of a number of different modules, often separated into packages to supply more granular namespaces. Importing code from one module to another is a simple matter, but that's only part of the story. There are several additional features available for more specific situations that you're likely to run into.

Fallback Imports

By now, you've seen several points where Python changes over time, sometimes in backward-incompatible ways. One particular change that tends to come up occasionally is when a module gets moved or renamed, but still does essentially the same thing as before. The only update needed to make your code work with it is to change to the import location, but you'll often need to maintain compatibility with versions both before and after the change.

The solution to this problem exploits Python's exception handling to determine whether the module exists at the new location. Because imports are processed at runtime, like any other statement, you can wrap them in a `try` block and catch an `ImportError`, which is raised if the import failed. Here's how you might import a common hash algorithm both before and after the change in Python 2.5, which moved its import location:

```
try:
    # Use the new library if available. Added in Python 2.5
    from hashlib import md5
except ImportError:
    # Compatible functionality provided prior to Python 2.5
    from md5 import new as md5
```

Notice here that the import prefers the newer library first. That's because changes like this usually have a grace period, where the old location is still available but deprecated. If you check for the older module first, you'll find it long after the new module became available. By checking for the new one first, you take advantage of any newer features or added behaviors as soon as they're available, falling back to older functionality only when necessary. Using the `as` keyword allows the rest of the module to simply reference the name `md5` either way.

This technique is just as applicable to third-party modules as it is to Python's own standard library, but third-party applications often require different handling. Rather than determining which module to use, it's often necessary to distinguish whether the application is available at all. This is determined the same way as the previous example, by wrapping the import statement in a `try` block.

What happens next, however, depends on how your application should behave if the module is unavailable. Some modules are strictly required, so if it's missing, you should raise an exception directly inside the `except ImportError` block or simply forgo exception handling altogether. Other times, a missing third-party module simply means a reduction in functionality. In this case, the most common approach is to assign `None` to the variable that would otherwise contain the imported module:

```
try:
    import docutils  # Common Python-based documentation tools
except ImportError:
    docutils = None
```

Then, when your code needs to utilize features in the imported module, it can use something like if docutils to see if the module is available, without having to reimport it.

Importing from the Future

Python's release schedule often incorporates new features, but it's not always a good idea to just introduce them out of nowhere. In particular, syntax additions and behavior changes may break existing code, so it's often necessary to provide a bit of a grace period. During the transition, these new features are made available by way of a special kind of import, letting you choose which features are updated for each module.

The special __future__ module allows you to name specific features that you'd like to use in a given module. This provides a simple compatibility path for your modules, since some modules can rely on new features while other modules can use existing features. Typically, the next release after a feature was added to __future__, and it becomes a standard feature available to all modules.

As a quick example, Python 3.0 changed the way integer division worked. In earlier versions, dividing one integer from another always resulted in an integer, which often resulted in a loss of precision if the result would normally produce a remainder. That makes sense to programmers who are familiar with the underlying C implementation, but it's different than what happens if you perform the same calculation on a standard calculator, so it caused a lot of confusion.

The behavior of division was changed to return floating point values if the division would contain a remainder, thus matching how a standard calculator would work. Before making the change across all of Python, however, the division option was added to the __future__ module, allowing the behavior to be changed earlier if necessary. Here's how an interactive interpreter session might look in Python 2.5. Python 3.x, however, by default handles it as if you promoted one to a floating point value as in >>> 5 / 2.0:

```
>>> 5 / 2  # Python 2.5 uses integer-only division by default
2
>>> from __future__ import division  # This updates the behavior of division
>>> 5 / 2
2.5
```

The __future__ module supports a number of such features, and new options are added with each release of Python. Rather than trying to list them all here, in the rest of this book I will mention them when the features being described were recent enough to need a __future__ import in older versions of Python, back to Python 2.5. Full details on these feature changes can always be found on the "What's New" page of the Python documentation.[1]

Note   If you try to import a feature from __future__ that already exists in the version of Python you're using, it doesn't do anything. The feature is already available, so no changes have to be made, but it also doesn't raise any exceptions.

Using __all__ to Customize Imports

One of the lesser-used features of Python imports is the ability to import the namespace from one module into that of another. This is achieved by using an asterisk as the portion of the module to import:

```
>>> from itertools import *
>>> list(chain([1, 2, 3], [4, 5, 6]))
[1, 2, 3, 4, 5, 6]
```

---

[1]See the "What's New" page at http://propython.com/whats-new.

Ordinarily, this would just take all the entries in the imported module's namespace that don't begin with an underscore and dump them into the current module's namespace. It can save some typing in modules that make heavy use of the imported module, because it saves you from having to include the module name every time you access one of its attributes.

Sometimes, however, it doesn't make sense for every object to be made available in this way. In particular, frameworks often include a number of utility functions and classes that are useful within the framework's module, but don't make much sense when exported to external code. In order to control what objects get exported when you import a module like this, you can specify __all__ somewhere in the module.

All that you need to do is supply a list—or some other sequence—that contains the names of objects that should get imported when the module is imported using an asterisk. Additional objects can still be imported either by importing the name directly or by just importing the module itself, rather than anything inside of it. Here's how an example module might supply its __all__ option:

```python
__all__ = ['public_func']

def public_func():
    pass

def utility_func():
    pass
```

Of course, there would be useful code in both of those functions in the real world. For the purposes of illustration, though, here's a quick rundown of the different ways that you could import that module, which we'll call example:

```
>>> import example
>>> example.public_func
<function public_func at 0x...>
>>> example.utility_func
<function utility_func at 0x...>
```

```
>>> from example import *
>>> public_func
<function public_func at 0x...>
>>> utility_func
Traceback (most recent call last):
  ...
NameError: name 'utility_func' is not defined
>>> from example import utility_func
>>> utility_func
<function utility_func at 0x...>
```

Notice how, in the final case, you can still import it directly using the from syntax, as long as you specify it explicitly. The only time __all__ comes into play is if you use an asterisk. So depending on if you want all functions available, or only one, you have choices.

EXPLICIT IS BETTER THAN IMPLICIT

It's generally considered bad form to import using the asterisk notation in the first place; PEP 8, the Python Style Guide, specifically recommends against it. The main issue with it is that it's not immediately obvious where the contents of that module came from. If you see a function used without a module namespace, you can usually look at the top of the module to see if it was imported; if not, you can safely assume that it was defined in the module. If it was imported with the asterisk notation, you'd have to either scan the entire module to see if it was defined or open up the source for the related module to see if it was defined there.

On occasion, it can still be useful to import using an asterisk, but it's best to only do so when you're wrapping it in another namespace. As illustrated in Chapter 11, you might allow your users to import a single root namespace that incorporates objects from several different modules. Rather than having to update the imports every time something new is added, you can use asterisk imports in the main module, without introducing any ambiguity in your users' modules.

Relative Imports

When starting out with a project, you'll spend most of your time importing from external packages, so every import is absolute; its path is rooted in your system's PYTHONPATH. Once your projects start growing to several modules, you'll be importing from one another regularly. And once you establish a hierarchy, you might realize that you don't want to include the full import path when sharing code between two modules at similar parts of the tree.

Python allows you to specify a relative path to the module you'd like to import, so you can move around an entire package, if necessary, with minimal modifications required. The preferred syntax for this is to specify part of the module's path with one or more periods, indicating how far up the path to look for the module. For example, if the `acme.shopping.cart` module needs to import from `acme.billing`, the two following import patterns are identical:

```
from acme import billing
from .. import billing
```

A single period allows you to import from the current package, so `acme.shopping.gallery` could be imported as `from . import gallery`. Alternatively, if you're looking to just import something from that module, you could instead simply prefix the module path with the necessary periods, then specify the names to import as usual: `from .gallery import Image`.

The __import__() Function

You don't always have to place your imports at the top of a module. In fact, sometimes you might not be able to write some of your imports in advance at all. You might be making decisions about which module to import based on user-supplied settings, or perhaps you're even allowing users to specify modules directly. These user-supplied settings are a convenient way to allow for extensibility without resorting to automatic discovery.

In order to support this functionality, Python allows you to import code manually using the `__import__()` function. It's a built-in function, so it's available everywhere, but using it requires some explanation because it's not as straightforward as some of the other features provided by Python. You can choose from five arguments to customize how a module gets imported and what contents are retrieved:

- `name`: The only argument that is always required, this accepts the name of the module that should be loaded. If it's part of a package, just separate each part of the path with a period, as when using `import path.to.module`.

- `globals`: A namespace dictionary that is used to define the context in which the module name is resolved. In standard `import` cases, the return value from the built-in `globals()` function is used to populate this argument.

- `locals`: Another namespace dictionary, ideally used to help define the context in which the module name is resolved. In reality, however, current implementations of Python simply ignore it. In the event of future support, the standard import provides the return value from the built-in `locals()` function for this argument.

- `fromlist`: A list of individual names that should be imported from the module, rather than importing the full module.

- `level`: An integer indicating how the path should be resolved with respect to the module that calls `__import__()`. A value of -1 allows both absolute and implicit relative imports; 0 allows only absolute imports; positive values indicate how many levels up the path to use for an explicit relative import.

Even though that may seem simple enough, the return value contains a few traps that can cause quite a bit of confusion. It always returns a module object, but it can be surprising to see which module is returned and what attributes are available on it. Because there are a number of different ways to import modules, these variations are worth understanding. First, let's examine how different types of module names impact the return value.

In the simplest case, you'd pass in a single module name to __import__(), and the return value is just what you'd expect: the module referenced by the name provided. The attributes available on that module object are the same as you'd have available if you imported that name directly in your code: the entire namespace that was declared in that module's code.

When you pass in a more complex module path, however, the return value may not match expectations. Complex paths are provided using the same dot-separated syntax used in your source files, so importing os.path, for instance, would be achieved by passing in "os.path". The returned value in that case is os, but the path attribute lets you access the module you're really looking for.

The reason for that variation is that __import__() mimics the behavior of Python source files, in which import os.path makes the os module available under that name. You can still access os.path, but the module that goes into the main namespace is os. Because __import__() works essentially the same way as a standard import, what you get in the return value is what you would have in the main module namespace ordinarily.

In order to get just the module at the end of the module path, you can take a couple of different approaches. The most obvious, although not necessarily direct, would be to split the given module name on periods, using each portion of the path to get each attribute layer from the module returned by __import__(). Here's a simple function that would do the job:

```
>>> def import_child(module_name):
...     module = __import__(module_name)
...     for layer in module_name.split('.')[1:]:
...         module = getattr(module, layer)
...     return module
...
>>> import_child('os.path')
<module 'ntpath' from 'C:\Python31\lib\ntpath.py'>
>>> import_child('os')
<module 'os' from 'C:\Python31\lib\os.py'>
```

Note   The exact name of the module referenced by `os.path` will vary based on the operating system under which it's imported. For example, it's called `ntpath` on Windows, whereas most Linux systems use `posixpath`. Most of the contents are the same, but they may behave slightly differently depending on the needs of the operating system, and each may have additional attributes that are unique to that environment.

As you can see, it works for the simple case as well as more complex situations, but it still goes through a bit more work than is really necessary to do the job. Of course, the time spent on the loop is fairly insignificant compared to the import itself, but if the module had already been imported, our `import_path()` function comprises most of the process. An alternate approach takes advantage of Python's own module caching mechanism to take the extra processing out of the picture:

```
>>> import sys
>>> def import_child(module_name):
...     __import__(module_name)
...     return sys.modules[module_name]
...
>>> import_child('os.path')
<module 'ntpath' from 'C:\Python31\lib\ntpath.py'>
>>> import_child('os')
<module 'os' from 'C:\Python31\lib\os.py'>
```

The `sys.modules` dictionary maps import paths to the module objects that were generated when importing them. By looking up the module in that dictionary, there's no need to mess around with the particulars of the module name.

Of course, this is really only applicable to absolute imports. Relative imports, no matter how they are referenced, are resolved relative to the module where the import statement—or in this case, the `__import__()` function call—is located. Because the most common case is to place `import_path()` in a common location, relative imports would be resolved relative to that, rather than the module that called `import_path()`. That could mean importing the completely wrong module.

The importlib Module

In order to address the issues that are raised by using __import__() directly, Python also includes the importlib module, which provides a more intuitive interface to import modules. The import_module() function is a much simpler way to achieve the same effect as __import__(), but in a way that more closely matches expectations.

For absolute imports, import_module() accepts the module path, just like __import__(). The difference, however, is that import_module() always returns the last module in the path, while __import__() returns the first one. The extra handling that was added in the previous section is made completely unnecessary because of this functionality, so this is a much better approach to use:

```
>>> from importlib import import_module
>>> import_module('os.path')
<module 'ntpath' from 'C:\Python31\lib\ntpath.py'>
>>> import_module('os')
<module 'os' from 'C:\Python31\lib\os.py'>
```

In addition, import_module() takes relative imports into account by also accepting a package attribute that defines the reference point from which the relative path should be resolved. This is easily done when calling the function, simply by passing in the always-global __name__ variable, which holds the module path that was used to import the current module in the first place:

```
import_module('.utils', package=__name__)
```

Caution   Relative imports don't work directly inside the interactive interpreter. The module the interpreter runs in isn't actually in the filesystem, so there are no relative paths to work with.

Exciting Python Extensions: Random Number Beacon at NIST

Most programming languages implement some form of random and pseudo-random number generator. Python does as well; however, the base algorithm which generates these random numbers is less robust than could be had elsewhere. As such, the National Institute of Standards and Technology (NIST) has implemented a randomness beacon which sends out every 60 seconds to connected users a true random number.

From May 2018, NIST states: "NIST is implementing a source of public randomness. The service (at `https://beacon.nist.gov/home`) uses two independent commercially available sources of randomness, each with an independent hardware entropy source and SP 800-90-approved components. The Beacon is designed to provide *unpredictability, autonomy, and consistency. Unpredictability* means that users cannot algorithmically predict bits before they are made available by the source. *Autonomy* means that the source is resistant to attempts by outside parties to alter the distribution of the random bits. *Consistency* means that a set of users can access the source in such a way that they are confident they all receive the same random string."[2]

You could think of the randomness beacon as a good way to obtain somewhat reliable randomness every 60 seconds for applications requiring a random value, such as a game. The term "somewhat" is used here to note that NIST says not to use their service for cryptographic needs, and certainly many people assert that the beacon is not really secure due to connections between NIST and NSA, and the fact that within the 60-second window the "randomness" could be compromised. However, all that being said, it is still an interesting and, the authors feel, valid service to have in your toolbox. To use the service you will need to install the library's required `https://www.nist.gov/programs-projects/nist-randomness-beacon` for access first.

---

[2]NIST, "NIST Randomness Beacon," `https://www.nist.gov/programs-projects/nist-randomness-beacon`, accessed May 22, 2018.

How to Install the NIST Beacon Library

Regardless of your platform, you can use the NIST beacon with Python. Information about versions and updates can be found at NIST or `https://pypi.org/project/nistbeacon/0.9.2`. Assuming you are using MS Windows and have pip installed and are online, it is as easy to install as:

`pip install nistbeacon  (press enter)`

Assuming you received no errors from the install, try a few of the following examples to get a feel for how the beacon works.

Simple Example to Get a Value

In the following example a 512 Hexadecimal (base 16) value is obtained from the beacon, displayed and converted to decimal. A random value is also obtained, in the range of 1 through 10, and displayed. Typing *record.* will display many other function options if using IDLE or other full-functioning IDEs.

```
#Get a 512 hex value from the beacon and display it
from nistbeacon import NistBeacon

record = NistBeacon.get_last_record()
v = record.output_value # 512 hex
r = record.pseudo_random # pick a pseudo random number
print ('Your random follows: ')
print (r.randint(1,10))  #print 1 - 10 random  #random())for floats .0 to 1.0
print()
print ('Hex original value:\n', v, '\n')
d=int(v,16) #convert to decimal
print ('Hex value converted to decimal:\n', d)
```

Example to Simulate Rolling Coin Flipping a Certain # Times and Display Heads or Tails

In this example a record is obtained every 66 seconds, converted to decimal, then run against modulus (remainder of integer division) to see if it is "odd" for "even," to simulate "heads" or "tails":

```
#Coin flip-O-matic
from nistbeacon import NistBeacon
import time
print()
print ('Coin flip 0 or 1 tails or heads')
print()
print ('Run five times')
for count in range (5):
    time.sleep(66)  #wait for new beacon every 66 seconds
    h = NistBeacon.get_last_record()
    v = h.output_value #512 hex
    d=int(v,16) #convert to decimal
    coin = d% 2 #modulus of record (0 or 1)
    if coin == 0:
        print ('tails')
    else:
        print ('heads')
```

Taking It With You

The features laid out in this chapter are just a taste of what Python has to offer if you're willing to take the time to learn the language. The rest of this book will rely heavily on what was laid out here, but each chapter will add another layer for future chapters to build on as well. In that spirit, let's continue with what you thought was one of the most basic, unassuming features of Python: *functions*.

CHAPTER 3

Functions

At the core of any programming language is the notion of functions, but we tend to take them for granted. Sure, there's the obvious fact that functions allow code to be encapsulated into individual units, which can be reused rather than being duplicated all over the place. But Python takes this beyond just the notion of what some languages allow, with functions being full-fledged objects that can be passed around in data structures, wrapped in other functions, or replaced entirely by new implementations.

In fact, Python provides enough flexibility with functions that there are actually several different types of functions, reflecting the various forms of declaration and purposes. Understanding each of these types of functions will help you decide which is appropriate for each situation you encounter while working with your own code. This chapter explains each of them in turn, as well as a variety of features you can take advantage of to extend the value of each function you create, regardless of its type.

At their core all functions are essentially equal, regardless of which of the following sections they fit into. The built-in function type forms their basis, containing all the attributes necessary for Python to understand how to use them:

```
>>> def example():
...     pass
...
>>> type(example)
<type 'function'>
>>> example
<function example at 0x...>
```

Of course, there are still a number of different types of functions and as many different ways of declaring them. First off, let's examine one of the most universal aspects of functions.

© J. Burton Browning and Marty Alchin 2019
J. B. Browning and M. Alchin, *Pro Python 3*, https://doi.org/10.1007/978-1-4842-4385-5_3

Arguments

Most functions need to take some arguments in order to do anything useful. Normally, that means defining them in order in the function (the declaration's) signature, and then supplying them in the same order when calling that function later. Python supports that model, but also supports passing keyword arguments and even arguments that won't be known until the function is called.

One of the most common advantages of Python's keyword arguments is that you can pass arguments in a different order than the way they were defined in the function. You can even skip arguments entirely, as long as they have a default value defined. This flexibility helps encourage the use of functions that support lots of arguments with default values.

EXPLICIT IS BETTER THAN IMPLICIT

One way that Python's keyword arguments encourage being explicit is to only allow arguments to be passed out of order if they're passed by keyword. Without keywords, Python needs to use the position of the argument to know which parameter name to bind to it when the function runs. Because keywords are just as explicit as positions, the ordering requirement can be lifted without introducing ambiguity.

In fact, keywords are even more explicit than positions when working with arguments, because the function call documents the purpose of each argument. Otherwise, you'd have to look up the function definition in order to understand its arguments. Some arguments may be understandable in context, but most optional arguments aren't obvious at a glance, so passing them with keywords makes for more readable code.

Planning for Flexibility

Planning parameter names, order, and default values is particularly important for functions intended to be called by someone who didn't write them, such as those in distributed applications. If you don't know the exact needs of the users who will eventually be using your code, it's best to move any assumptions you may have into arguments that can be overridden later.

As an extremely simple example, consider a function that appends a prefix to a string:

```
def add_prefix(my_string):
    """Adds a 'pro_' prefix before the new string is returned."""
    return 'pro_' + my_string
final_string=input('Enter a string so we can put pro_ in front of it!:  ')
print(add_prefix(final_string))
```

The 'pro_' prefix here may make sense for the application it was written for, but what happens when anything else wants to use it? Right now, the prefix is hard-coded into the body of the function itself, so there's no available alternative. Moving that assumption into an argument makes for an easy way to customize the function later:

```
def add_prefix(my_string, prefix='pro_'):
    """Adds a 'pro_' prefix before the string provided, a default value."""
    return prefix + my_string
final_string=input("Enter a string so we can put pro_ in front of it!:  ")
print(add_prefix(final_string))
```

The function call without the prefix argument doesn't need to change, so existing code works just fine. The section on preloading arguments later in this chapter shows how even the prefix can be changed and still be used by code that doesn't know about it.

Of course, this example is far too simple to provide much real-world value, but the functions illustrated throughout the rest of this book will take advantage of plenty of optional arguments, showing their value in each situation.

Variable Positional Arguments

Most functions are designed to work on a specific set of arguments, but some can handle any number of arguments, acting on each in turn. These may be passed into a single argument as a tuple, list, or other iterable.

Take a typical shopping cart, for example. Adding items to the cart could be done one at a time or in batches. Using a definition of a class, with a function inside, here's how it *could* be done, using a standard argument:

```
class ShoppingCart:
    def add_to_cart(items):
        self.items.extend(items)
```

That would certainly do the trick, but now consider what that means for all the code that has to call it. The common case would be to add just a single item, but as the function always accepts a list, it would end up looking something like this:

```
cart.add_to_cart([item])
```

So we've basically sabotaged the majority case in order to support the minority. Worse yet, if add_to_cart() originally supported just one item and was changed to support multiples, this syntax would break any existing calls, requiring you to rewrite them just to avoid a TypeError.

Ideally, the method should support the standard syntax for single arguments, while still supporting multiple arguments. By adding an asterisk before an argument name, you can specify that that all remaining positional arguments are collected into one tuple bound to the argument prefixed with an asterisk that didn't get assigned to anything before it. In this case there are no other arguments, so variable positional arguments can make up the entire argument list:

```
    def add_to_cart(*items):
        self.items.extend(items)
```

Now, the method can be called with any number of positional arguments rather than having to group those arguments first into a tuple or list. The extra arguments are bundled in a tuple automatically before the function starts executing. This cleans up the common case, while still enabling more arguments as needs require. Here are a few examples of how the method could be called:

```
cart.add_to_cart(item)
cart.add_to_cart(item1, item2)
cart.add_to_cart(item1, item2, item3, item4, item5)
```

There is still one more way to call this function that allows the calling code to support any number of items as well, but it's not specific to functions that are designed to accept variable arguments. See the section on invoking functions with variable arguments for all the details.

Variable Keyword Arguments

Functions may need to take extra configuration options, particularly if passing those options to some other library further down the line. The obvious approach would be to accept a dictionary, which can map configuration names to their values:

```
class ShoppingCart:
    def __init__(self, options):
        self.options = options
```

Unfortunately, that ends up with a problem similar to the one we encountered with positional arguments described in the previous section. The simple case in which you only override one or two values gets fairly complicated. Here are two ways the function call could look, depending on preference:

```
options = {'currency': 'USD'}
cart = ShoppingCart(options)

cart = ShoppingCart({'currency': 'USD'})
```

Of course, this approach doesn't scale any prettier than the list provided in the positional argument problem from the previous section. Also, like the previous problem, this can be problematic. If the function you're working with were previously set up to accept some explicit keyword arguments, the new dictionary argument would break compatibility.

Instead, Python offers the ability to pass a variable number of keyword arguments by adding two asterisks before the name of the argument that will accept them. This allows for the much friendlier keyword argument syntax, while still allowing for a fully dynamic function call. Examine the following stub:

```
def __init__(self, **options):
    self.options = options
```

Now consider what that same stub function from earlier would look like, given that the function now takes arbitrary keyword arguments:

```
cart = ShoppingCart(currency='USD')
```

Caution   When working with variable arguments, there's one difference between positional and keyword arguments that can cause problems. Positional arguments are grouped into a tuple, which is immutable, while keyword arguments are placed into a dictionary, which is mutable (changeable).

BEAUTIFUL IS BETTER THAN UGLY

The second function call example here is a classic example of code that would generally be considered ugly by many Python programmers. The sheer volume of punctuation—quotation marks around both the key and value, a colon between them, and curly braces around the whole thing—inside the already necessary parentheses make it very cluttered and difficult to process at a glance.

E.g. `cart = ShoppingCart({'currency': 'USD'})`

By switching to keyword arguments, as shown in this section, the appearance of the code is considerably better aligned with Python's core values and philosophy. Beauty may be subjective in its very nature, but certain subjective decisions are praised by the vast majority of the programmers.

Combining Different Kinds of Arguments

These options for variable arguments combine with the standard options, such as required and optional arguments. In order to make sure everything meshes nicely, Python has some very specific rules for defining parameters in a function signature. There are only four types of arguments, listed here in the order they generally appear in functions:

- Required arguments
- Optional arguments
- Variable number of positional arguments
- Variable keyword arguments

Putting the required arguments first in the list ensures that positional arguments satisfy the required arguments prior to getting into the optional arguments. Variable arguments can only pick up values that didn't fit into anything else, so they naturally get defined at the end. Here's how this stub would look in a typical function definition:

```
def create_element(name, editable=True, *children, **attributes):
```

This same ordering can be used when calling functions, but it has one shortcoming. In this example, you'd have to supply a value for editable as a positional argument in order to pass in any children at all. It'd be better to be able to supply them right after the name, avoiding the optional editable argument entirely most of the time.

To support this, Python also allows variable positional arguments to be placed among standard arguments. Both required and optional arguments can be positioned after the variable argument, but now they must be passed by keyword. All the arguments are still available, but the less common ones become more optional when not required and more explicit when they do make sense.

IN THE FACE OF AMBIGUITY, REFUSE THE TEMPTATION TO GUESS

By allowing positional arguments in the middle of a list of explicit arguments, Python might have introduced a considerable ambiguity. Consider a function defined to pass commands through to an arbitrary argument: perform_action(action, *args, log_output=False). Ordinarily, you can supply enough positional arguments to reach even the optional arguments, but in this case, what would happen if you supplied three or more values?

One possible interpretation is to give the first value to the first argument, the last value to the last argument, and everything else to the variable argument. That could work, but then it comes down to a guess as to the intent of the programmer making the call. Once you consider a function with even more arguments behind the variable argument, the possible interpretations become quite numerous.

Instead, Python strictly enforces that everything after the variable argument becomes accessible by keyword only. Positional argument values beyond those explicitly defined in the function go straight into the variable argument, whether just one or dozens were provided. The implementation becomes easy to explain by having just one way to do it, and it's even more explicit by enforcing the use of keywords.

An added feature of this behavior is that explicit arguments placed after variable positional arguments can still be required. The only real difference between the two types of placement is the requirement of using keyword arguments; whether the argument requires a value still depends on whether you define a default argument:

```
>>> def join_with_prefix(prefix, *segments, delimiter):
...     return delimiter.join(prefix + segment for segment in segments)
...
>>> join_with_prefix('P', 'ro', 'ython')
Traceback (most recent call last):
  ...
TypeError: join_with_prefix() needs keyword-only argument delimiter
>>> join_with_prefix('P', 'ro', 'ython', ' ')
Traceback (most recent call last):
  ...
TypeError: join_with_prefix() needs keyword-only argument delimiter
>>> join_with_prefix('P', 'ro', 'ython', delimiter=' ')
'Pro Python'
```

Note   If you want to accept keyword-only arguments but you don't have a good use for variable positional arguments, simply specify a single asterisk without an argument name. This tells Python that everything after the asterisk is keyword-only, without also accepting potentially long sets of positional arguments. One caveat is that if you also accept variable keyword arguments, you must supply at least one explicit keyword argument. Otherwise, there's really no point in using the bare asterisk notation, and Python will raise a SyntaxError.

In fact, remember that the ordering requirements of required and optional arguments are solely intended for the case of positional arguments. With the ability to define arguments as being keyword-only, you're now free to define them as required and optional in any order, without any complaints from Python. Ordering isn't important when calling the function, so it's also not important when defining the function. Consider rewriting the previous example to require the prefix as a keyword argument, while also making the delimiter optional:

```
>>> def join_with_prefix(*segments, delimiter=' ', prefix):
...     return delimiter.join(prefix + segment for segment in segments)
>>> join_with_prefix('ro', 'ython', prefix='P')
'Pro Python'
```

Caution   Be careful taking advantage of this level of flexibility, because it's not very straightforward compared to how Python code is typically written. It's certainly possible, but it runs contrary to what most Python programmers will expect, which can make it difficult to maintain in the long run.

In all cases, however, variable keyword arguments must be positioned at the end of the list, after all other types of arguments.

Invoking Functions with Variable Arguments

In addition to being able to define arguments that can accept any number of values, the same syntax can be used to pass values into a function call. The big advantage to this is that it's not restricted to arguments that were defined to be variable in nature. Instead, you can pass variable arguments into any function, regardless of how it was defined. The * unpacks an iterable and passes its contents as separate arguments.

The same asterisk (*) notation is used to specify variable arguments, which are then expanded into a function call as if all the arguments were specified directly. A single asterisk specifies positional arguments, while two asterisks specify keyword arguments. This is especially useful when passing in the return value of a function call directly as an argument, without assigning it to individual variables first:

```
>>> value = 'ro ython'
>>> join_with_prefix(*value.split(' '), prefix='P')
```

This example seems obvious on its own, because it's a variable argument being passed in to a variable argument, but the same process works just fine on other types of functions as well. Because the arguments get expanded before getting passed to the function, it can be used with any function, regardless of how its arguments were specified. It can even be used with built-in functions and those defined by extensions written in C.

Note   You can only pass in one set of variable positional arguments and one set of variable keyword arguments in a function call. If you have two lists of positional arguments, for example, you'll need to join them together yourself and pass that combined list into the function instead of trying to use the two separately.

Passing Arguments

When you start adding a number of arguments to function calls, many of which are optional, it becomes fairly common to know some of the argument values that will need to be passed, even if it's still long before the function will actually be called. Rather than having to pass in all the arguments at the time the call is made, it can be quite useful to apply some of those arguments in advance, so fewer can be applied later.

This concept is officially called partial application of the function, but the function doesn't get called at all yet, so it's really more a matter of preloading some of the arguments in advance. When the preloaded function is called later, any arguments passed along are added to those that were provided earlier.

WHAT ABOUT CURRYING?

If you're familiar with other forms of functional programming, you may have heard of *currying*, which may look very similar to preloading arguments. Some frameworks have even provided functions named `curry()` that can preload arguments on a function, which leads to even more confusion. The difference between the two is subtle but important.

With a truly curried function, you must call it as many times as necessary to fill up all of the arguments. If a function accepts three arguments and you call it with just one argument, you'd get back a function that accepts two more arguments. If you call that new function, it still won't execute your code but will instead load the next argument and return another function that takes the last remaining argument. Calling that function will finally satisfy all the arguments, so the actual code will be executed and return a useful value.

Partial application returns a function which, when called later, will at least try to execute code, no matter how many arguments may remain. If there are required arguments that haven't gotten a value yet, Python will raise a TypeError just like it would if you had called it with missing arguments any other time. So even though there are certainly similarities between the two techniques, it's important to understand the difference.

This behavior is provided as part of the built-in functools module, by way of its partial() function. By passing in a callable and any number of positional and keyword arguments, it will return a new callable that can be used later to apply those arguments:

```
>>> import os
>>> def load_file(file, base_path='/', mode='rb'):
...     return open(os.path.join(base_path, file), mode)
...
>>> f = load_file('example.txt')
>>> f.mode
'rb'
>>> f.close()

>>> import functools
>>> load_writable = functools.partial(load_file, mode='w')
>>> f = load_writable('example.txt')
>>> f.mode
'w'
>>> f.close()
```

Note   The technique of preloading arguments is true for the partial() function, but the technique of passing one function into another to get a new function back is generally known as a *decorator or higher order function*. Decorators, as you'll see later in this chapter, can perform any number of tasks when called; preloading arguments is just one example.

This is commonly used to customize a more flexible function into something simpler, so it can be passed into an API that doesn't know how to access that flexibility. By preloading the custom arguments beforehand, the code behind the API can call your function with the arguments it knows how to use, but all the arguments will still come into play.

Caution   When using `functools.partial()`, you won't be able to provide any new values for those arguments that were previously loaded. This is, of course, standard behavior any time you try to supply multiple values for a single argument, but the situation comes up much more often when you're not supplying them all in the same function call. For an alternative approach that addresses this issue, see the "Decorators" section of this chapter.

Introspection

Python is very transparent, allowing code to inspect many aspects of objects at runtime. Because functions are objects like any others, there are several things that your code can glean from them, including the function signature, which specifies parameters. Obtaining a function's arguments directly requires going through a fairly complicated set of attributes that describe Python's bytecode structures, but thankfully Python also provides some functions to make it easier.

Many of Python's introspection features are available as part of the standard `inspect` module, with its `getfullargspec()` function being of use for function arguments. It accepts the function to be inspected and returns a named tuple of information about that function's arguments. The returned tuple contains values for every aspect of an argument specification:

- `args`: A list of explicit argument names

- `varargs`: The name of the variable positional argument

- `varkw`: The name of the variable keyword argument

- `defaults`: A tuple of default values for explicit arguments

- `kwonlyargs`: A list of keyword-only argument names

- kwonlydefaults: A dictionary of default values for keyword-only arguments

- annotations: A dictionary of argument annotations, which will be explained later in this chapter

To better illustrate what values are present in each part of the tuple, here's how it maps out to a basic function declaration:

```
>>> def example(a=1, b=1, *c, d, e=2, **f) -> str:
...     pass
...
>>> import inspect
>>> inspect.getfullargspec(example)
FullArgSpec(args=['a', 'b'], varargs='c', varkw='f', defaults=(1,),
kwonlyargs=[
'd', 'e'], kwonlydefaults={'e': 2}, annotations={'a': <class 'int'>,
'return': <
class 'str'>})
```

Example: Identifying Argument Values

Sometimes it can be useful to log what arguments a function will receive, regardless of which function it is or what its arguments look like. This behavior often comes into play in systems that generate argument lists based on something other than a Python function call. Some examples include instructions from a template language and regular expressions that parse text input.

Unfortunately, positional arguments present a bit of a problem because their values don't include the name of the argument they'll be sent to. Default values also pose a problem because the function call doesn't need to include any values at all. Because the log should include all the values that will be given to the function, both of these problems will need to be addressed.

First, the easy part. Any argument values passed by keyword don't need to be matched up with anything manually, as the argument names are provided right with the values. Rather than concerning ourselves with logging at the outset, let's start with a function to get all the arguments in a dictionary that can be logged. The function accepts a function, a tuple of positional arguments, and a dictionary of keyword arguments:

```python
def example(a=1, b=1, *c, d, e=2, **f) -> str:
    pass

def get_arguments(func, args, kwargs):
    """
    Given a function and a set of arguments, return a dictionary
    of argument values that will be sent to the function.
    We are modifying get_arguments by adding new parts to it.
    """
    arguments = kwargs.copy()
    return arguments

print(get_arguments(example, (1,), {'f': 4}))  #will yield a result
of:  {'f': 4}
```

That really was easy. The function makes a copy of the keyword arguments instead of just returning it directly because we'll be adding entries to that dictionary soon enough. Next, we have to deal with positional arguments. The trick is to identify which argument names map to the positional argument values, so that those values can be added to the dictionary with the appropriate names. This is where `inspect.getfullargspec()` comes into play, using `zip()` to do the heavy lifting:

```python
def example(a=1, b=1, *c, d, e=2, **f) -> str:
    pass

import inspect
def get_arguments(func, args, kwargs):
```

97

```
    """
    Given a function and a set of arguments, return a dictionary
    of argument values that will be sent to the function.
    """
    arguments = kwargs.copy()
    spec = inspect.getfullargspec(func)
    arguments.update(zip(spec.args, args))

    return arguments

print(get_arguments(example, (1,), {'f': 4}))  # will output {'a': 1, 'f': 4}
```

Now that the positional arguments have been dealt with, let's move on to figuring out default values. If there are any default values that weren't overridden by the arguments provided, the defaults should be added to the argument dictionary, as they will be sent to the function:

```
import inspect
def example(a=1, b=1, *c, d, e=2, **f) -> str:
    pass
def get_arguments(func, args, kwargs):
    """
    Given a function and a set of arguments, return a dictionary
    of argument values that will be sent to the function.
    """
    arguments = kwargs.copy()
    spec = inspect.getfullargspec(func)
    arguments.update(zip(spec.args, args))

    if spec.defaults:
        for i, name in enumerate(spec.args[-len(spec.defaults):]):
            if name not in arguments:
                arguments[name] = spec.defaults[i]

    return arguments

print(get_arguments(example, (1,), {'f': 4})) # will output  {'a': 1, 'b': 1, 'f': 4}
```

Because optional arguments must come after required arguments, this addition uses the size of the `defaults` tuple to determine the names of the optional argument. Looping over them, it then assigns only those values that weren't already provided. Unfortunately, this is only half of the default value situation. Because keyword-only arguments can take default values as well, `getfullargspec()` returns a separate dictionary for those values:

```python
import inspect
def example(a=1, b=1, *c, d, e=2, **f) -> str:
    pass
def get_arguments(func, args, kwargs):
    """
    Given a function and a set of arguments, return a dictionary
    of argument values that will be sent to the function.
    """
    arguments = kwargs.copy()
    spec = inspect.getfullargspec(func)
    arguments.update(zip(spec.args, args))

    for i, name in enumerate(spec.args[-len(spec.defaults)]):
        if name not in arguments:
            arguments[name] = spec.defaults[i]

    if spec.kwonlydefaults:
        for name, value in spec.kwonlydefaults.items():
            if name not in arguments:
                arguments[name] = value

    return arguments

print(get_arguments(example, (1,), {'f': 4})) # will yield {'a': 1, 'b': 1,
'e': 2, 'f': 4}
```

Because default values for keyword-only arguments also come in dictionary form, it's much easier to apply those because the argument names are known in advance. With that in place, `get_arguments()` can produce a more complete dictionary of arguments that will be passed to the function. Unfortunately, because this returns a dictionary and variable positional arguments have no names, there's no way to add them to the dictionary. This limits its usefulness a bit, but it's still valid for a great many function definitions.

Example: A More Concise Version

The previous example is certainly functional, but it's a bit more code than is really necessary. In particular, it takes a fair amount of work supplying default values when explicit values aren't provided. That's not very intuitive, however, because we usually think about default values the other way around: they're provided first, then overridden by explicit arguments.

The `get_arguments()` function can be rewritten with that in mind by bringing the default values out of the function declaration first, before replacing them with any values passed in as actual arguments. This avoids a lot of the checks that have to be made to make sure nothing gets overwritten accidentally.

The first step is to get the default values out. Because the `defaults` and `kwonlydefaults` attributes of the argument specification are set to None if no default values were specified, we actually have to start by setting up an empty dictionary to update. Then the default values for positional arguments can be added in.

Because this only needs to update a dictionary this time, without regard for what might be in it already, it's a bit easier to use a different technique to get the positional defaults. Rather than using a complex slice that's fairly difficult to read, we can use a similar `zip()` to what was used to get the explicit argument values. By first reversing the argument list and the default values, they still match up starting at the end:

```
def example(a=1, b=1, *c, d, e=2, **f) -> str:
    pass
def get_arguments(func, args, kwargs):
    """

    Given a function and a set of arguments, return a dictionary
    of argument values that will be sent to the function.
    """
```

```
    arguments = {}
    spec = inspect.getfullargspec(func)

    if spec.defaults:
        arguments.update(zip(reversed(spec.args), reversed(spec.defaults)))

    return arguments

print(get_arguments(example, (1,), {'f': 4}))  # will output  {'b': 1}
```

Adding default values for keyword arguments is much easier because the argument specification already supplies them as a dictionary. We can just pass that straight into an update() of the argument dictionary and move on:

```
def example(a=1, b=1, *c, d, e=2, **f) -> str:
    pass
def get_arguments(func, args, kwargs):
    """

    Given a function and a set of arguments, return a dictionary
    of argument values that will be sent to the function.
    """
    arguments = {}
    spec = inspect.getfullargspec(func)

    if spec.defaults:
        arguments.update(zip(reversed(spec.args), reversed(spec.defaults)))
    if spec.kwonlydefaults:
        arguments.update(spec.kwonlydefaults)

    return arguments

print(get_arguments(example, (1,), {'f': 4})) # will output {'b': 1, 'e': 2}
```

Now all that's left is to add the explicit argument values that were passed in. The same techniques used in the earlier version of this function will work here, with the only exception being that keyword arguments are passed in an update() function instead of being copied to form the argument dictionary in the first place:

```python
def example(a=1, b=1, *c, d, e=2, **f) -> str:
    pass
def get_arguments(func, args, kwargs):
    """
    Given a function and a set of arguments, return a dictionary
    of argument values that will be sent to the function.
    """
    arguments = {}
    spec = inspect.getfullargspec(func)

    if spec.defaults:
        arguments.update(zip(reversed(spec.args), reversed(spec.defaults)))
    if spec.kwonlydefaults:
        arguments.update(spec.kwonlydefaults)
    arguments.update(zip(spec.args, args))
    arguments.update(kwargs)

    return arguments
print(get_arguments(example, (1,), {'f': 4}))  # will output {'a': 1, 'b':
1, 'e': 2, 'f': 4}
```

With that, we have a much more concise function that works the way we normally think of default argument values. This type of refactoring is fairly common after you get more familiar with the advanced techniques available to you. It's always useful to look over old code to see if there's an easier, more straightforward way to go about the task at hand. This will often make your code faster as well as more readable and maintainable going forward. Now we'll extend our solution to also validate arguments.

Example: Validating Arguments

Unfortunately, that doesn't mean that the arguments returned by get_arguments() are capable of being passed into the function without errors. As it stands, get_arguments() assumes that any keyword arguments supplied are in fact valid arguments for the function, but that isn't always the case. In addition, any required arguments that didn't get a value will cause an error when the function is called. Ideally, we should be able to validate the arguments as well.

We can start with get_arguments(), so we have a dictionary of all the values that will be passed to the function, then we have two validation tasks: make sure all arguments have values and make sure no arguments were provided that the function doesn't know about. The function itself may impose additional requirements on the argument values, but as a generic utility, we can't make any assumptions about the content of any of the provided values.

Let's start off with making sure all the necessary values were provided. We don't have to worry as much about required or optional arguments this time around, since get_arguments() already makes sure optional arguments have their default values. Any argument left without a value is therefore required:

```
import itertools

def validate_arguments(func, args, kwargs):
    """

    Given a function and its arguments, return a dictionary
    with any errors that are posed by the given arguments.
    """
    arguments = get_arguments(func, args, kwargs)
    spec = inspect.getfullargspec(func)
    declared_args = spec.args[:]
    declared_args.extend(spec.kwonlyargs)
    errors = {}

    for name in declared_args:
        if name not in arguments:
            errors[name] = "Required argument not provided."

    return errors
```

With the basics in place to validate that all required arguments have values, the next step is to make sure the function knows how to deal with all the arguments that were provided. Any arguments passed in that aren't defined in the function should be considered an error:

```
import itertools

def validate_arguments(func, args, kwargs):
    """
    Given a function and its arguments, return a dictionary
    with any errors that are posed by the given arguments.
    """
    arguments = get_arguments(func, args, kwargs)
    spec = inspect.getfullargspec(func)
    declared_args = spec.args[:]
    declared_args.extend(spec.kwonlyargs)
    errors = {}

    for name in declared_args:
        if name not in arguments:
            errors[name] = "Required argument not provided."

    for name in arguments:
        if name not in declared_args:
            errors[name] = "Unknown argument provided."

    return errors
```

Of course, because this relies on get_arguments(), it inherits the same limitation of variable positional arguments. This means validate_arguments() may sometimes return an incomplete dictionary of errors. Variable positional arguments present an additional challenge that can't be addressed with this function. A more comprehensive solution is provided in the section on function annotations.

Decorators

When dealing with a large codebase, it's very common to have a set of tasks that need to be performed by many different functions, usually before or after doing something more specific to the function at hand. The nature of these tasks is as varied as the projects that use them, but here are some of the more common examples of where decorators are used:

- Access control

- Cleanup of temporary objects

- Error handling

- Caching

- Logging

In all of these cases, there's some boilerplate code that needs to be executed before or after what the function's really trying to do. Rather than copying that code into each function, it would be better if it could be written once and simply applied to each function that needs it. This is where decorators come in.

Technically, decorators are just simple functions designed with one purpose: accept a function and return a function. The function returned can be the same as the one passed in, or it could be completely replaced by something else along the way. The most common way to apply a decorator is using a special syntax designed just for this purpose. Here's how you could apply a decorator designed to suppress any errors during the execution of a function:

```
import datetime
from myapp import suppress_errors

@suppress_errors
def log_error(message, log_file='errors.log'):
    """Log an error message to a file."""

    log = open(log_file, 'w')
    log.write('%s\t%s\n' % (datetime.datetime.now(), message))
```

This syntax tells Python to pass the `log_error()` function as an argument to the `suppress_errors()` function, which then returns a replacement to use instead. It's easier to understand what happens behind the scenes by examining the process used in older versions of Python, before the @ syntax was introduced in Python 2.4:

```
#Python 2.x example
import datetime
from myapp import suppress_errors

def log_error(message, log_file='errors.log'):
    """Log an error message to a file."""

    log = open(log_file, 'w')
    log.write('%s\t%s\n' % (datetime.datetime.now(), message))
log_error = suppress_errors(log_error)
```

DON'T REPEAT YOURSELF/READABILITY COUNTS

When using the older decoration approach, notice that the name of the function is written three different times. Not only is this some extra typing that seems unnecessary; it complicates matters if you ever need to change the function name, and it only gets worse the more decorators you add. The newer syntax can apply a decorator without repeating the function name, no matter how many decorators you use.

Of course, the @ syntax does have one other benefit, which greatly helps its introduction: it keeps decorators right near the function's signature. This makes it easy to see at a glance which decorators are applied, which more directly conveys the total behavior of the function. Having them at the bottom of the function requires more effort to understand the complete behavior, so by moving decorators up to the top, readability is greatly enhanced.

The older option is still available and behaves identically to the @ syntax. The only real difference is that the @ syntax is only available when defining the function in the source file. If you want to decorate a function that was imported from elsewhere, you'll have to pass it into the decorator manually, so it's important to remember both ways it can work:

```
from myapp import log_error, suppress_errors

log_error = suppress_errors(log_error)
```

To understand what commonly goes on inside decorators like `log_error()`, it's necessary to first examine one of the most misunderstood and underutilized features of Python, and many other languages as well: closures.

Closures

Despite their usefulness, closures can seem to be an intimidating topic. Most explanations assume prior knowledge of things such as lexical scope, free variables, upvalues, and variable extent. Also, because so much can be done without ever learning about closures, the topic often seems mysterious and magical, as if it's the domain of experts, unsuitable for the rest of us. Thankfully, closures really aren't as difficult to understand as the terminology may suggest.

In a nutshell, *a closure is a function that's defined inside another function but is then passed outside that function where it can be used by other code.* There are some other details to learn as well, but it's still fairly abstract at this point, so here's a simple example of a closure:

```
def multiply_by(factor):
    """Return a function that multiplies values by the given factor"""
    def multiply(value):
        """Multiply the given value by the factor already provided"""
        return value * factor
    return multiply
times2=multiply_by(2)
print(times2(2))
```

As you can see, when you call `multiply_by()` with a value to use as a multiplication factor, the inner `multiply()` gets returned to be used later on. Here's how it would actually be used, which may help explain why this is useful. If you key in the previous code line by line from a Python prompt, the following would give you an idea about how this works:

```
>>> times2 = multiply_by(2)
>>> times2(5)
10
>>> times2(10)
20
>>> times3 = multiply_by(3)
>>> times3(5)
15
>>> times2(times3(5))
30
```

This behavior looks a bit like the argument preloading feature of `functools.partial()`, but you don't need to have a function that takes both arguments at once. The interesting part of about how this works, however, is that the inner function doesn't need to accept a `factor` argument of its own; it essentially inherits that argument from the outer function.

The fact that an inner function can reference the values of an outer function often seems perfectly normal when looking at the code, but there are a couple of rules about how it works that might not be as obvious. First, the inner function must be defined within the outer function; simply passing in a function as an argument won't work:

```
def multiply(value):
    return value * factor

def custom_operator(func, factor):
    return func

multiply_by = functools.partial(custom_operator, multiply)
```

On the surface, this looks mostly equivalent to the working example shown previously, but with the added benefit of being able to provide a callable at runtime. After all, the inner function gets placed inside the outer function and gets returned for use by other code. The problem is that closures only work if the inner function is actually defined inside the outer function, not just anything that gets passed in:

```
>>> times2 = multiply_by(2)
>>> times2(5)
Traceback (most recent call last):
  ...
NameError: global name 'factor' is not defined
```

This almost contradicts the functionality of `functools.partial()`, which works much like the `custom_operator()` function described here, but remember that `partial()` accepts all of the arguments at the same time as it accepts the callable to be bundled with them. It doesn't try to pull in any arguments from anywhere else.

Wrappers

Closures come into play heavily in the construction of wrappers, the most common use of decorators. Wrappers are functions designed to contain another function, adding some extra behavior before or after the wrapped function executes. In the context of the closure discussion, a wrapper is the inner function, while the wrapped function is passed in as an argument to the outer function. Here's the code behind the `suppress_errors()` decorator shown in the previous section:

```
def suppress_errors(func):
    """Automatically silence any errors that occur within a function"""

    def wrapper(*args, **kwargs):
        try:
            return func(*args, **kwargs)
```

```
    except Exception:
        pass

  return wrapper
```

A few things are going on here, but most of them have already been covered. The decorator takes a function as its only argument, which isn't executed until the inner wrapper function executes. By returning the wrapper instead of the original function, we form a closure, which allows the same function name to be used even after suppress_errors() is done.

Because the wrapper has to be called as if it were the original function, regardless of how that function was defined, it must accept all possible argument combinations. This is achieved by using variable positional and keyword arguments together and passing them straight into the original function internally. This is a very common practice with wrappers because it allows maximum flexibility, without caring what type of function it's applied to.

The actual work in the wrapper is quite simple: just execute the original function inside a try/except block to catch any exceptions that are raised. In the event of any errors it just continues merrily along, implicitly returning None instead of doing anything interesting. It also makes sure to return any value returned by the original function, so that everything meaningful about the wrapped function is maintained.

In this case the wrapper function is fairly simple, but the basic idea works for many more complex situations as well. There could be several lines of code both before and after the original function is called, perhaps with some decisions about whether it is called at all. Authorization wrappers, for instance, will typically return or raise an exception without ever calling the wrapped function, if the authorization failed for any reason.

Unfortunately, wrapping a function means some potentially useful information is lost. Chapter 5 shows how Python has access to certain attributes of a function, such as its name, docstring, and argument list. By replacing the original function with a wrapper, we've actually replaced all of that other information as well. In order to bring some of it back, we turn to a decorator in the functools module called wraps.

It may seem odd to use a decorator inside a decorator, but it really just solves the same problem as anything else: there's a common need that shouldn't require duplicate code everywhere it takes place. The functools.wraps() decorator copies the name, docstring, and some other information over to the wrapped function, so at least some of it gets retained. It does not copy over the argument list, but it's better than nothing:

```
import functools

def suppress_errors(func):
    """Automatically silence any errors that occur within a function"""

    @functools.wraps(func)
    def wrapper(*args, **kwargs):
        try:
            return func(*args, **kwargs)
        except Exception:
            pass

    return wrapper
```

What may seem most odd about this construction is that functools.wraps() takes an argument in addition to the function to which it's applied. In this case, that argument is the function to copy attributes from, which is specified on the line with the decorator itself. This is often useful for customizing decorators for specific tasks, so next we'll examine how to take advantage of custom arguments in your own decorators.

Decorators with Arguments

Ordinarily decorators only take a single argument, the function to be decorated. Behind the scenes, though, Python evaluates the @ line as an expression before applying it as a decorator. The result of the expression is what's actually used as a decorator. In the simple case, the decorator expression is just a single function, so it evaluates easily. Adding arguments in the form used by functools.wraps() makes the whole statement evaluate like this:

```
wrapper = functools.wraps(func)(wrapper)
```

Looking at it this way, the solution becomes clear: one function returns another. The first function accepts the extra arguments and returns another function, which is used as the decorator. This makes implementing arguments on a decorator more complex because it adds another layer to the whole process, but it's easy to deal with once you see it in context. Here's how everything works together in the longest chain you're likely to see:

- A function to accept and validate arguments, and also return a function that decorates the original

- A decorator to accept a user-defined function

- A wrapper to add extra behavior

- The original function that was decorated

Not all of that will happen for every decorator, but that's the general approach of the most complex scenarios. Anything more complicated is simply an expansion of one of those four steps. As you'll notice, three of the four have already been covered, so the extra layer imposed by decorator arguments is really the only thing left to discuss.

This new outermost function accepts all the arguments for the decorator, optionally validates them, and returns a new function as a closure over the argument variables. That new function must take a single argument, functioning as the decorator. Here's how the suppress_errors() decorator might look if it instead accepted a logger function to report the errors to, rather than completely silencing them:

```
import functools

def suppress_errors(log_func=None):
    """Automatically silence any errors that occur within a function"""

    def decorator(func):
        @functools.wraps(func)
        def wrapper(*args, **kwargs):
            try:
                return func(*args, **kwargs)
            except Exception as e:
                if log_func is not None:
                    log_func(str(e))

        return wrapper

    return decorator
```

This layering allows `suppress_errors()` to accept arguments prior to being used as a decorator, but it removes the ability to call it without any arguments. Because that was the previous behavior, we've now introduced a backward incompatibility. The closest we can get to the original syntax is to actually call `suppress_errors()` first, but without any arguments.

Here's an example function that processes updates files in a given directory. This is a task that's often performed on an automated schedule, so that if something goes wrong, it can just stop running and try again at the next appointed time:

```python
import datetime
import os
import time
from myapp import suppress_errors

@suppress_errors()
def process_updated_files(directory, process, since=None):
    """
    Processes any new files in a `directory` using the `process` function.
    If provided, `since` is a date after which files are considered updated.

    The process function passed in must accept a single argument: the absolute
    path to the file that needs to be processed.
    """
    if since is not None:
        # Get a threshold that we can compare to the modification time later
        threshold = time.mktime(since.timetuple()) + since.microsecond / 1000000
    else:
        threshold = 0

    for filename in os.listdir(directory):
        path = os.path.abspath(os.path.join(directory, filename))
        if os.stat(path).st_mtime > threshold:
            process(path)
```

Unfortunately, this is still a strange situation to end up with, and it really doesn't look like anything that Python programmers are used to. Clearly, we need a better solution.

Decorators with—or without—Arguments

Ideally, a decorator with optional arguments would be able to be called without parentheses if no arguments are provided, while still being able to provide the arguments when necessary. This means supporting two different flows in a single decorator, which can get tricky if you're not careful. The main problem is that the outermost function must be able to accept arbitrary arguments *or* a single function, and it must be able to tell the difference between the two and behave accordingly.

That brings us to the first task: determining which flow to use when the outer function is called. One option would be to inspect the first positional argument and check to see if it's a function, since decorators always receive the function as a positional argument.

Interestingly, a pretty good distinction can be made based on something mentioned briefly in the previous paragraph. Decorators always receive the decorated function as a positional argument, so we can use that as its distinguishing factor. For all other arguments we can instead rely on keyword arguments, which are generally more explicit anyway, thus making it more readable as well.

We could do this by way of using *args and **kwargs, but because we know the positional argument list is just a fixed single argument, it's easier to just make that the first argument and make it optional. Then, any additional keyword arguments can be placed after it. They'll all need default values, of course, but the whole point here is that all arguments are optional, so that's not a problem.

With the argument distinction squared away, all that's left is to branch into a different code block if arguments are provided, rather than a function to be decorated. By having an optional first positional argument, we can simply test for its presence to determine which branch to go through:

```
import functools

def suppress_errors(func=None, log_func=None):
    """Automatically silence any errors that occur within a function"""

    def decorator(func):
        @functools.wraps(func)
        def wrapper(*args, **kwargs):
            try:
```

```
            return func(*args, **kwargs)
        except Exception as e:
            if log_func is not None:
                log_func(str(e))

    return wrapper

if func is None:
    return decorator
else:
    return decorator(func)
```

This now allows `suppress_errors()` to be called with or without arguments, but it's still important to remember that arguments *must* be passed with keywords. This is an example in which an argument looks identical to the function being decorated. There's no way to tell the difference by examining them, even if we tried.

If a logger function is provided as a positional argument, the decorator will assume it's the function to be decorated, so it'll actually execute the logger immediately, with the function to be decorated as its argument. In essence, you'll end up logging the function you wanted to decorate. Worse yet, the value you're left with after decorating the function is actually the return value from the logger, not the decorator. Because most loggers don't return anything, it'll probably be None—that's right, your function has vanished. Given that you keyed in the aforementioned functions, you can try the following from a prompt:

```
>>> def print_logger(message):
...     print(message)
...
>>> @suppress_errors(print_logger)
... def example():
...     return variable_which_does_not_exist
...
<function example at 0x...>
>>> example
>>>
```

This is a side effect of the way the decorator works, and there's little to be done other than documenting it and making sure you always specify keywords when applying arguments.

Example: Memoization

To demonstrate how decorators can copy out common behavior into any function you like, consider what could be done to improve the efficiency of deterministic functions. Deterministic functions always return the same result given the same set of arguments, no matter how many times they're called. Given such a function, it should be possible to cache the results of a given function call so if it's called with the same arguments again, the result can be looked up without having to call the function again.

Using a cache, a decorator can store the result of a function using the argument list as its key. Dictionaries can't be used as keys in a dictionary, so only positional arguments can be taken into account when populating the cache. Thankfully, most functions that would take advantage of memoization are simple mathematical operations, which are typically called with positional arguments anyway:

```
def memoize(func):
    """
    Cache the results of the function so it doesn't need to be called
    again, if the same arguments are provided a second time.
    """
    cache = {}

    @functools.wraps(func)
    def wrapper(*args):
        if args in cache:
            return cache[args]

        # This line is for demonstration only.
        # Remove it before using it for real.
        print('Calling %s()' % func.__name__)

        result = func(*args)
        cache[args] = result
        return result

    return wrapper
```

Now, whenever you define a deterministic function, you can use the `memoize()` decorator to automatically cache its result for future use. Here's how it would work for some simple mathematical operations. Again, given you keyed in the aforelisted stub, try the following:

```
>>> @memoize
... def multiply(x, y):
...     return x * y
...
>>> multiply(6, 7)
Calling multiply()
42
>>> multiply(6, 7)
42
>>> multiply(4, 3)
Calling multiply()
12
>>> @memoize
... def factorial(x):
...     result = 1
...     for i in range(x):
...         result *= i + 1
...     return result
...
>>> factorial(5)
Calling factorial()
120
>>> factorial(5)
120
>>> factorial(7)
Calling factorial()
5040
```

Caution   Memoization is best suited for functions with a few arguments, which are called with relatively few variations in the argument values. Functions that are called with a large number of arguments or have a lot of variety in the argument values that are used will quickly fill up a lot of memory with the cache. This can slow down the entire system, with the only benefit being the minority of cases where arguments are reused. Also, functions that aren't truly deterministic will actually cause problems because the function won't be called every time.

Example: A Decorator to Create Decorators

Astute readers will have noticed something of a contradiction in the descriptions of the more complex decorator constructs. The purpose of decorators is to avoid a lot of boilerplate code and simplify functions, but the decorators themselves end up getting quite complicated just to support features such as optional arguments. Ideally, we could put that boilerplate into a decorator as well, simplifying the process for new decorators.

Because decorators are Python functions, just like those they decorate, this is quite possible. As with the other situations, however, there's something that needs to be taken into account. In this case, the function you define as a decorator will need to distinguish between the arguments meant for the decorator and those meant for the function it decorates:

```python
def decorator(declared_decorator):
    """Create a decorator out of a function, which will be used as a wrapper."""

    @functools.wraps(declared_decorator)
    def final_decorator(func=None, **kwargs):
        # This will be exposed to the rest
        # of your application as a decorator

        def decorated(func):
            # This will be exposed to the rest
            # of your application as a decorated
```

118

```
        # function, regardless how it was called
        @functools.wraps(func)
        def wrapper(*a, **kw):
            # This is used when actually executing
            # the function that was decorated
            return declared_decorator(func, a, kw, **kwargs)

        return wrapper

    if func is None:
        # The decorator was called with arguments,
        # rather than a function to decorate
        return decorated
    else:
        # The decorator was called without arguments,
        # so the function should be decorated immediately
        return decorated(func)

    return final_decorator
```

With this in place, you can define your decorators in terms of the wrapper function directly; then, just apply this decorator to manage the overhead behind the scenes. Your declared functions must always accept three arguments now, with any additional arguments added on beyond that. The three required arguments are shown in the following list:

- The function that will be decorated, which should be called if appropriate

- A tuple of positional arguments that were supplied to the decorated function

- A dictionary of keyword arguments that were supplied to the decorated function

With these arguments in mind, here's how you might define the suppress_errors() decorator described previously in this chapter:

```
>>> @decorator
... def suppress_errors(func, args, kwargs, log_func=None):
...     try:
...         return func(*args, **kwargs)
...     except Exception as e:
...         if log_func is not None:
...             log_func(str(e))
...
>>> @suppress_errors
... def example():
...     return variable_which_does_not_exist
...
>>> example() # Doesn't raise any errors
>>> def print_logger(message):
...     print(message)
...
>>> @suppress_errors(log_func=print_logger)
... def example():
...     return variable_which_does_not_exist
...
>>> example()
global name 'variable_which_does_not_exist' is not defined
```

Function Annotations

There are typically three aspects of a function that don't deal with the code within it: a name, a set of arguments, and an optional docstring. Sometimes, however, that's not quite enough to fully describe how the function works or how it should be used. Static-typed languages—such as Java, for example—also include details about what type of values are allowed for each of the arguments, as well as what type can be expected for the return value.

Python's response to this need is the concept of function annotations. Each argument, as well as the return value, can have an expression attached to it, which describes a detail that can't be conveyed otherwise. This could be as simple as a type, such as int or str, which is analogous to static-typed languages, as shown in the following example stub:

```python
def prepend_rows(rows:list, prefix:str) -> list:
    return [prefix + row for row in rows]
```

The biggest difference between this example and traditional static-typed languages isn't a matter of syntax; it's that in Python annotations can be *any* expression, not just a type or a class. You could annotate your arguments with descriptive strings, calculated values, or even inline functions—see this chapter's section on lambdas for details. Here's what the previous example might look like if annotated with strings as additional documentation:

```python
def prepend_rows(rows:"a list of strings to add to the prefix",
                 prefix:"a string to prepend to each row provided",
                 ) -> "a new list of strings prepended with the prefix":
    return [prefix + row for row in rows]
```

Of course, this flexibility might make you wonder about the intended use for function annotations, but there isn't one, and that's deliberate. Officially, the intent behind annotations is to encourage experimentation in frameworks and other third-party libraries. The two examples shown here could be valid for use with type checking and documentation libraries, respectively.

Example: Type Safety

To illustrate how annotations can be used by a library, consider a basic implementation of a type safety library that can understand and utilize the function described previously. It would expect argument annotations to specify a valid type for any incoming arguments, while the return annotation would be able to validate the value returned by the function.

Because type safety involves verifying values before and after the function is executed, a decorator is the most suitable option for the implementation. Also, because all of the type-hinting information is provided in the function declaration, we don't need to worry about any additional arguments, so a simple decorator will suffice. The first task, however, is to validate the annotations themselves, as they must be valid Python types in order for the rest of the decorator to work properly:

```python
import inspect

def typesafe(func):
    """
    Verify that the function is called with the right argument types and
    that it returns a value of the right type, according to its annotations
    """

    spec = inspect.getfullargspec(func)

    for name, annotation in spec.annotations.items():
        if not isinstance(annotation, type):
            raise TypeError("The annotation for '%s' is not a type." % name)

    return func
```

So far this doesn't do anything to the function, but it does check to see that each annotation provided is a valid type, which can then be used to verify the type of the arguments referenced by the annotations. This uses `isinstance()`, which compares an object to the type it's expected to be. More information on `isinstance()` and on types and classes in general can be found in Chapter 4.

Now that we can be sure all the annotations are valid, it's time to start validating some arguments. Given how many types of arguments there are, let's take them one at a time. Keyword arguments are the easiest to start out with, since they already come with their name and value tied together, so that's one less thing to worry about. With a name, we can get the associated annotation and validate the value against that. This would also be a good time to start factoring out some things, as we'll end up having to use some of the same things over and over again. Here's how the wrapper would look to begin with:

```
import functools
import inspect

def typesafe(func):
    """

    Verify that the function is called with the right argument types and
    that it returns a value of the right type, according to its annotations
    """

    spec = inspect.getfullargspec(func)
    annotations = spec.annotations

    for name, annotation in annotations.items():
        if not isinstance(annotation, type):
            raise TypeError("The annotation for '%s' is not a type." % name)

    error = "Wrong type for %s: expected %s, got %s."

    @functools.wraps(func)
    def wrapper(*args, **kwargs):
        # Deal with keyword arguments
        for name, arg in kwargs.items():
            if name in annotations and not isinstance(arg, annotations[name]):
                raise TypeError(error % (name,
                                         annotations[name].__name__,
                                         type(arg).__name__))
        return func(*args, **kwargs)
    return wrapper
```

By now, this should be fairly self-explanatory. Any keyword arguments provided will be checked to see if there's an associated annotation. If there is, the provided value is checked to make sure it's an instance of the type found in the annotation. The error message is factored out because it'll get reused a few more times before we're done.

Next up is dealing with positional arguments. Once again, we can rely on zip() to line up the positional argument names with the values that were provided. Because the result of zip() is compatible with the items() method of dictionaries, we can actually use chain() from the itertools module to link them together into the same loop:

Part one: add part two to this to see it in action as a script:

```python
import functools
import inspect
from itertools import chain

def typesafe(func):
    """
    Verify that the function is called with the right argument types and
    that it returns a value of the right type, according to its annotations
    """
    spec = inspect.getfullargspec(func)
    annotations = spec.annotations
    for name, annotation in annotations.items():
        if not isinstance(annotation, type):
            raise TypeError("The annotation for '%s' is not a type." % name)

    error = "Wrong type for %s: expected %s, got %s."

    @functools.wraps(func)
    def wrapper(*args, **kwargs):
        # Deal with keyword arguments
        for name, arg in chain(zip(spec.args, args), kwargs.items()):
            if name in annotations and not isinstance(arg, annotations[name]):
                raise TypeError(error % (name,
                                         annotations[name].__name__,
                                         type(arg).__name__))
        return func(*args, **kwargs)
    return wrapper
```

Although that takes care of both positional and keyword arguments, it's not everything. Because variable arguments can also accept annotations, we have to account for argument values that don't line up as nicely with defined argument names. Unfortunately, there's something else that must be dealt with before we can do much of anything on that front.

If you're paying really close attention, you might notice a very subtle bug in the code as it stands. In order to make the code a bit easier to follow and to account for any arguments that are passed by keywords, the wrapper iterates over the kwargs dictionary in its entirely, checking for associated annotations. Unfortunately, that leaves us with the possibility of an unintentional name conflict.

To illustrate how the bug could be triggered, first consider what would be expected when dealing with variable arguments. Because we can only apply a single annotation to the variable argument name itself, that annotation must be assumed to apply to all arguments that fall under that variable argument, whether passed positionally or by keyword. Without explicit support for that behavior yet, variable arguments should just be ignored, but here's what happens with the code as it stands:

Part two: put this at the end of the script you just keyed in:

```
@typesafe
def example(*args:int, **kwargs:str):
    pass

print(example(spam='eggs'))  #fine
print(example(kwargs='spam'))  #fine
print(example(args='spam'))  # not fine!
# output will be:
#Traceback (most recent call last):
#TypeError: Wrong type for args: expected int, got str.
```

Interestingly, everything works fine unless the function call includes a keyword argument with the same name as the variable positional argument. Although it may not seem obvious at first, the problem is actually in the set of values to iterate over in the wrapper's only loop. It assumes that the names of all the keyword arguments line up nicely with annotations.

Basically, the problem is that keyword arguments that are meant for the variable argument end up getting matched up with annotations from other arguments. For the most part, this is acceptable because two of the three types of arguments won't ever cause problems. Matching it with an explicit argument name simply duplicates what Python already does, so using the associated annotation is fine, and matching the variable keyword argument name ends up using the same annotation that we were planning on using anyway.

So the problem only crops up when a keyword argument matches the variable positional argument name, because that association never makes sense. Sometimes if the annotation is the same as that of the variable keyword argument, the problem might never show up, but it's still there, regardless. Because the code for the wrapper function is still fairly minimal, it's not too difficult to see where the problem is occurring.

In the main loop, the second part of the iteration chain is the list of items in the kwargs dictionary. That means everything passed in by keyword is checked against named annotations, which clearly isn't always what we want. Instead, we only want to loop over the explicit arguments at this point, while still supporting both positions and keywords. That means we'll have to construct a new dictionary based on the function definition, rather than taking the easy way out and relying on kwargs, as we are now. The outer typesafe() function has been removed from the listing here to make the code easier to digest in print:

```
def wrapper(*args, **kwargs):
    # Populate a dictionary of explicit arguments passed positionally
    explicit_args = dict(zip(spec.args, args))

    # Add all explicit arguments passed by keyword
    for name in chain(spec.args, spec.kwonlyargs):
        if name in kwargs:
            explicit_args[name] = kwargs[name]

    # Deal with explicit arguments
    for name, arg in explicit_args.items():
        if name in annotations and not isinstance(arg, annotations[name]):
            raise TypeError(error % (name,
                                     annotations[name].__name__,
                                     type(arg).__name__))

    return func(*args, **kwargs)
```

With that bug out of the way, we can focus on properly supporting variable arguments. Because keyword arguments have names but positional arguments don't, we can't manage both types in one pass like we could with the explicit arguments. The processes are fairly similar to the explicit arguments, but the values to iterate over are different in each case. The biggest difference, however, is that the annotations aren't referenced by the name of the arguments.

In order to loop over just the truly variable positional arguments, we can simply use the number of explicit arguments as the beginning of a slice on the positional arguments tuple. This gets us all positional arguments provided after the explicit arguments or an empty list if only explicit arguments were provided.

For keyword arguments, we have to be a bit more creative. Because the function already loops over all the explicitly declared arguments at the beginning, we can use that same loop to exclude any matching items from a copy of the kwargs dictionary. Then we can iterate over what's left over to account for all the variable keyword arguments:

```
def wrapper(*args, **kwargs):
    # Populate a dictionary of explicit arguments passed positionally
    explicit_args = dict(zip(spec.args, args))
    keyword_args = kwargs.copy()

    # Add all explicit arguments passed by keyword
    for name in chain(spec.args, spec.kwonlyargs):
        if name in kwargs:
            explicit_args[name] = keyword_args.pop(name)

    # Deal with explicit arguments
    for name, arg in explicit_args.items():
        if name in annotations and not isinstance(arg, annotations[name]):
            raise TypeError(error % (name,
                                     annotations[name].__name__,
                                     type(arg).__name__))

    # Deal with variable positional arguments
    if spec.varargs and spec.varargs in annotations:
        annotation = annotations[spec.varargs]
        for i, arg in enumerate(args[len(spec.args):]):
```

```
            if not isinstance(arg, annotation):
                raise TypeError(error % ('variable argument %s' % (i + 1),
                                         annotation.__name__,
                                         type(arg).__name__))

    # Deal with variable keyword arguments
    if spec.varkw and spec.varkw in annotations:
        annotation = annotations[spec.varkw]
        for name, arg in keyword_args.items():
            if not isinstance(arg, annotation):
                raise TypeError(error % (name,
                                         annotation.__name__,
                                         type(arg).__name__))

    return func(*args, **kwargs)
```

This covers all explicit arguments as well as variable arguments passed in by position and keyword. The only thing left is to validate the value returned by the target function. Thus far the wrapper just calls the original function directly without regard for what it returns, but by now, it should be easy to see what needs to be done:

```
def wrapper(*args, **kwargs):
    # Populate a dictionary of explicit arguments passed positionally
    explicit_args = dict(zip(spec.args, args))
    keyword_args = kwargs.copy()

    # Add all explicit arguments passed by keyword
    for name in chain(spec.args, spec.kwonlyargs):
        if name in kwargs:
            explicit_args[name] = keyword_args(name)

    # Deal with explicit arguments
    for name, arg in explicit_args.items():
        if name in annotations and not isinstance(arg, annotations[name]):
```

```
            raise TypeError(error % (name,
                                     annotations[name].__name__,
                                     type(arg).__name__))

    # Deal with variable positional arguments
    if spec.varargs and spec.varargs in annotations:
        annotation = annotations[spec.varargs]
        for i, arg in enumerate(args[len(spec.args):]):
            if not isinstance(arg, annotation):
                raise TypeError(error % ('variable argument %s' % (i + 1),
                                         annotation.__name__,
                                         type(arg).__name__))

    # Deal with variable keyword arguments
    if spec.varkw and spec.varkw in annotations:
        annotation = annotations[spec.varkw]
        for name, arg in keyword_args.items():
            if not isinstance(arg, annotation):
                raise TypeError(error % (name,
                                         annotation.__name__,
                                         type(arg).__name__))

    r = func(*args, **kwargs)
    if 'return' in annotations and not isinstance(r, annotations['return']):
        raise TypeError(error % ('the return value',
                                 annotations['return'].__name__,
                                 type(r).__name__))
    return r
```

With that, we have a fully functional type safety decorator, which can validate all
arguments to a function as well as its return value. There's one additional safeguard
we can include to find errors even more quickly, however. In the same way as the outer
typesafe() function already validates that the annotations are types, that part of the
function is also capable of validating the default values for all provided arguments.
Because variable arguments can't have default values, this is much simpler than dealing
with the function call itself:

```
import functools
import inspect
from itertools import chain

def typesafe(func):
    """
    Verify that the function is called with the right argument types and
    that it returns a value of the right type, according to its annotations
    """
    spec = inspect.getfullargspec(func)
    annotations = spec.annotations

    for name, annotation in annotations.items():
        if not isinstance(annotation, type):
            raise TypeError("The annotation for '%s' is not a type." % name)

    error = "Wrong type for %s: expected %s, got %s."
    defaults = spec.defaults or ()
    defaults_zip = zip(spec.args[-len(defaults):], defaults)
    kwonlydefaults = spec.kwonlydefaults or {}

    for name, value in chain(defaults_zip, kwonlydefaults.items()):
        if name in annotations and not isinstance(value, annotations[name]):
            raise TypeError(error % ('default value of %s' % name,
                                     annotations[name].__name__,
                                     type(value).__name__))

    @functools.wraps(func)
    def wrapper(*args, **kwargs):
        # Populate a dictionary of explicit arguments passed positionally
        explicit_args = dict(zip(spec.args, args))
        keyword_args = kwargs.copy()

        # Add all explicit arguments passed by keyword
        for name in chain(spec.args, spec.kwonlyargs):
            if name in kwargs:
                explicit_args[name] = keyword_args.pop(name)
```

```
    # Deal with explicit arguments
    for name, arg in explicit_args.items():
        if name in annotations and not isinstance(arg, annotations[name]):
            raise TypeError(error % (name,
                                     annotations[name].__name__,
                                     type(arg).__name__))

    # Deal with variable positional arguments
    if spec.varargs and spec.varargs in annotations:
        annotation = annotations[spec.varargs]
        for i, arg in enumerate(args[len(spec.args):]):
            if not isinstance(arg, annotation):
                raise TypeError(error % ('variable argument %s' % (i + 1),
                                         annotation.__name__,
                                         type(arg).__name__))

    # Deal with variable keyword arguments
    if spec.varkw and spec.varkw in annotations:
        annotation = annotations[spec.varkw]
        for name, arg in keyword_args.items():
            if not isinstance(arg, annotation):
                raise TypeError(error % (name,
                                         annotation.__name__,
                                         type(arg).__name__))

    r = func(*args, **kwargs)
    if 'return' in annotations and not isinstance(r, annotations['return']):
        raise TypeError(error % ('the return value',
                                 annotations['return'].__name__,
                                 type(r).__name__))
    return r
return wrapper
```

Factoring Out the Boilerplate

Looking over the code as it stands, you'll notice a lot of repetition. Each form of annotation ends up doing the same things: checking to see if the value is appropriate and raising an exception if it's not. Ideally, we'd be able to factor that into a separate

131

function that can focus solely on the actual task of validation. The rest of the code is really just boilerplate, managing the details of finding the different types of annotations.

Because the common code will be going into a new function, the obvious way to tie it into the rest of the code is to create a new decorator. This new decorator will be placed on a function that will process the annotation for each value, so we'll call it annotation_ processor. The function passed into annotation_processor will then be used for each of the annotation types throughout the existing code:

```
import functools
import inspect
from itertools import chain

def annotation_decorator(process):
    """
    Creates a decorator that processes annotations for each argument passed
    into its target function, raising an exception if there's a problem.
    """
    @functools.wraps(process)
    def decorator(func):
        spec = inspect.getfullargspec(func)
        annotations = spec.annotations

        defaults = spec.defaults or ()
        defaults_zip = zip(spec.args[-len(defaults):], defaults)
        kwonlydefaults = spec.kwonlydefaults or {}

        for name, value in chain(defaults_zip, kwonlydefaults.items()):
            if name in annotations:
                process(value, annotations[name])
        @functools.wraps(func)
        def wrapper(*args, **kwargs):
            # Populate a dictionary of explicit arguments passed positionally
            explicit_args = dict(zip(spec.args, args))
            keyword_args = kwargs.copy()
```

```
        # Add all explicit arguments passed by keyword
        for name in chain(spec.args, spec.kwonlyargs):
            if name in kwargs:
                explicit_args[name] = keyword_args.pop(name)

        # Deal with explicit arguments
        for name, arg in explicit_args.items():
            if name in annotations:
                process(arg, annotations[name])

        # Deal with variable positional arguments
        if spec.varargs and spec.varargs in annotations:
            annotation = annotations[spec.varargs]
            for arg in args[len(spec.args):]:
                process(arg, annotation)

        # Deal with variable keyword arguments
        if spec.varkw and spec.varkw in annotations:
            annotation = annotations[spec.varkw]
            for name, arg in keyword_args.items():
                process(arg, annotation)

        r = func(*args, **kwargs)
        if 'return' in annotations:
            process(r, annotations['return'])
        return r

    return wrapper

    return decorator
```

Note   Because we're making it a bit more generic, you'll notice that the initial portion of the decorator no longer checks that the annotations are valid types. The decorator itself no longer cares what logic you apply to the argument values, as that's all done in the decorated function.

Now we can apply this new decorator to a much simpler function to provide a new typesafe() decorator, which functions just like the one in the previous section:

```
@annotation_decorator
def typesafe(value, annotation):
    """
    Verify that the function is called with the right argument types and
    that it returns a value of the right type, according to its annotations
    """
    if not isinstance(value, annotation):
        raise TypeError("Expected %s, got %s." % (annotation.__name__,
                                                  type(value).__name__))
```

The benefit of doing this is that it's much easier to modify the behavior of the decorator in the future. In addition, you can now use annotation_processor() to create new types of decorators that use annotation for different purposes, such as type coercion.

Example: Type Coercion

Rather than strictly requiring that the arguments all be the types specified when they're passed into the function, another approach is to coerce them to the required types inside the function itself. Many of the same types that are used to validate values can also be used to coerce them directly into the types themselves. In addition, if a value can't be coerced, the type it's passed into raises an exception, usually a TypeError, just like our validation function.

ROBUSTNESS PRINCIPLE

This is one of the more obvious applications of the robustness principle. Your function requires an argument be of a specific type, but it's much nicer to accept some variations, knowing that they can be converted to the right type before your function needs to deal with them. Likewise, coercion also helps ensure that the return value is always of a consistent type that the external code knows how to deal with.

The decorator presented in the previous section provides a good starting point for adding this behavior to a new decorator, and we can use it to modify the incoming value according to the annotation that was provided along with it. Because we're relying on a type constructor to do all the necessary type checking and raise exceptions appropriately, this new decorator can be much simpler. In fact, it can be expressed in just one actual instruction:

```
@annotation_decorator
def coerce_arguments(value, annotation):
    return annotation(value)
```

This is so simple that it doesn't even require the annotation be a type at all. Any function or class that returns an object will work just fine, and the value returned will be passed into the function decorated by `coerce_arguments()`. Or will it? If you look back at the `annotation_decorator()` function as it stands, there's a minor problem that prevents it from working the way this new decorator would need it to.

The problem is that in the lines that call the `process()` function that was passed into the outer decorator, the return value is thrown away. If you try to use `coerce_arguments()` with the existing decorator, all you'll get is the exception-raising aspect of the code, not the value coercion aspect. So, in order to work properly, we'll need to go back and add that feature to `annotation_processor()`.

There are a few things that need to be done overall, however. Because the annotation processor will be modifying the arguments that will be eventually sent to the decorated function, we'll need to set up a new list for positional arguments and a new dictionary for keyword arguments. Then we have to split up the explicit argument handling, so that we can distinguish between positional and keyword arguments. Without that, the function wouldn't be able to apply variable positional arguments correctly:

```
def wrapper(*args, **kwargs):
    new_args = []
    new_kwargs = {}
    keyword_args = kwargs.copy()
```

```
        # Deal with explicit arguments passed positionally
        for name, arg in zip(spec.args, args):
            if name in annotations:
                new_args.append(process(arg, annotations[name]))

        # Deal with explicit arguments passed by keyword
        for name in chain(spec.args, spec.kwonlyargs):
            if name in kwargs and name in annotations:
                new_kwargs[name] = process(keyword_args.pop(name),
                                                annotations[name])

        # Deal with variable positional arguments
        if spec.varargs and spec.varargs in annotations:
            annotation = annotations[spec.varargs]
            for arg in args[len(spec.args):]:
                new_args.append(process(arg, annotation))

        # Deal with variable keyword arguments
        if spec.varkw and spec.varkw in annotations:
            annotation = annotations[spec.varkw]
            for name, arg in keyword_args.items():
                new_kwargs[name] = process(arg, annotation)

        r = func(*new_args, **new_kwargs)
        if 'return' in annotations:
            r = process(r, annotations['return'])
        return r
```

With those changes in place, the new coerce_arguments() decorator will be able to replace the arguments on the fly, passing the replacements into the original function. Unfortunately, if you're still using typesafe() from before, this new behavior causes problems because typesafe() doesn't return a value. Fixing that is a simple matter of returning the original value, unchanged, if the type check was satisfactory:

```
@annotation_decorator
def typesafe(value, annotation):
```

```
"""
Verify that the function is called with the right argument types and
that it returns a value of the right type, according to its annotations
"""
if not isinstance(value, annotation):
    raise TypeError("Expected %s, got %s." % (annotation.__name__,
                                              type(value).__name__))
return value
```

Annotating with Decorators

The natural question to ask is: what happens if you want to use two libraries together?
One might expect you to supply valid types, whereas the other expects a string to use for
documentation. They're completely incompatible with each other, which forces you to
use one or the other, rather than both. Furthermore, any attempt to merge the two, using
a dictionary or some other combined data type, would have to be agreed on by both
libraries, as each would need to know how to get at the information it cares about.

Once you consider how many other frameworks and libraries might take advantage
of these annotations, you can see how quickly the official function annotations fall
apart. It's still too early to see which applications will actually use it or how they'll work
together, but it's certainly worth considering other options that can bypass the problems
completely.

Because decorators can take arguments of their own, it's possible to use them to
provide annotations for the arguments of the functions they decorate. This way, the
annotations are separate from the function itself and provided directly to the code that
makes sense of them. And because multiple decorators can be stacked together on a
single function, it's already got a built-in way of managing multiple frameworks.

Example: Type Safety as a Decorator

To illustrate the decorator-based approach to function annotations, let's consider the
type safety example from earlier. It already relied on a decorator, so we can extend that
to take arguments, using the same types that the annotations provided previously.
Essentially, it'll look something like this:

```
>>> @typesafe(str, str)
... def combine(a, b):
...     return a + b
...
>>> combine('spam', 'alot')
'spamalot'
>>> combine('fail', 1)
Traceback (most recent call last):
  ...
TypeError: Wrong type for b: expected str, got int.
```

It works almost exactly like the true annotated version, except that the annotations are supplied to the decorator directly. In order to accept arguments, we're going to just change the first portion of the code a bit so that we can get the annotations from the arguments instead of inspecting the function itself.

Because annotations come in through arguments to the decorator, we have a new outer wrapper for receiving them. When the next layer receives the function to be decorated it can match up the annotations with the function's signature, providing names for any annotations passed positionally. Once all the available annotations have been given the right names, they can be used by the rest of the inner decorator without any further modifications:

```
import functools
import inspect
from itertools import chain
def annotation_decorator(process):
    """

    Creates a decorator that processes annotations for each argument passed
    into its target function, raising an exception if there's a problem.
    """
    def annotator(*args, **kwargs):
```

```
annotations = kwargs.copy()
@functools.wraps(process)
def decorator(func):
    spec = inspect.getfullargspec(func)
    annotations.update(zip(spec.args, args))

    defaults = spec.defaults or ()
    defaults_zip = zip(spec.args[-len(defaults):], defaults)
    kwonlydefaults = spec.kwonlydefaults or {}

    for name, value in chain(defaults_zip, kwonlydefaults.items()):
        if name in annotations:
            process(value, annotations[name])

    @functools.wraps(func)
    def wrapper(*args, **kwargs):
        new_args = []
        new_kwargs = {}
        keyword_args = kwargs.copy()

        # Deal with explicit arguments passed positionally
        for name, arg in zip(spec.args, args):
            if name in annotations:
                new_args.append(process(arg, annotations[name]))

        # Deal with explicit arguments passed by keyword
        for name in chain(spec.args, spec.kwonlyargs):
            if name in kwargs and name in annotations:
                new_kwargs[name] = process(keyword_args.pop(name),
                                           annotations[name])

        # Deal with variable positional arguments
        if spec.varargs and spec.varargs in annotations:
            annotation = annotations[spec.varargs]
            for arg in args[len(spec.args):]:
                new_args.append(process(arg, annotation))

        # Deal with variable keyword arguments
        if spec.varkw and spec.varkw in annotations:
```

```
                    annotation = annotations[spec.varkw]
                    for name, arg in keyword_args.items():
                        new_kwargs[name] = process(arg, annotation)
            r = func(*new_args, **new_kwargs)
            if 'return' in annotations:
                r = process(r, annotations['return'])
            return r

        return wrapper

    return decorator
```

return annotator

That handles most of the situation, but it doesn't handle return values yet. If you try to supply a return value using the right name, `return`, you'll get a syntax error because it's a reserved Python keyword. Trying to provide it alongside the other annotations would require each call to pass annotations using an actual dictionary, where you can provide the return annotation without upsetting Python's syntax.

Instead, you'll need to provide the return value annotation in a separate function call, where it can be the sole argument without any reserved name issues. When working with most types of decorators, this would be easy to do: just create a new decorator that checks the return value and be done with it. Unfortunately, as the eventual decorator you're working with is created outside the control of our code, it's not so easy.

If you completely detached the return value processing from the argument processing, the programmer who's actually writing something like the `typesafe()` decorator would have to write it twice; once to create the argument-processing decorator and again to create the return-value–processing decorator. Because that's a clear violation of DRY, let's reuse as much of their work as possible.

Here's where some design comes into play. We're looking at going beyond just a simple decorator, so let's figure out how to best approach it so that it makes sense to those who have to use it. Thinking about the available options, one solution springs to mind fairly quickly. If we can add the extra annotation function as an attribute of the final decorator, you'd be able to write the return value annotator on the same line as the other decorator, but right afterward, in its own function call. Here's what it might look like, if you went that route:

```
@typesafe(int, int).returns(int)
def add(a, b):
    return a + b
```

Unfortunately this isn't an option, for reasons that can be demonstrated without even adding the necessary code to support it. The trouble is, this formation isn't allowed as Python syntax. If typesafe() hadn't taken any arguments it would work, but there's no support for calling two separate functions as part of a single decorator. Instead of supplying the return value annotation in the decorator itself, let's look somewhere else.

Another option is to use the generated typesafe() decorator to add a function as an attribute to the wrapper around the add() function. This places the return value annotation at the end of the function definition, closer to where the return value is specified. In addition, it helps clarify the fact that you can use typesafe() to supply argument decorators without bothering to check the return value, if you want to. Here's how it would look:

```
@typesafe(int, int)
def add(a, b):
    return a + b
add.returns(int)
```

It's still very clear and perhaps even more explicit than the syntax that doesn't work anyway. As an added bonus, the code to support it is very simple, requiring just a few lines be added to the end of the inner decorator() function:

```
def decorator(func):
    from itertools import chain

    spec = inspect.getfullargspec(func)
    annotations.update(zip(spec.args, args))

    defaults = spec.defaults or ()
    defaults_zip = zip(spec.args[-len(defaults):], defaults)
    kwonlydefaults = spec.kwonlydefaults or {}
```

```
            for name, value in chain(defaults_zip, kwonlydefaults.items()):
                if name in annotations:
                    process(value, annotations[name])
        @functools.wraps(func)
        def wrapper(*args, **kwargs):
            new_args = []
            new_kwargs = {}
            keyword_args = kwargs.copy()

            # Deal with explicit arguments passed positionally
            for name, arg in zip(spec.args, args):
                if name in annotations:
                    new_args.append(process(arg, annotations[name]))

            # Deal with explicit arguments passed by keyword
            for name in chain(spec.args, spec.kwonlyargs):
                if name in kwargs and name in annotations:
                    new_kwargs[name] = process(keyword_args.pop(name),
                                               annotations[name])

            # Deal with variable positional arguments
            if spec.varargs and spec.varargs in annotations:
                annotation = annotations[spec.varargs]
                for arg in args[len(spec.args):]:
                    new_args.append(process(arg, annotation))

            # Deal with variable keyword arguments
            if spec.varkw and spec.varkw in annotations:
                annotation = annotations[spec.varkw]
                for name, arg in keyword_args.items():
                    new_kwargs[name] = process(arg, annotation)

            r = func(*new_args, **new_kwargs)
            if 'return' in annotations:
                r = process(r, annotations['return'])
            return r
```

```
def return_annotator(annotation):
    annotations['return'] = annotation
wrapper.returns = return_annotator

return wrapper
```

Because this new `returns()` function will be called before the final `typesafe()` function ever will, it can simply add a new annotation to the existing dictionary. Then, when `typesafe()` does get called later, the internal wrapper can just continue working like it always did. This just changes the way the return value annotation is supplied, which is all that was necessary.

Because all of this behavior was refactored into a separate decorator, you can apply this decorator to `coerce_arguments()` or any other similarly purposed function. The resulting function will work the same way as `typesafe()`, only swapping out the argument handling with whatever the new decorator needs to do.

Generators

Chapter 2 introduced the concept of generator expressions and stressed the importance of iteration. Whereas generator expressions are useful for simple situations, you'll often need more sophisticated logic to determine how the iteration should work. You may need finer-grained control over the duration of the loop, the items getting returned, possible side effects that get triggered along the way, or any number of other concerns you may have.

Essentially, you need a real function, but with the benefits of a proper iterator and without the cognitive overhead of creating the iterator yourself. This is where generators come in. By *allowing you to define a function that can produce individual values one at a time, rather than just a single return value*, you have the added *flexibility of a function and the performance of an iterator*.

Generators are set aside from other functions by their use of the `yield` statement. This is somewhat of an analog to the typical `return` statement, except that `yield` doesn't cause the function to stop executing completely. It pushes one value out of the function, which gets consumed by the loop that called the generator; then, when that loop starts over, the generator starts back up again. It picks up right where it left off, running until it finds another yield statement or the function simply finishes executing.

The basics are best illustrated by an example, so consider a simple generator that returns the values in the classic Fibonacci sequence. The sequence begins with 0 and 1; each following number is produced by adding up the two numbers before it in the sequence. Therefore, the function only ever needs to keep two numbers in memory at a time, no matter how high the sequence goes. In order to keep it from continuing on forever, however, it's best to require a maximum number of values it should return, making a total of three values to keep track of.

It's tempting to set up the first two values as special cases, yielding them one at a time before even starting into the main loop that would return the rest of the sequence. That adds some extra complexity, however, which can make it pretty easy to accidentally introduce an infinite loop. Instead, we'll use a couple other seed values, –1 and 1, which can be fed right into the main loop directly. They'll generate 0 and 1 correctly when the loop's logic is applied.

Next, we can add a loop for all the remaining values in the sequence, up until the count is reached. Of course, by the time the loop starts two values have already been yielded, so we have to decrease count by 2 before entering the loop. Otherwise, we'd end up yielding two more values than were requested:

Part one: add part two to see it in action:

```
def fibonacci(count):
    # These seed values generate 0 and 1 when fed into the loop
    a, b = -1, 1

    while count > 0:
        # Yield the value for this iteration
        c = a + b
        yield c

        # Update values for the next iteration
        a, b = b, c
        count -= 1
```

With the generator in place, you can iterate over the values it produces, simply by treating it like you would any other sequence. Generators are iterable automatically, so a standard for loop already knows how to activate it and retrieve its values. Before you add part two, do a hand trace of -1 and 1 through the structure you and can see exactly how it operates.

Part two: add to end of previous code and run:

```
for x in fibonacci(3):
        print(x)
# output is
#0
#1
#1
for x in fibonacci(7):
        print(x)
#output is
#0
#1
#1
#2
#3
#5
#8
```

Unfortunately, the main benefit of generators can also, at times, be somewhat of a burden. Because there's no complete sequence in memory at any given time, generators always have to pick up where they left off. Most of the time, however, you'll completely exhaust the generator when you iterate over it the first time, so when you try to put it into another loop, you won't get anything back at all.

Add this to the end after part two and run:

```
fib = fibonacci(7)
print(list(fib)) # output [0, 1, 1, 2, 3, 5, 8]
print(list(fib)) # output []
```

This behavior can seem a bit misleading at first, but most of the time, it's the only behavior that makes sense. Generators are often used in places where the entire sequence isn't even known in advance or it may change after you iterate over it. For example, you might use a generator to iterate over the users currently accessing a system. Once you've identified all the users, the generator automatically becomes stale and you need to create a new one, which refreshes the list of users.

Note   If you've used the built-in `range()` function (or `xrange()` prior to Python 3.0) often enough, you may have noticed that it does restart itself if accessed multiple times. That behavior is provided by moving one level lower in the iteration process, by implementing the iterator protocol explicitly. It can't be achieved with simple generators, but Chapter 5 shows that you can have greater control over iteration of the objects you create.

Lambdas

In addition to providing features on their own, functions are often called on to provide some extra minor bit of functionality to some other feature. For example, when sorting a list, you can configure Python's behavior by supplying a function that accepts a list item and returns a value that should be used for comparison. This way, given a list of House objects, for instance, you can sort by price:

```
>>> def get_price(house):
...     return house.price
...
>>> houses.sort(key=get_price)
```

Unfortunately, this seems like a bit of a waste of the function's abilities, plus it requires a couple of extra lines of code and a name that never gets used outside of the `sort()` method call. A better approach would be if you could specify the key function directly in line with the method call. This not only makes it more concise, it also places the body of the function right where it will be used, so it's a lot more readable for these types of simple behaviors.

146

In these situations, Python's lambda form is extremely valuable. Python provides a separate syntax, identified by the keyword lambda. This allows you to define a function without a name as a single expression, with a much simpler feature set. Before diving into the details of the syntax, here's what it looks like in the house-sorting example. Think of it as a one-line minifunction. Try the following:

```
>>> g=lambda x: x*x
>>> g(8)  # which returns 8 * 8
```

As you can see, this is a considerably compressed form of a function definition. Following the lambda keyword is a list of arguments, separated by commas. In the sort example only one argument is needed, and it can be named anything you like, such as any other function. They can even have default values if necessary, using the same syntax as regular functions. Arguments are followed by a colon, which notes the beginning of the lambda's body. If no arguments are involved, the colon can be placed immediately after the lambda keyword:

```
>>> a = lambda: 'example'
>>> a
<function <lambda> at 0x. .>
>>> a()
'example'
>>> b = lambda x, y=3: x + y
>>> b()
Traceback (most recent call last):

TypeError: <lambda>() takes at least 1 positional argument (0 given)
>>> b(5)
8
>>> b(5, 1)
6
```

As you'll have likely discovered by now, the body of the lambda is really just its return value. There's no explicit return statement, so the entire body of the function is really just a single expression used to return a value. That's a big part of what makes the lambda form so concise, yet easily readable, but it comes at a price: only a single expression is allowed. You can't use any control structures, such as try, with, or while blocks; you can't assign variables inside the function body; and you can't perform multiple operations without them also being tied to the same overall expression.

This may seem extremely limiting, but in order to still be readable, the function body must be kept as simple as possible. In situations in which you need the additional control flow features, you'll find it much more readable to specify it in a standard function, anyway. Then you can pass that function in where you might otherwise use the lambda. Alternatively, if you have a portion of the behavior that's provided by some other function, but not all of it, you're free to call out to other functions as part of the expression.

Introspection

One of the primary advantages of Python is that nearly everything can be examined at runtime, from object attributes and module contents to documentation and even generated bytecode. Peeking at this information is called introspection, and it permeates nearly every aspect of Python. The following sections define some of the more general introspection features that are available, while more specific details are given in the remaining chapters.

The most obvious attribute of a function that can be inspected is its name. It's also one of the simplest, made available at the __name__ attribute. The return is the string used to define the function. In the case of lambdas, which have no names, the __name__ attribute is populated with the standard string '<lambda>':

```
>>> def example():
...     pass
...
>>> example.__name__
'example'
>>> (lambda: None).__name__
'<lambda>'
```

Identifying Object Types

Python's dynamic nature can sometimes make it seem difficult to ensure you're getting the right type of value or to even know what type of value it is. Python does provide some options for accessing that information, but it's necessary to realize those are two separate tasks, so Python uses two different approaches.

The most obvious requirement is to identify what type of object your code was given. For this Python supplies its built-in `type()` function, which accepts an object to identify. The return value is the Python class that was used to create the given object, even if that creation was done implicitly, by way of a literal value:

```
>>> type('example')
<type 'str'>
>>> class Test:
...     pass
...
>>> type(Test)
<type 'classobj'>
>>> type(Test())
<type 'instance'>
```

Chapter 4 explains in detail what you can do with that class object once you have it, but the more common case is to compare an object against a particular type you expect to receive. This is a different situation because it doesn't really matter exactly what type the object is. As long as the value is an instance of the right type, you can make correct assumptions about how it behaves.

There are a number of different utility functions available for this purpose, most of which are covered in Chapter 4. This section and the next chapter will make use of one of them fairly frequently, so it merits some explanation here. The `isinstance()` function accepts two arguments: the object to check and the type you're expecting it to be. The result is a simple `True` or `False`, making it suitable for if blocks:

```
>>> def test(value):
...     if isinstance(value, int):
...         print('Found an integer!')
...
>>> test('0')
>>> test(0)
Found an integer!
```

Modules and Packages

Functions and classes that are defined in Python are placed inside of modules, which in turn are often part of a package structure. Accessing this structure when importing code is easy enough, using documentation or even just peeking at the source files on disk. Given a piece of code, however, it's often useful to identify where it was defined in the source code.

For this reason, all functions and classes have a __module__ attribute, which contains the import location of the module where the code was defined. Rather than just supplying the name of the module, the math.sin._module__ also includes the full path to where the module resides. Essentially, it's enough information for you to pass it straight into any of the dynamic importing features shown in Chapter 2.

Working with the interactive interpreter is something of a special case because there's no named source file to work with. Any functions or classes defined there will have the special name '__main__' returned from the __module__ attribute:

```
>>> def example():
...     pass
...
>>> example
<function example at 0x...>
>>> example.__module__
'__main__'
```

Docstrings

Because you can document your functions with docstrings included right alongside the code, Python also stores those strings as part of the function object. By accessing the __doc__ attribute of a function, you can read a docstring into code, which can be useful for generating a library's documentation on the fly. Consider the following example, showing simple docstring access on a simple function:

```
def example():
    """This is just an example to illustrate docstring access."""
    pass
print(example.__doc__)  # which outputs This is just an example to
illustrate docstring access.
```

Next, try the following from a prompt:

```
>>> def divide(x, y):
...     """
...     divide(integer, integer) -> floating point
...
...     This is a more complex example, with more comprehensive documentation.
...     """
...     return float(x) / y # Use float()for compatibility prior to 3.0
...
>>> divide.__doc__
'\n    divide(integer, integer) -> floating point\n\n    This is a more
complex example, with more comprehensive documentation.\n    '
>>> print(divide.__doc__)

    divide(integer, integer) -> floating point
```

This is a more complex example, with more comprehensive documentation.

As you can see, simple docstrings are easy to handle just by reading in __doc__ and using it however you need to. Unfortunately, more complex docstrings will retain all whitespace, including newlines, making them more challenging to work with. Worse yet, your code can't know which type of docstring you're looking at without scanning it for certain characters. Even if you're just printing it out to the interactive prompt, you still have an extra line before and after the real documentation, as well as the same indentation as was present in the file.

To handle complex docstrings more gracefully, like the one shown in the example, the inspect module mentioned previously also has a getdoc() function, designed to retrieve and format docstrings. It strips out whitespace both before and after the documentation, as well as any indentation that was used to line up the docstring with the code around it. Here's that same docstring again, but formatted with inspect.getdoc():

```
>>> import inspect
>>> print(inspect.getdoc(divide))

divide(integer, integer) -> floating point
This is a more complex example, with more comprehensive documentation.
```

We still have to use print() at the interactive prompt because the newline character is still retained in the result string. All inspect.getdoc() strips out is the whitespace that was used to make the docstring look right alongside the code for the function. In addition to trimming the space at the beginning and end of the docstring, getdoc() uses a simple technique to identify and remove whitespace used for indentation.

Essentially, getdoc() counts the number of spaces at the beginning of each line of code, even if the answer is 0. Then it determines the lowest value of those counts and removes that many characters from each line that remains after the leading and trailing whitespace has been removed. This allows you to keep other indentation in the docstring intact, as long as it's greater than what you need to align the text with the surrounding code. Here's an example of an even more complex docstring, so you can see how inspect.getdoc() handles it:

```
>>> def clone(obj, count=1):
...     """
...     clone(obj, count=1) -> list of cloned objects
...
...     Clone an object a specified number of times, returning the cloned
...     objects as a list. This is just a shallow copy only.
...
...     obj
...         Any Python object
...     count
...         Number of times the object will be cloned
...
...         >>> clone(object(), 2)
...         [<object object at 0x12345678>, <object object at 0x87654321>]
...     """
...     import copy
...     return [copy.copy(obj) for x in count]
...
>>> print(inspect.getdoc(clone))
clone(obj, count=1) -> list of cloned objects
Clone an object a specified number of times, returning the cloned
objects as a list. This is just a shallow copy only.
obj
    Any Python object
count
    Number of times the object will be cloned

  >>> clone(object(), 2)
  [<object object at 0x12345678>, <object object at 0x87654321>]
```

Notice how the descriptions of each argument are still indented four spaces, just like they appeared to be in the function definition. The shortest lines had just four total spaces at the beginning, while those had eight, so Python stripped out the first four, leaving the rest intact. Likewise, the example interpreter session was indented by two extra spaces, so the resulting string maintains a two-space indentation.

Oh, and don't worry too much about the `copy function` just yet. Chapter 6 describes in detail how to make and manage copies of objects when necessary.

Exciting Python Extensions: Statistics

Most people working with statistical analysis might not consider Python as a first choice. Since Python is a general-purpose language and other languages such as R, SAS, or SPSS are aimed at statistics directly, this makes sense. However, Python, via it's rich set of libraries, might be a good choice, especially since it is so user-friendly and handles data acquisition with ease. It is integrated well with other languages. However, let's see how easy it is to work with statistical analysis with Python. One library to use is Pandas (Python Data Analysis Library).

Install Pandas and Matplotlib

Use *PIP* to install Pandas.

1) From an escalated command prompt, type: **pip install pandas** (enter)

   This will also install NumPy and datautils, which will be needed. Assuming you had no errors, make a file and try a test read to make sure it works.

2) Type: pip install matplotlib (enter)

Make a Text File of Data

First, we will make a CSV (comma separated values) text file with some hypothetical data. This could be data from the Internet, or a database, and so on. You might well have a spreadsheet (e.g., Excel or OpenOffice) of data you want to work with. These packages make it easy to "save as" CSV format. For now, use your favorite text editor.

1) Start Notepad (Windows) and enter the following, saving as a text file to the same folder where you are going to save your Python file to read it. Make sure the text file and Python file are in the same folder!

```
"Subject","Gender","Level","GPA","Major","Age"
"1","female","Freshmen",3.9,"History",23
"2","male","Senior",3.9,"History",18
"3","male","Senior",2.5,"Psy",21
"4","male","Freshmen",2.0,"Math",32
"5","female","Junior",3.5,"Chem",19
"6","male","Freshmen",3.0,"History",20
```

2) Save the file as "students.csv" and make sure a txt extension is not appended to the file name; the complete file name should only be "students.csv".

Use Pandas to Display Data

Now, let's test and see if we can read our CSV data and display it to the screen. Once this works, we can work with the data a bit. Create a Python script and run the following, giving the Python file a valid name of your own choice:

```
import pandas
data = pandas.read_csv('students.csv', sep=',', na_values=".")
print (data)
```

Your output should be similar to the following:

```
   Subject   Gender      Level  GPA     Major  Age
0        1   female   Freshmen  3.9   History   23
1        2     male     Senior  3.9   History   18
2        3     male     Senior  2.5       Psy   21
3        4     male   Freshmen  2.0      Math   32
4        5   female     Junior  3.5      Chem   19
5        6     male   Freshmen  3.0   History   20
```

Output from reading students.csv data file using Pandas.

Running Some Data Analysis

In this next example, let's look at the average age of the students who are in different majors. The statistics library's make this easy, in this case the function is *mean()* and *groupby()*:

```
import pandas
data = pandas.read_csv('students.csv', sep=',', na_values=".")
print (data)
groupby_major = data.groupby('Major')
for major, student_age in groupby_major['Age']:
        print( 'The average age for', major, 'majors is: ', student_age.mean())
```

```
   Subject   Gender      Level  GPA     Major  Age
0        1   female   Freshmen  3.9   History   23
1        2     male     Senior  3.9   History   18
2        3     male     Senior  2.5       Psy   21
3        4     male   Freshmen  2.0      Math   32
4        5   female     Junior  3.5      Chem   19
5        6     male   Freshmen  3.0   History   20
The average age for Chem majors is:  19.0
The average age for History majors is:  20.333333333333332
The average age for Math majors is:  32.0
The average age for Psy majors is:  21.0
```

Average student age output for various majors.

The *unique()* function will show you only unique values for a given column of data. For example, using our students.csv file, we can list only the majors that are in the dataset. Note that the column field is case-sensitive, so you would want to either display or view the original CSV file to make sure your case is correct. In this case a capital M is needed in Major, or it would not function properly:

```
import pandas
data = pandas.read_csv('students.csv', sep=',', na_values=".")
dif_majors = data.Major.unique()
print(dif_majors)
```

Next, you might want to only access certain columns of data. Consider the following, where only the Major and GPA columns of data will be extracted and displayed:

```
import pandas
data = pandas.read_csv('students.csv', sep=',', na_values=".")
major_gpa = data[['Major','GPA']].head(10)
print (major_gpa)
```

Plotting with Matplotlib

The Matplotlib library will allow you to visualize your numeric data, which is very important with trying to convey information to the general population. In fact, visualizing data can help even data experts to find hidden meaning from the information. Try the following example to see how easy it is to visualize a series of data values graphically:

```
import matplotlib.pyplot as plt
plt.plot([1,8,2,9,6]) # x values
plt.ylabel('Data readings for five hours') #y values
plt.show()
```

Types of Charts

There are many types of charts available. A quick visit to Matplotlib.org will show new additions and features of the library for pyplot, which are evolving at a rapid pace. Consider the following to see just a few of the many types of charts available to you from this library:

```
#Pie chart example
import matplotlib.pyplot as plt
#Data sets 1 - 5
sets = 'D 1', 'D 2', 'D 3', 'D 4', 'D 5'
data = [5, 10, 15, 20, 50]
plt.pie(data, labels=sets)
plt.show()
```

There are many others such as bar, hist (histogram), box, density, area, scatter, and XKCD-style charts (comic web site with Pythonish humor). The format is similar to pie.

Combine Matplotlib with Pandas

Now that we have the basics down for visualizing data let's visualize a larger data set, which would be a bit more practical: you would not normally type every value into your code, but would be reading from a CSV file or similar, perhaps obtained from an Internet site. We will combine data visualization with Pandas. In the following example we add a few functions such as *tick* and *title* and make a histogram of students in age ranges from the students.csv data set. Pandas and Matplotlib with pyplot are good tools to use in combination:

```
import pandas
import matplotlib.pyplot as plt
data = pandas.read_csv('students.csv', sep=',', na_values=".")

age = data[['Age']]
print(age)
plt.hist(age)
plt.xticks(range(18,33))
plt.title('Ages of students')
plt.show()
```

The Pandas and Matplotlib documentation and main web site of course will describe other functions available, but this will get you using Pandas features so that you can easily integrate other features you might need into your applications as needed.

Taking It with You

Although Python functions may seem to be quite simple on the surface, you now know how to define and manage them in ways that really fit your needs. Of course, you're probably looking to incorporate functions into a more comprehensive object-oriented program, and for that, we'll need to look at how Python's classes work.

CHAPTER 4

Classes

In Chapter 3 you reviewed how *functions* allow you to define code that can be reused. This allowed for general code streamlining by not having to retype "chunks" of code. However, it's often more useful to combine those same functions into logical groupings that define the behavior and attributes of a particular type of object. This is standard object-oriented (OO) programming, which is implemented in Python by way of *types* and *classes*. These, like functions, may seem simple enough on the surface, but there's a considerable amount of power behind them that you can leverage.

The most basic idea of a class is that it encapsulates the behavior of an object, whereas an *instance* of the class *represents the data for the object*. Therefore, even though data may well change from one instance to another, behavior determined by the underlying class will remain the same across those instances. Defining, extending, and altering that behavior is the focus of this chapter.

Inheritance

The simplest way to use classes is to define a single class for a single type of object. That works well for many simple applications, but you're likely to find the need for finer-grained control over the behavior of objects. In particular, it's common to have a single common set of behaviors for a large collection of objects, but you then need to modify them or add new ones for a smaller set of more specific objects.

To facilitate this, Python allows each class to specify one or more base classes that will provide the fundamental behavior. Then, the new class being defined can add new behaviors or override any existing ones. By default, all objects descend from the built-in `object` type, although that doesn't really do anything useful on its own. It's really just a foundation type that underpins the entire system, as everything else inherits from it.

© J. Burton Browning and Marty Alchin 2019
J. B. Browning and M. Alchin, *Pro Python 3*, https://doi.org/10.1007/978-1-4842-4385-5_4

Like most object-oriented languages, Python lets you define as many subclasses as you'd like for a given class, and you can subclass those as well, going as many levels deep as necessary. This vertical approach to inheritance is appropriate for most applications, because it maximizes the usefulness of the base classes. When a single, typically large, set of behaviors needs to be reused across a variety of other classes, vertical inheritance proves quite useful. Try a very simple Python class with an explicit constructor:

```python
class Contact:
    def __init__(self, lName, fName): # explicit constructor for class
        self.lastName = lName
        self.firstName = fName

worker1 = Contact("Smith", "James")
print(worker1.lastName, worker1.firstName)
```

Python also has some built-in functions to modify your classes.. This is a peek ahead to the "Attributes" section of this chapter, but these functions are *getattr(obj, name)* to access the attribute of an object; *setattr(obj, name, value)* to set the attribute of an object; *hasattr(obj, name)* to check for existence; and, finally, *delattr(obj, name)* to delete an attribute in an object. Public properties are, of course, accessible once the object is created:

```python
class Contact:
    def __init__(self, lName, fName): # explicit constructor for class
        self.lastName = lName
        self.firstName = fName
worker1 = Contact('Smith', 'James')
print(worker1.lastName, worker1.firstName) # object.public_property
newLast=raw_input('Enter new last name: ')
setattr(worker1,'lastName',newLast) # set attribute with new value
print(worker1.lastName, worker1.firstName)
print(getattr(worker1, 'lastName')) # get existing attribute
```

As yet another example, consider a common scenario involving a contact management application. At the root of all else you would have a Contact class, because, by definition, everything in the application is a contact. It would have a set of fields and behaviors associated with it, which cover only those things that are pertinent to all contacts, according to the needs of your application:

```python
class Contact:
    name = TextField()
    email = EmailAddressField()
    phone = PhoneNumberField()

    def send_mail(self, message):
        # Email sending code would go here
```

For now, don't worry about the specifics of where each of the field classes come from or how they work in the application. If you're interested, Chapter 11 demonstrates one possible framework for writing classes like this. The key for now is that each of the fields represents a single piece of data relating to the class at hand. Values might be provided by user input, results from a database query, or even random value generator; what's important is the structure of the class and how subclasses will work with it.

Even with just a contact in place, you can create a useful application based on those core fields and behaviors. Providing additional features means adding support for different types of contacts. For instance, real people have a first name, last name, and perhaps a cell phone, whereas companies will often have only a single name and phone number. Likewise, companies will do business in particular industries, which wouldn't make any sense in the case of individuals:

```python
class Person(Contact):
    first_name = TextField()
    last_name = TextField()
    name = ComputedString('%(last_name)s, %(first_name)s')
    cell_phone = PhoneNumberField()

class Company(Contact):
    industry = TextField()
```

Now we have a basic hierarchy beginning to take shape. People are different from companies, and they each have different fields that are appropriate to each case. Python's inheritance system automatically pulls the fields from the Contact class and makes them available on the Person and Company classes. You can subclass these as well, providing such Person types as Employee, Friend, and FamilyMember:

```python
class Employee(Person):
    employer = RelatedContact(Company)
    job_title = TextField()
    office_email = EmailAddressField()
    office_phone = PhoneNumberField()
    extension = ExtensionField()

class Friend(Person):
    relationship = TextField()

class FamilyMember(Person):
    relationship = TextField()
    birthday = DateField()
```

Notice here that even though both Friend and FamilyMember have relationship fields that work identically to each other, FamilyMember doesn't inherit from Friend. It's not necessarily true that a family member will also be a friend, so the class structure reflects that. Each new subclass is automatically considered to be a more specific example of the class it extends, so it's important that the inheritance scheme reflects the actual relationships being codified.

This may seem like a philosophical detail, but it has real ramifications in code as well. As will be shown in the "Introspection" section in this chapter, Python code can take a look at the inheritance structure of classes, so any mismatches can cause your code to confuse one type of class for another. The best way to avoid those problems is to think about how the objects you're representing actually relate to one another and try to recreate those relationships in code.

Multiple Inheritance

Python also supports a horizontal approach to class inheritance, by allowing a subclass to define more than one base class at a time. This way, a class can obtain behaviors from many various classes without having to go several levels deep. Of course, that means taking a different logical approach because you're no longer defining classes by increasing specificity. Instead, in some uses of multiple inheritance, you're essentially building up each class as a set of components.

Building up classes like this is particularly well suited for applications in which your classes share some common behaviors but are not otherwise related to each other in a hierarchical manner. In order to make sense, this typically requires a large number of classes to be built from a reasonably large number of components. Because that's not the way most applications are put together, it's rarely used this way in the wild.

Instead, multiple inheritance is often called on to apply support classes, called mixins. Mixin classes don't provide full functionality on their own; they instead supply just a small add-on feature that could be useful on a wide range of different classes. One example might be a mixin that returns None when you try to access any attribute that isn't available on the object, rather than raising an AttributeError:

```
class NoneAttributes:
    def __getattr__(self, name):
        return None
```

The __getattr__() method, which will be described in more detail in the "Magic Methods" section later in this chapter, is called whenever an attribute is requested that isn't available on the object. Because it works as a fallback, it's an obvious choice for a mixin; the real class provides its own functionality, with the mixin adding onto that where applicable:

```
class Example(BaseClass, NoneAttributes):
    pass

e = Example()
e.does_not_exist
```

In typical applications, a vertical hierarchy will provide most of the functionality, with mixins adding some extras where necessary. Because of the potential number of classes involved when accessing attributes, it becomes even more important to fully understand how Python decides which class is used for each attribute and method that was accessed. To put it another way, you need to know the order in which Python resolves which method to use.

Method Resolution Order

Given a class hierarchy, Python needs to determine which class to use when attempting to access an attribute by name. To do this, Python has rules that govern how to order a set of base classes when a new class is defined. For most basic usage of classes you don't really need to know how this works, but if you work with multilevel or multiple inheritance, the details in this section will help you understand what's really going on.

In the simple vertical-only scenario, it's easy to imagine how the Method Resolution Order (MRO) would be created. The class you're actually working with would be first in line, followed by its base class, followed by the base class of the base class, and so on up the line until you get back to the root object type.

At each step in the chain, Python checks to see if the class has an attribute with the name being requested, and if it does, that's what you get. If not, it moves on to the next one. This is easy to see with a simple example. Key this in from a prompt and try it:

```
>>> class Book:
...     def __init__(self, title):
...         self.title = title
...         self.page = 1
...     def read(self):
...         return 'There sure are a lot of words on page %s.' % self.page
...     def bookmark(self, page):
...         self.page = page
...
>>> class Novel(Book):
...     pass
```

```
...
>>> class Mystery(Novel):
...     def read(self):
...         return "Page %s and I still don't know who did it!" % self.page
...
>>> book1 = Book('Pro Python')
>>> book1.read()
'There sure are a lot of words on page 1.'
>>> book1.bookmark(page=52)
>>> book1.read()
'There sure are a lot of words on page 52.'
>>> book2 = Novel('Pride and Prejudice')
>>> book2.read()
'There sure are a lot of words on page 1.'
>>> book3 = Mystery('Murder on the Orient Express')
>>> book3.read()
"Page 1 and I still don't know who did it!"
>>> book3.bookmark(page=352)
>>> book3.read()
"Page 352 and I still don't know who did it!"
```

As you can see, when calling `read()` on a `Mystery` object, you get the method that's defined directly on that class, while using `bookmark()` on that same class uses the implementation from `Book`. Likewise, `Novel` doesn't define anything on its own—it's just there to make for a more meaningful hierarchy—so all of the methods you have access to actually come from `Book`. To put it more directly, the MRO for `Mystery` is [`Mystery`, `Novel`, `Book`], while the MRO for `Novel` is simply [`Novel`, `Book`].

So what happens when you take a horizontal approach using multiple inheritance? For the sake of simplicity, we'll start with just a single layer of inheritance for each of the supplied base classes so that it's a purely horizontal approach. In this case Python goes from left to right, in the order the classes were defined as base classes. Here's what the previous example looks like once we add a `purchase()` method, which would allow the user to buy a copy of the book. If you still have the previous terminal session open, try the next bit to add on to what we have done:

```
>>> class Product:
...     def purchase(self):
...         return 'Wow, you must really like it!'
...
>>> class BookProduct(Book, Product):
...     pass
...
>>> class MysteryProduct(Mystery, Product):
...     def purchase(self):
...         return 'Whodunnit?'
...
>>> product1 = BookProduct('Pro Python')
>>> product1.purchase()
'Wow, you must really like it!'
>>> product2 = MysteryProduct('Murder on the Orient Express')
>>> product2.purchase()
'Whodunnit?'
```

Thus far, each MRO has been very straightforward and easy to understand, even if you didn't know what was going on behind the scenes. Unfortunately, things get more complex when you start combining both forms of inheritance. It doesn't even take a very complicated example to illustrate the problem; consider what happens when you inherit from one class that has a base class of its own and a mixin that stands alone:

```
class A:
    def test(self):
        return 'A'
class B(A):
    pass
class C:
    def test(self):
        return 'C'
```

This is simple enough, but if you create a new class, D, which subclasses both B and C, what would happen if you call its `test()` method? As always, it's easy enough to test this out in the interactive interpreter, where you'll see that the answer depends on which one you put first. Make sure you are in the same session, and have keyed in the aforementioned code, and then try the following to see the results:

```
>>> class D(B, C):
...     pass
...
>>> D().test()
'A'
>>> class D(C, B):
...     pass
...
>>> D().test()
'C'
```

On the surface, it seems easy to assume that Python simply goes depth first; it looks at the first base class and follows it all the way down, looking for the requested attribute, moving on to the next base class only when it can't find what it needs. That observation is certainly true for this and many other cases, but it's still not the whole story. What's really going on takes the whole inheritance scheme into account.

Before clarifying the full algorithm, however, let's get one thing out of the way. The first namespace Python looks at is always the instance object. If the attribute isn't found there, it goes to the actual class that provides that object's behavior. These two namespaces are always the first two to be checked, regardless of any inheritance structure that may be in use. Python try to locate it through class inheritance only if the attribute isn't found there.

Rather than looking at the whole inheritance structure as a kind of tree, Python tries to flatten it out to a single list, with each class appearing just once. This is an important distinction because it's possible for two base classes to subclass the same class deeper in the chain, but looking at that class twice would only cause confusion later on. To resolve this and other potential issues, there needs to be a single, flat list to work with.

The first step is to identify all the different paths that can be taken to get from a class to its basemost class. There will always be at least one path, even if there's no base class, for two reasons. For one, the MRO for a given class always includes the class itself in the first position. This may seem obvious from earlier descriptions, but the rest of the algorithm will make it clear why this is important to state explicitly. Also, every class implicitly inherits from object, so that's at the end of every MRO.

So, for just a simple class, A, which doesn't inherit from anything, its MRO is just a simple two-element list: [A, object]. If you have another class, B, which subclasses A, its MRO becomes fairly obvious as well, being [B, A, object]. Once you introduce a bit of multiple inheritance, it's possible for the same class to appear more than once in the overall tree, so we need some extra work in order to sort out the MRO.

Consider a new class, C, which inherits from both B and A. Now A shows up under two different branches and at two different distances from the new class, C.

Note   It might not make sense to do this because B already inherits from A. Remember, however, that you may not always know in advance what the base classes are doing behind the scenes. You might extend classes that were passed into your code from elsewhere or were generated dynamically, such as will be shown later in this chapter. Python doesn't know how your classes are laid out, so it has to be able to account for all the possibilities.

```
>>> class A:
...     pass
...
>>> class B(A):
...     pass
...
>>> class C(B, A):
...     pass
...
```

The MRO for object is obviously just [object], and A has already been shown to be [A, object], as you would expect. B is clearly [B, A, object], but what about C? Looking at it depth-first, you might guess [C, B, A, object] once the duplicate A is removed. Taking a breadth-first (horizontal before vertical) approach, you'd come up with [C, A, B, object].

So which way does Python go? The truth is, neither of those is accurate; Python uses an algorithm called C3. This algorithm takes all the inheritance into account, reducing it by one layer at a time, until only a single list remains. At each level, C3 processes the class lists that were created for all of that level's parent classes. Because of this, it starts at the most generic class, object, and continues outward from there.

With C in place, we can finally see how the algorithm works in detail. By the time Python encounters C, both A and B have already been processed, so their MROs are known. In order to combine them, C3 looks at the first class in each of the parent MROs to see if it can find a candidate for inclusion in the MRO for C. Of course, that begs the question of what exactly constitutes a valid candidate.

The only criteria used to identify a candidate class is whether it exists in only the first position in any of the MRO lists being considered. It doesn't have to be in all of them, but if it's present, it must be the first in the list. If it's in any other position in any of the lists, C3 will skip it until its next pass. Once it finds a valid entry, it pulls that into the new MRO and looks for the next one using the same procedure.

Example: C3 Algorithm

Because algorithms are really just code, let's put together a simple C3 function that will perform the necessary linearization—reducing the inheritance tree into a single list. Before diving into the full implementation, however, let's first take a look at what the function call would look like, so we know what data it'll be working with. For C, it would look like this:

```
C3(C, [B, A, object], [A, object], [B, A])
```

The first argument is the class itself, which is followed by the known MRO lists for its parent classes, in the order they were defined on the class. The last argument, however, is simply the list of parent classes themselves, without their full MROs. As will be shown in a slight modification of C later, this extra argument is necessary to resolve some ambiguities.

As with any function, there are a few boring details that need to be put in place before the real heavy lifting can be done. In the case of C3, there will be some modification of the MRO lists along the way, and we don't want those modifications to affect the code that called the C3 function, so we have to make copies of them to work with. In addition, we need to set up a new list to contain the final MRO being generated by the algorithm:

```
def C3(cls, *mro_lists):
    # Make a copy so we don't change existing content
    mro_lists = [list(mro_list[:]) for mro_list in mro_lists]
    # Set up the new MRO with the class itself
    mro = [cls]

    # The real algorithm goes here.

    return mro
```

We can't just use mro_list[:] here because that only copies the outer list. All the other lists that were contained inside that list would remain, so any modifications to them would be visible outside the function. By using a list comprehension and copying each of the internal lists, we get copies of all the lists involved, so they can be safely altered.

THE ROBUSTNESS PRINCIPLE

If you're already aware of Python's copy module—or you've skipped ahead to Chapter 6—you may wonder why we don't just use copy.deepcopy(mro_list) instead. At the very least, you may be wondering what that extra list(mro_list[:]) is for, because we're passing in lists already. By explicitly casting each of the internal sequences to lists and wrapping it all in a list comprehension, we can allow the function to accept any valid sequence types, including tuples, which aren't able to be modified after being created (like a constant perhaps). This makes the C3 function much more liberal in what it accepts.

With the housekeeping out of the way, we can move on to the main algorithm. Because we don't know in advance how many classes are in each MRO, it's best to wrap the main workload in a simple while True loop, which will execute indefinitely, so we can control its flow using break and continue. Of course, this means you shouldn't try executing this code until a bit later on, until we have the necessary control code in place.

The first task inside that loop will be to loop over each MRO list, get its first class, and see if it's in any position other than first in any of the other lists. If it is, that class isn't a valid candidate yet and we need to move on to the first class in the next list. Here's the loop necessary to perform those first steps:

```python
import itertools

def C3(cls, *mro_lists):
    # Make a copy so we don't change existing content
    mro_lists = [list(mro_list[:]) for mro_list in mro_lists]

    # Set up the new MRO with the class itself
    mro = [cls]

    while True:
        for mro_list in mro_lists:
            # Get the first item as a potential candidate for the MRO.
            candidate = mro_list[0]

            if candidate in itertools.chain(*(x[1:] for x in mro_lists)) :
                # The candidate was found in an invalid position, so we
                # move on to the next MRO list to get a new candidate.
                continue

    return mro
```

The chain used here reduces all the non–first classes in all the MRO lists down to a single list, so it's easier to test whether the current candidate is valid or not. Of course, the current code only responds if the candidate is invalid. If it wasn't found in that chain, it's a valid candidate and can be promoted to the final MRO right away.

In addition, we need to remove that candidate from the MRO list where it was found, as well as any of the others it might be found in. This is made a bit easier by the fact that we know it can only be the first item in any of the lists and that it won't be in any of them that were already processed in this round. We can therefore just look at each of the remaining candidates and remove the class that was promoted. In any case, none of the other MRO lists should be processed for a new candidate this time around, so we also need to add a continue:

```python
while True:
# Reset for the next round of tests
    candidate_found = False

    for mro_list in mro_lists:
        if not len(mro_list):
            # Any empty lists are of no use to the algorithm.
            continue

        # Get the first item as a potential candidate for the MRO.
        candidate = mro_list[0]

        if candidate_found:
            # Candidates promoted to the MRO are no longer of use.
            if candidate in mro:
                mro_list.pop(0)
            # Don't bother checking any more candidates if one was found.
            continue

        if candidate in itertools.chain(*(x[1:] for x in mro_lists)) :
            # The candidate was found in an invalid position, so we
            # move on to the next MRO list to get a new candidate.
            continue

        else:
            # The candidate is valid and should be promoted to the MRO.
            mro.append(candidate)
            mro_list.pop(0)
            candidate_found = True
```

Note   Now that we're removing items from the MRO lists, we also have to add in an extra bit of code to handle the situation in which one of the lists was completely emptied. Because there's nothing of value in an empty list, the loop just moves on to the next one.

With the candidate selection now complete, the only things left are to tell the algorithm when its job is done and it should exit the loop. As it stands it will empty the lists completely, but continue looping through them forever, without ever returning the new MRO. The key to identifying this situation is that it will indeed empty all the lists. Therefore, we can check the remaining MRO lists to see if any classes remain. If not, it's done and can end the loop:

```
while True:
    # Reset for the next round of tests
    candidate_found = False

    for mro_list in mro_lists:
        if not len(mro_list):
            # Any empty lists are of no use to the algorithm.
            continue
        # Get the first item as a potential candidate for the MRO.
        candidate = mro_list[0]

        if candidate_found:
            # Candidates promoted to the MRO are no longer of use.
            if candidate in mro:
                mro_list.pop(0)
            # Don't bother checking any more candidates if one was found.
            continue

        if candidate in itertools.chain(*(x[1:] for x in mro_lists)) :
            # The candidate was found in an invalid position, so we
            # move on to the next MRO list to get a new candidate.
            continue
```

```
        else:
            # The candidate is valid and should be promoted to the MRO.
            mro.append(candidate)
            mro_list.pop(0)
            candidate_found = True

    if not sum(len(mro_list) for mro_list in mro_lists):
        # There are no MROs to cycle through, so we're all done.
        # note any() returns false if no items so it could replace sum(len)
        break
```

This loop, inside the C3 function mentioned already, can successfully create an MRO for any valid Python inheritance scheme. Going back to the function call for the C class mentioned previously, we'd get the following result. Notice that we're using strings here instead of the actual classes, to make it easier to illustrate. Nothing about the C3 algorithm is actually tied to classes anyway; it's all just about flattening out a hierarchy that may contain duplicates:

```
>>> C3('C', ['B', 'A', 'object'], ['A', 'object'], ['B', 'A'])
['C', 'B', 'A', 'object']
```

That's all well and good, but there's another related situation that needs some attention as well: what happens when C inherits from A before B? One would logically assume that any attributes found on A would be used before those on B, even though B's MRO puts B before A. That would violate an important consistency in class inheritance: the order of items in an MRO should be preserved in all of its future subclasses.

Those subclasses are allowed to add new items to their MRO, even inserting them in between items in the MRO of the base class, but all the MROs involved should still retain the same ordering they had originally. So when doing something like C(A, B), the correct result would actually be inconsistent with user expectations.

That's why the C3 algorithm requires that the base classes themselves be added to the list of MROs that are passed in. Without them, we could invoke the C3 algorithm with this new construct and get the same result that was obtained with the original ordering:

```
>>> C3('C', ['B', 'A', 'object'], ['A', 'object'])
['C', 'B', 'A', 'object']
>>> C3('C', ['A', 'object'], ['B', 'A', 'object'])
['C', 'B', 'A', 'object']
```

Even though it seems like the two should do different things, they would actually end up doing the same thing. By adding in the extra class list at the end, however, the behavior of C3 changes a bit. The first candidate is A, which is found in the second position in the MRO of B, so A is skipped for this round. The next candidate is B, which is found in the list added in the final argument, so that's skipped, too. When the final list is examined, A is skipped once again.

This means C3 completes a full loop without finding any valid candidates, which is how it detects inappropriate constructs like C(A, B). Without a valid candidate, no items are removed from any of the lists and the main loop would run again with exactly the same data. Without any extra handling for the invalid case, our current Python implementation of C3 will simply continue on indefinitely. It would be better to raise an exception. First, however, let's validate this assumption by examining Python's own behavior with C(A, B). Assuming that you keyed in the previous examples, try the following:

```
>>> class A:
...     pass
...
>>> class B(A):
...     pass
...
>>> class C(A, B):
...     pass
...
Traceback (most recent call last):
  ...
TypeError:  Cannot create a consistent method resolution
order (MRO)  for bases B, A
```

Sure enough, Python's class system disallows this construct in an effort to force developers to only make classes that make sense. Duplicating this functionality in our own C3 class is fairly easy now that we know how to identify an invalid situation. All we have to do is check at the end of the loop and see whether a valid candidate was found. If not, we can raise a TypeError:

```
import itertools

def C3(cls, *mro_lists):
    # Make a copy so we don't change existing content
    mro_lists = [list(mro_list[:]) for mro_list in mro_lists]

    # Set up the new MRO with the class itself
    mro = [cls]

    while True:
        # Reset for the next round of tests
        candidate_found = False

        for mro_list in mro_lists:
            if not len(mro_list):
                # Any empty lists are of no use to the algorithm.
                continue

            # Get the first item as a potential candidate for the MRO.
            candidate = mro_list[0]

            if candidate_found:
                # Candidates promoted to the MRO are no longer of use.
                if candidate in mro:
                    mro_list.pop(0)
                # Don't bother checking any more candidates if one was found.
                continue

            if candidate in itertools.chain(*(x[1:] for x in mro_lists)) :
                # The candidate was found in an invalid position, so we
                # move on to the next MRO list to get a new candidate.
                continue

            else:
                # The candidate is valid and should be promoted to the MRO.
                mro.append(candidate)
                mro_list.pop(0)
                candidate_found = True
```

```
    if not sum(len(mro_list) for mro_list in mro_lists):
        # There are no MROs to cycle through, so we're all done.
        break

    if not candidate_found:
        # No valid candidate was available, so we have to bail out.
        break
        raise TypeError("Inconsistent MRO")

return mro
```

With this last piece in place, our C3 implementation matches the behavior of Python's own, covering all the bases. Most arbitrary class inheritance structures can be reduced to a valid MRO, so you typically don't need to worry too much about how the algorithm works. There is one feature of classes, however—the super() function—that relies on the MRO extensively.

Using super() to Pass Control to Other Classes

One of the most common reasons to create a subclass is to override the behavior of some existing method. It could be as simple as logging every time the method is called, or as complex as completely replacing its behavior with a different implementation. In the case of the former, where you're simply tweaking existing behavior, it's quite useful to be able to use the original implementation directly so that you don't have to reinvent the wheel just to make some minor changes.

To achieve this, Python supplies the built-in super() function, which is all too often misunderstood. The common explanation of super() is that it allows you to call a method on a base class within the overridden method on a subclass. That description works to a point, but before explaining it more fully let's examine how it behaves in the simple case, to see what that even means:

```
class A(object):
    def afunction(self):
        print('afunction from Class A')
class B(A):
```

```
    def __init__(self):
        print('B is constructed!!!') # constructor for B
    def afunction(self):
        return super(B, self).afunction()
sample1=B()
print(sample1.afunction())
```

In this simple example, `super()` returns the base class of the method. To build on what we just read about, `super()` looks at the next class in the MRO, in this case class A. Notice that we say "overridden," as we have two functions named *afunction*.

Next, consider an application that needs to create a dictionary that automatically returns None for any keys that don't already have a value associated with them. This is fairly similar to `defaultdict`, but it doesn't have to create a new value each time; it just returns None:

```
>>> class NoneDictionary(dict):
...        def __getitem__(self, name):
...            try:
...                return super(NoneDictionary, self).__getitem__(name)
...            except KeyError:
...                return None
...
>>> d = NoneDictionary()
>>> d['example']
>>> d['example'] = True
>>> d['example']
True
```

Before getting too much further, it's important to realize what `super()` is really doing here. In some languages, `super()` is simply a language feature that gets compiled into some special code to access methods from other classes. In Python, however, `super()` returns an actual object, which has a set of attributes and methods that are based on where it was used.

From this simple example, it does seem that super() just provides access to a method on the base class, but remember that there can be any number of base classes involved, with more than one specified on each class. Given the complex nature of some inheritance structures, it should be clear by now that Python would use the MRO to determine which method to use. What may not be obvious, however, is which MRO is used when looking up the method.

Just looking at it, you might think that Python uses the MRO of the class where super() was used, which would be NoneDictionary in the example given here. Because most cases will look very much like that example, that assumption will be accurate enough to account for most cases. However, more complicated class hierarchies raise the question of what happens when the MRO gets changed in subclasses. Consider the following set of classes; however, start a new Python session, as these class definitions are a bit different than our first example:

```
>>> class A:
...     def test(self):
...         return 'A'
...
>>> class B(A):
...     def test(self):
...         return 'B->' + super(B, self). test()
...
>>> B().test()
'B->A'
```

In this example, using super() inside of B refers to its base class, A, as expected. Its test() method includes a reference to itself, so we'll be able to see along the way if things change. Along with B, we could define another class, C, which also subclasses A. To illustrate things a bit better down the road, C will implement its own test() method, without using super():

```
>>> class C(A):
...     def test(self):
...         return 'C'
...
>>> C().test()
'C'
```

Of course, there's nothing unusual or problematic about this so far, as it doesn't interact with A or B in any way. Where things get interesting is when we create a new class, D, which subclasses both B and C. It doesn't need a test() method, so we just leave its body blank, making it as simple as a class can be. Let's see what happens to test() now:

```
>>> class D(B, C):
...     pass
...
>>> D().test()
'B->C'
```

Now we can finally see what's going on. We can see that test() is called on B, causing its reference in the output, but when it calls super().test(), it refers to the method of C, rather than the one on A. If Python simply used the MRO of the class where the method was defined, it would reference A, not C. Instead, because it uses C, we can gain some insight into how super() really works.

In the most common case, which includes the usage shown here, super() takes two arguments: a class and an instance of that class. As our example has shown, the instance object determines which MRO will be used to resolve any attributes on the resulting object. The provided class determines a subset of that MRO, because super() only uses those entries in the MRO that occur after the class provided.

The recommended usage is to provide the class where super() was used as the first argument, and the standard self as the second argument. The resulting object will retain the instance namespace dictionary of self, but it only retrieves attributes that were defined on the classes found later in the MRO than the class provided. Technically, however, you could pass in a different class and get different results:

```
>>> class B(A):
...     def test(self):
...         return 'B->' + super(C, self). test()
...
>>> class D(B, C):
...     pass
...
>>> D().test()
'B->A'
```

In this example, where B actually references C in its invocation of super(), the resulting MRO skips C, moving straight onto A, which is shown by calling test() again. This is a dangerous thing to do in common practice, however, as shown when trying to use B on its own:

```
>>> B().test()
Traceback (most recent call last):
  ...
TypeError:  super(type, obj):  obj must be an instance or subtype of type
```

Because self isn't a subclass of C in this case, C isn't anywhere in the MRO, so super() can't determine where it should start looking for attributes. Rather than creating a useless object that just throws an AttributeError for everything, super() fails when first called, providing a better error message.

WARNING: BE CAREFUL WITH YOUR ARGUMENTS

One common mistake when using `super()` is to use it on a method that won't always have the same signature across all the various classes. In our examples here, the test() method doesn't take any arguments, so it's easy to make sure it's the same across the board. Many other cases, such as `__getitem__()`, shown previously, are standard protocols that should never have their function signatures significantly changed by any subclass. Chapter 5 shows many of these cases in more detail.

Unfortunately you can't always know what another class will do, so using super() can sometimes cause problems by providing the wrong arguments to the class given. Of course, this really isn't any different than passing in an object that has a different protocol than what another function expects.

The reason it's worth noting with super() is that it's easy to assume you know what function you're actually calling. Without a solid understanding of how MROs work and how `super()` determines which attributes to use, problems can seem to come up out of nowhere. Even with a thorough knowledge of these topics, however, the only real defense against such problems is an agreement among all the classes involved to not change method signatures.

Introspection

Given all the different inheritance options available, it's appropriate that Python provides a number of tools to identify what structure a class uses. The most obvious introspection task for use with classes is to determine whether an object is an instance of a given class. This behavior is provided using the built-in `isinstance() function`, which takes any arbitrary object as its first argument and a Python class as its second argument. Only if the given class is anywhere in the inheritance chain of the object's class will `isinstance()` return True:

```
>>> isinstance(10, int)
True
>>> isinstance('test', tuple)
False
```

A natural complement to `isinstance()` is the ability to determine whether one class has another class somewhere in its inheritance chain. This feature, provided by the built-in `subclass() function`, works just like `isinstance()`, except that it operates on a class rather than an instance of it. If the first class contains the second anywhere in its inheritance chain, `issubclass()` returns `True`:

```
>>> issubclass(int, object)
True
>>> class A:
...     pass
...
>>> class B(A):
...     pass
...
>>> issubclass(B, A)
True
>>> issubclass(B, B)
True
```

That last example may seem odd, as B clearly can't be a subclass of itself, but this behavior is to remain consistent with `isinstance()`, which returns `True` if the type of the provided object is the exact class provided along with it. In a nutshell, the relationship between the two can be described using a simple expression, which is always true:

```
isinstance(obj, cls) == issubclass(type(obj), cls)
```

If you'd like more information about the inheritance structure for a particular class, there are a few different tools at your disposal. If you'd like to know what base classes were defined for a particular class, simply access its __bases__ attribute, which will contain those base classes in a tuple. It only provides the immediate base classes, however, without any of the classes that were extended deeper than that:

```
>>> B.__bases__
(<class '__main__.A'>,)
```

On the other side of the coin, every class also has a __subclasses__() method, which returns a list of all the subclasses of the class you're working with. Like __bases__, this only goes one level away from the class you're working with. Any further subclasses need to use some other mechanism to keep track of subclasses, some of which will be discussed later in this book:

```
>>> A.__subclasses__()
[<class '__main__.B'>]
```

If you'd like even more information and control, every class also has an __mro__ attribute, which contains the full MRO for that class, in a tuple. As mentioned previously, this also includes the actual class you pass in along with any of its parent classes. You might even try this on the first example with super() used earlier:

```
>>> B.__mro__
(<class '__main__.B'>, <class '__main__.A'>, <class 'object'>)
```

How Classes Are Created

Defining a class in Python works differently than in many other languages, although the differences are not always apparent. It seems quite simple: you supply a name, possibly a base class to inherit from, some attributes, and some methods. But when Python encounters that declaration, the process that takes place actually has more in common with functions than you may realize.

To start with, the body of a class declaration is a code block. Just like if, for, and while, the body of a class block can contain any valid Python code, which will execute from top to bottom. It will follow function calls, perform error handling, read files, or anything else you ask it to do. In fact, if blocks can be quite useful inside of a class declaration:

```
>>> try:
...     import custom_library
... except ImportError:
...     custom_library = None
...
>>> class Custom:
...     if custom_library is not None:
...         has_library = True
...     else:
...         has_library = False
...
>>> Custom.has_library
False
```

Tip   This example is useful for demonstration purposes only. If you're looking to achieve the exact effect shown here, it's much more pragmatic to simply assign the expression `custom_library is not None` directly to the `has_library` attribute. It returns a Boolean value anyway, so the end result is identical, but it's a much more common approach to the task at hand.

After Python finishes executing the inner code, you'll notice that `has_library` becomes an attribute of the class object that's made available to the rest of your code. This is possible because Python's class declarations work a little bit like functions. When a new class is found, Python starts by creating a new namespace for the block of code inside it. While executing the code block, any assignments are made in that new namespace. Then the namespace created is used to populate a new object, which implements the new class.

Creating Classes at Runtime

The previous section alluded to the fact that Python creates type objects while executing code, compiling and interpreting. As with nearly everything else that happens at runtime, you can hook into that process yourself and use it to your advantage. Doing so takes advantage of what Python does behind the scenes when encountering a class.

The really important stuff happens just after the contents of the class are processed. At this point Python takes the class namespace and passes it, along with some other pieces of information, to the built-in type(), which creates or "instantiates" the new class object. This means that all classes are actually subclasses of type(), which sits at the base of all of them. Specifically, there are three pieces of information that type() uses to instantiate a class:

- The name of the class that was declared

- The base classes the defined class should inherit from

- The namespace dictionary populated when executing the class body

This information is all that's necessary to represent the entire class, and even though Python obtains this information automatically by inspecting the class declaration, you can create a type by passing in these values directly.

The name is easiest, as it's just a string with the name of the class. Base classes get slightly more involved, but they're still fairly simple: just supply a sequence containing existing class objects that the new class should inherit from. The namespace dictionary is just that: a dictionary, which happens to contain everything that should be attached to the new class by name. Here's an example of how the same class could be created in two different ways:

```
>>> class Example(int):
...     spam = 'eggs'
...
>>> Example
<class '__main__.Example'>
>>> Example = type('Example', (int,), {'spam': 'eggs'})
>>> Example
<class '__main__.Example'>
```

DON'T REPEAT YOURSELF

You'll notice that this example ends up having to write the name `Example` twice, which may seem to violate the DRY principle. Remember, however, that there are really two things going on here, and the two aren't tied to each other. First, the class is being created, which requires us to supply a name. Second, the new class gets bound to a name in the namespace.

This example uses the same name for both operations, partly for convenience and partly for compatibility with the native class declaration above it. However, the namespace assignment is completely separate from class creation, so any name could be used. In fact, most of the time you won't even know the name of the class in advance, so you'll almost always use a different name in practice anyway.

Like most times, you have low-level access to a common feature, `type()`, which gives you plenty of chances to create problems. One of the three arguments to `type()` is the name of the class to create, so it's possible to create multiple classes with the same name.

In addition, by passing in the attribute namespace, you can supply a new `__module__` attribute to mimic its presence in a different module. It won't actually put the class in the specified module, but it will fool any code that introspects the module later on. Having two classes with both the same name and module could potentially cause problems with tools that introspect modules to determine their structure and hierarchy.

Of course, it's possible to encounter these problems even without using `type()` directly. If you create a class, assign it to a different name, and then create a new class with the same name as the original, you can have the exact same naming problem. Also, Python lets you supply a `__module__` attribute within a standard class declaration, so you can even create clashes in code that's not under your control.

Even though it's possible to run into these problems without resorting to `type()` directly, the warning here is that `type()` makes it much easier to accidentally encounter problems. Without it, you'd have to write code that specifically exploits the preceding points in order to create naming conflicts. With `type()`, however, the values supplied might come from user input, customization settings, or any number of other places, and the code won't look like it has any problems of this nature.

Unfortunately there are no real safeguards against these types of problems, but there are some things you can do to help reduce the risks. One approach would be to wrap all custom class creation inside of a function that keeps track of which names have been assigned and reacts appropriately when a duplicate is created. A more pragmatic option is simply to make sure any introspecting code is capable of handling a case where duplicates are encountered. Which approach to use will depend on the needs of your code.

Metaclasses

Thus far, classes have been defined as being processed by the built-in type, which accepts the class name, its base classes, and a namespace dictionary. But type is just a class like anything else; it's only special in that it's a class used to create classes—a metaclass. Like any other class, though, it can be subclassed to provide customized behavior for our application. Because the metaclass receives the full class declaration as soon as Python encounters it, you can unlock some pretty powerful features.

By subclassing type you can create your own metaclass, which can customize the creation of new classes to better suit the needs of your application. Like any class-based customization, this is done by creating a subclass of type and overriding any methods that make sense for the task at hand. In most cases, this is either __new__() or __init__(). The "Magic Methods" section later in this chapter will explain the difference between the two, but for this discussion we'll just use __init__(), since it's easier to work with.

As mentioned previously, type() takes three arguments, all of which must be accounted for in any subclasses. To start off simple, consider the following metaclass, which prints out the name of every class it encounters:

```python
>>> class SimpleMetaclass(type):
...     def __init__(cls, name, bases, attrs):
...         print(name)
...         super(SimpleMetaclass, cls).__init__(name, bases, attrs)
...
```

This alone is enough to capture a class declaration. Using `super()` here makes sure that any other necessary initialization also takes place. Even though `type` doesn't do anything in its own `__init__()`, remember from earlier in this chapter that this class could be part of a bigger inheritance structure. Using `super()` makes sure that the class gets initialized properly, regardless of what "properly" really means in the given context.

To apply this metaclass to a new class and print out its name, Python allows the class definition to specify a metaclass right alongside its parent classes. It looks like a keyword argument, but this isn't a function call, so it's actually part of the syntax of a class declaration. Here's an example of how our `SimpleMetaclass` would work:

```
>>> class Example(metaclass=SimpleMetaclass):
...     pass
...
>>> Example
```

All that was needed here was to supply the metaclass in the class definition, and Python automatically ships that definition off to the metaclass for processing. The only difference between this and a standard class definition is that it uses `SimpleMetaclass` instead of the `standard` type.

Note   The first argument to the `__init__()` method on a metaclass is typically called cls, although you might think it should be self because `__init__()` operates an instance object, rather than a class. That's true in general, and this case is actually no exception. The only difference here is that the instance is a class object itself, which is an instance of `type`, so using self would still be accurate. However, because of the differences between classes and objects, we still refer to class objects as `cls`, rather than `self`, so they stay well separated.

Metaclasses can be difficult to understand without real-world examples to illustrate their usefulness. Let's take a look at how a simple metaclass can be used to provide a powerful framework for registering and using plugins.

Example: Plugin Framework

As an application grows flexibility becomes increasingly important, so attention often turns to plugins and whether the application can accommodate that level of modularity. There are many ways to implement plugin systems and individual plugins, but they all have three core features in common.

First, you need a way to define a place where plugins can be used. In order to plug something in, there needs to be a socket for the plug to fit into. In addition, it should be very obvious how to implement individual plugins along the way. Lastly, the framework needs to provide an easy way to access all the plugins that were found, so they can all be used. Other features may be added on top, but these are what make a plugin framework.

There are several approaches that would satisfy these requirements, but because plugins are really a form of extension, it makes sense to have them extend a base class. This makes the first requirement fairly simple to define: the point where plugins can attach themselves would be a class. As a class it takes advantage of Python's own extension features, not only through the built-in subclass syntax but also by allowing the base class to provide some methods that constitute default functionality or offer help for common plugin needs. Here's how such a plugin mount point might look for an application that validates user input:

```
class InputValidator:
    """

    A plugin mount for input validation.
    Supported plugins must provide a validate(self, input) method, which
    receives
    input as a string and raises a ValueError if the input was invalid. If the
    input was properly valid, it should just return without error. Any return
    value will be ignored.
    """

    def validate(self, input):
        # The default implementation raises a NotImplementedError
        # to ensure that any subclasses must override this method.
        raise NotImplementedError
```

Even without any of the framework-level code that makes the plugins work, this example demonstrates one of the most important aspects of an extensible system: documentation. Only by properly documenting a plugin mount can you expect plugin authors to correctly adhere to its expectations. The plugin framework itself doesn't make any assumptions about what requirements your application will have, so it's up to you to document them.

With a mount point written, individual plugins can easily be created simply by writing a subclass of the mount point that's already in place. By providing new or overridden methods to satisfy the documented requirements, they can add their own little slice of functionality to the overall application. Here's an example validator that ensures the provided input only consists of ASCII characters:

```
class ASCIIValidator(InputValidator):
    """
    Validate that the input only consists of valid ASCII characters.

    >>> v = ASCIIValidator()
    >>> v.validate('sombrero')
    >>> v.validate('jalapeño')
    Traceback (most recent call last):
      ...
    UnicodeDecodeError: 'ascii' codec can't decode character '\xf1' in position
    6: ordinal not in range(128)
    """

    def validate(self, input):
        # If the encoding operation fails, str.enc  ode() raises a
        # UnicodeDecodeError, which is a subclass of ValueError.
        input.encode('ascii')
```

Tip   Notice that this also provides its own documentation. Because plugins are also classes all their own, they can be subclassed by even more specialized plugins down the road. This makes it important to include thorough documentation even at this level, to help ensure proper usage later.

Now that we have two of the three components out of the way, the only thing left before tying it all together is to illustrate how to access any plugins that were defined. Because our code will already know about the plugin mount point, that makes an obvious place to access them, and as there could be anywhere from zero to hundreds of plugins, it's optimal to iterate over them, without caring how many there are. Here's an example function that uses any and all available plugins to determine whether some input provided by a user is valid:

```
def is_valid(input):
    for plugin in InputValidator.plugins:
        try:
            plugin().validate(input)
        except ValueError:
            # A ValueError means invalidate input
            return False
    # All validators succeeded
    return True
```

Having plugins means you can extend the functionality of even a simple function like this without having to touch its code again later. Simply add a new plugin, make sure it gets imported, and the framework does the rest. With that, we finally get around to explaining the framework and how it ties all these pieces together. Because we're working with classes whose definitions specify more than just their behavior, a metaclass would be an ideal technique.

All the metaclass really needs to do is recognize the difference between a plugin mount class and a plugin subclass and register any plugins in a list on the plugin mount, where they can be accessed later. If that sounds too simple, it's really not. In fact, the entire framework can be expressed in just a few lines of code, and it only takes one extra line of code on the plugin mount to activate the whole thing:

```
class PluginMount(type):
    """
    Place this metaclass on any standard Python class to turn it into a plugin
    mount point. All subclasses will be automatically registered as plugins.
    """
    def __init__(cls, name, bases, attrs):
        if not hasattr(cls, 'plugins'):
            # The class has no plugins list, so it must be a mount point,
            # so we add one for plugins to be registered in later.
            cls.plugins = []
        else:
            # Since the plugins attribute already exists, this is an
            # individual plugin, and it needs to be registered.
            cls.plugins.append(cls)
```

That's all that's necessary to supply the entire plugin framework. When the metaclass is activated on the plugin mount, the __init__() method recognizes that the plugins attribute doesn't yet exist, so it creates one and returns without doing anything else. When a plugin subclass is encountered the plugins attribute is available by virtue of its parent class, so the metaclass adds the new class to the existing list, thus registering it for later use.

Adding this functionality to the inputValidator mount point described previously is as simple as adding the metaclass to its class definition.

```
class InputValidator(metaclass=PluginMount):
    ...
```

Individual plugins are still defined as standard plugins, without additional effort required. Because metaclasses are inherited by all subclasses, the plugin behavior is added automatically.

Controlling the Namespace

Metaclasses can also be used to help control how Python processes the class declaration. Rather than waiting for the class to be created before acting on it, another tactic is to process the raw components of the class while Python is going through them. This is made possible by a special metaclass called __prepare__().

By supplying a __prepare__() method on your metaclass, you can get early access to the class declaration. In fact, this happens so early that the body of the class definition hasn't even been processed yet. The __prepare__() method receives just the class name and a tuple of its base classes. Rather than getting the namespace dictionary as an argument, __prepare__() is responsible for returning that dictionary itself.

The dictionary returned by __prepare__() is used as the namespace while Python executes the body of the class definition. This allows you to intercept each attribute as soon as it's assigned to the class, so it can be processed immediately. Ordinarily this is used to return an ordered dictionary, so that attributes can be stored in the order they were declared within the class. For reference, take a look at how a metaclass would work without using __prepare__():

```
>>> from collections import OrderedDict
>>> class OrderedMeta(type):
...     def __init__(cls, name, bases, attrs):
...         print(attrs)
...
>>> class Example(metaclass=OrderedMeta):
...     b = 1
...     a = 2
...     c = 3
...
{'a': 2, '__module__': '__main__', 'b': 1, 'c': 3}
```

The default behavior returns a standard dictionary, which doesn't keep track of how the keys are added. Adding a simple __prepare__() method provides all that's needed to keep the ordering intact after the class is processed:

```
>>> class OrderedMeta(type):
...     @classmethod
...     def __prepare__(cls, name, bases):
...         return OrderedDict()
...     def __init__(cls, name, bases, attrs):
...         print(attrs)
...
>>> class Example(metaclass=OrderedMeta):
...     b = 1
...     a = 2
...     c = 3
...
OrderedDict([('__module__', '__main__'), ('B', 1), ('A', 2), ('c', 3)])
```

Note   The __module__ attribute is at the beginning of the attribute list because it gets added just after __prepare__() is called, before Python starts processing the body of the class.

WITH GREAT POWER COMES GREAT RESPONSIBILITY

By controlling the object used for the namespace dictionary, you can have a tremendous amount of control over how the entire class declaration behaves. Every time a line in a class references a variable or assigns an attribute, the custom namespace can intercede and change the standard behavior. One possibility is to provide decorators that can be used when defining methods within the class, without requiring a separate import to make them available to the class definition. Likewise, you can control how attributes are assigned by changing their names, wrapping them in helper objects, or removing them from the namespace completely.

This amount of power and flexibility can be easily abused to provide a level of magic not seen elsewhere. To a developer simply using your code without fully understanding how it's implemented, it'll look like Python itself is wildly inconsistent. Worse yet, any significant changes you make to the behavior of the class declaration could impact the behavior of other tools your users might try to combine with yours. Chapter 5 shows how you can enable these features by extending your dictionary, but be very careful when doing so.

Attributes

Once an object is instantiated, any data associated with it is kept within a new namespace dictionary that's specific to that instance. Access to this dictionary is handled by attributes, which make for easier access than using dictionary keys. Just like dictionary keys, attribute values can be retrieved, set, and deleted as necessary.

Typically, accessing an attribute requires you to know the name of the attribute in advance. The syntax for attributes doesn't offer the same flexibility as dictionary keys in providing variables instead of literals, so it can seem limited if you need to get or set an attribute with a name that came from somewhere else. Instead of offering a special syntax for working with attributes in this way, Python provides a trio of functions.

The first, `getattr()`, retrieves the value to which an attribute refers, given a variable that contains the name of the attribute. The next, `setattr()`, takes both the name of an attribute and its value and attaches that value to the attribute with the given name. Finally, `delattr()` allows you to delete an attribute value given the name as its argument. With these functions, you can work with any attribute on any object without knowing the attribute names when writing code.

Properties

Rather than only acting as a proxy to the standard namespace dictionary, properties allow attributes to be powered by methods that can access the full power of Python. Typically, properties are defined using the built-in `@property` decorator function. Applied to a method, it forces the method to be called whenever the function's name is accessed as an attribute name:

```
>>> class Person:
...     def __init__(self, first_name, last_name):
...         self.first_name = first_name
...         self.last_name = last_name
...     @property
...     def name(self):
...         return '%s, %s' % (self.last_name, self.first_name)
...
>>> p = Person('Marty', 'Alchin')
>>> p.name
'Alchin, Marty'
>>> p.name = 'Alchin, Martin'  # Update it to be properly legal
Traceback (most recent call last):
  ...
AttributeError: can't set attribute
```

That last error isn't terribly descriptive, but basically properties defined this way only retrieve attribute values, not set them. Function calls are only one way, so to set the value we'll need to add another method that handles that side of things. This new method would accept another variable: the value that should be set on the attribute.

In order to mark the new method as the setter for a property, it's decorated much like the getter property. Rather than using a built-in decorator, though, the getter gains a setter attribute that can be used to decorate the new method. This fits with the typical noun-based naming convention of decorators, while also describing which property will be managed:

```
>>> class Person:
...     def __init__(self, first_name, last_name):
...         self.first_name = first_name
...         self.last_name = last_name
...     @property
```

199

```
...        def name(self):
...            return '%s, %s' % (self.last_name, self.first_name)
...        @name.setter
...        def name(self, value):
...            return '%s, %s' % (self.last_name, self.first_name)
...
>>> p = Person('Marty', 'Alchin')
>>> p.name
'Alchin, Marty'
>>> p.name = 'Alchin, Martin'  # Update it to be properly legal
>>> p.name
'Alchin, Martin'
```

Just make sure that the setter method is named the same as the original getter method, or it won't work properly. The reason for this is that name.setter doesn't actually update the original property with the setter method. Instead, it copies the getter onto the new property and assigns them both to the name given to the setter method. Exactly what this means behind the scenes will be explained better in the next section on descriptors.

In addition to getting and setting values, a property can also delete the current value, using a decorator similar to the setter. By applying name.deleter to a method that only accepts the usual self, you can use that method to delete values from the attribute. For the Person class shown here, that means clearing out both first_name and last_name together:

```
>>> class Person:
...        def __init__(self, first_name, last_name):
...            self.first_name = first_name
...            self.last_name = last_name
...        @property
...        def name(self):
...            return '%s, %s' % (self.last_name, self.first_name)
...        @name.setter
```

```
...        def name(self, value):
...            return '%s, %s' % (self.last_name, self.first_name)
...        @name.deleter
...        def name(self):
...            del self.first_name
...            del self.last_name
...
>>> p = Person('Marty', 'Alchin')
>>> p.name
'Alchin, Marty'
>>> p.name = 'Alchin, Martin' # Update it to be properly legal
>>> p.name
'Alchin, Martin'
>>> del p.name
>>> p.name
Traceback (most recent call last):
  ...
AttributeError: 'Person' object has no attribute 'last_name'
```

Descriptors

One potential problem with properties is that they require all the methods to be defined as part of the class definition. It's great for adding functionality to a class if you have control over the class yourself, but when building a framework for inclusion in other code, we'll need another approach. Descriptors allow you to define an object that can behave in the same way as a property on any class to which it's assigned.

In fact, properties are implemented as descriptors behind the scenes, as are methods, which will be explained in the next section. This makes descriptors perhaps one of the most fundamental aspects of advanced class behavior. They work by implementing any of three possible methods, dealing with getting, setting, and deleting values.

The first, __get__(), manages retrieval of attribute values, but unlike a property, a descriptor can manage attribute access on both the class and its instances. In order to identify the difference, __get__() receives both the object instance and its owner class as arguments. The owner class will always be provided, but if the descriptor is accessed directly on the class instead of an instance, the instance argument will be None.

A simple descriptor using only the __get__() method can be used to always provide an up-to-date value when requested. The obvious example, then, is an object that returns the current date and time without requiring a separate method call:

```
>>> import datetime
>>> class CurrentTime:
...     def __get__(self, instance, owner):
...         return datetime.datetime.now()
...
>>> class Example:
...     time = CurrentTime()
...
>>> Example().time
datetime.datetime(2009, 10, 31, 21, 27, 5, 236000)
>>> import time
>>> time.sleep(5 * 60) # Wait five minutes
>>> Example().time
datetime.datetime(2009, 10, 31, 21, 32, 15, 375000)
```

The related __set__() method manages setting a value on the attribute managed by the descriptor. Unlike __get__(), this operation can only be performed on instance objects. If you assign a value to the given name on the class instead, you'll actually overwrite the descriptor with the new value, removing all of its functionality from the class. This is intentional, because without it, there would be no way to modify or remove a descriptor once it's been assigned to a class.

Because it doesn't need to accept the owner class, __set__() only receives the instance object and the value being assigned. The class can still be determined by accessing the __class__ attribute on the instance object provided, though, so there's no information lost. With both __get__() and __set__() defined on a descriptor, we can do something more useful. For example, here's a basic descriptor that behaves just like an attribute, except that it logs every time its value is changed:

```
>>> import datetime
>>> class LoggedAttribute:
...     def __init__(self):
...         self.log = []
...         self.value_map = {}
...     def __set__(self, instance, value):
...         self.value_map[instance] = value
...         log_value = (datetime.datetime.now(), instance, value)
...         self.log.append(log_value)
...     def __get__(self, instance, owner):
...         if not instance:
...             return self # This way, the log is accessible
...         return self.value_map[instance]
...
>>> class Example:
...     value = LoggedAttribute()
...
>>> e = Example()
>>> e.value = 'testing'
>>> e.value
'testing'
>>> Example.value.log
[(datetime.datetime(2009, 10, 31, 21, 49, 59, 933000), <__main__.Example object a
t 0x...>, 'testing')]
```

Before going on, there are a few important things to notice here. First, when setting a value on the descriptor, __set__() adds it to a dictionary on itself, using the instance as a key. The reason for this is that the descriptor object is shared among all the instances of the class it's attached to. If you were to set the value to the descriptor's self, that value would be shared among all those instances as well.

> **Note**   Using a dictionary is just one way to make sure that instances are handled,
> but it's not the best. It's used here because the preferred method, assigning
> directly to the instance's namespace dictionary, is only an option once you know
> the name of the attribute. Descriptors on their own don't have access to that name,
> so the dictionary is used here instead. Chapter 11 shows an approach to address
> this problem based on metaclasses.

Also, notice that `__get__()` returns self if no instance was passed in. Because the descriptor works based on setting values, it has no additional value to contribute when called on the class. Most of the time, when a descriptor is in this situation it makes more sense to raise an `AttributeError` to prevent users from trying something that doesn't make sense. Doing so here would mean the value log would never be available, so the descriptor returns itself.

In addition to getting and setting values, descriptors can also delete values from the attribute or the attribute itself. The `__delete__()` method manages this behavior, and because it only works on instances and doesn't care about the value, it receives the instance object as its only argument.

In addition to managing attributes, descriptors are also used to implement one of the most important aspects of object-oriented programming: methods.

Methods

When a function is defined in a class, it's considered to be a method. Even though it still works like a function in general, it has class information available to it because functions are actually descriptors as well. Within the category of methods, however, there are two distinct types: bound and unbound methods.

Unbound Methods

Because descriptors can be accessed from the class as well as its instances, methods can be accessed from both as well. When accessing a function on a class, it becomes an unbound method. The descriptor receives the class, but methods typically require the instance, so they're referred to as unbound when accessed without one.

Calling it an unbound method is really more of a naming convention than any formal declaration. What you get when accessing the method on a class is just the function object itself:

```
>>> class Example:
...     def method(self):
...         return 'done!'
...
>>> type(Example.method)
<class 'function'>
>>> Example.method
<function method at 0x...>

# self isn't passed automatically

>>> Example.method()
Traceback (most recent call last):
  ...
TypeError: method() takes exactly 1 position argument (0 given)
```

It's still callable just like any other standard function, but it also carries information about what class it's attached to. Notice that the self argument in an unbound method isn't passed automatically, as there's no instance object available to bind to it.

Bound Methods

Once the class is instantiated, each method descriptor returns a function that's bound to that instance. It's still backed by the same function, and the original unbound method is still available on the class, but the bound method now automatically receives the instance object as its first argument:

```
>>> ex = Example()
>>> type(ex.method)
<class 'method'>
>>> ex.method
<bound method Example.method of <__main__.Example object at 0x...>>

# self gets passed automatically now

>>> ex.method()
'done!'

# And the underlying function is still the same

>>> Example.method is ex.method.__func__
True
```

is and == have related yet different functionality and == could have
replaced *is* in this instance, yet since *is* checks to see if two arguments
refer to the same object versus == checks to see if two object have same
value, *is* works better for our needs.

As you can see, bound methods are still backed by the same function as unbound
methods. The only real difference is that bound methods have an instance to receive as
the first argument. It's important to realize also that the instance object is passed as a
positional argument, so the argument name doesn't need to be self to work properly,
but it's a well-established standard that you should follow whenever possible.

Tip   Because bound methods accept an instance as the first argument, method
binding can be faked by explicitly providing an instance as the first argument to
an unbound method. It all looks the same to the method, and it can be a useful
approach when passing functions around as callbacks.

Sometimes, however, the method doesn't need access to the instance object,
regardless of whether the class has been instantiated. These methods fall into two
separate types.

Class Methods

When a method only needs access to the class it's attached to, it's considered a class method, which Python supports through the use of a built-in @classmethod decorator. This ensures that the method will always receive the class object as its first positional argument, regardless of whether it's called as an attribute of the class or one of its instances:

```
>>> class Example:
...     @classmethod
...     def method(cls):
...         return cls
...
>>> Example.method()
<class __main__.Example at 0x...>
>>> Example().method()
<class __main__.Example at 0x...>
```

Once the @classmethod decorator has been applied—see the section later in this chapter for information on decorators—the method() method will never receive an instance of Example as its first argument, but will always be the class itself or one of its subclasses. The cls argument will always be whatever class was used to call the method, rather than just the one where the method was defined.

Although it may not be clear from the previous example, class methods are actually bound instance methods, just like those described in the previous sections. Because all classes are actually instances of a built-in type, class methods are bound to the class itself:

```
>>> Example.method
<bound method type.method of <class '__main__.Example'>>
```

Class methods can also be created in another, slightly more indirect way. Because all classes are really just instances of metaclasses, you can define a method on a metaclass. All instance classes will then have access to that method as a standard bound method. There's no need to use the @classmethod decorator, because the method is already bound to the class using the standard behavior described previously. Here's how it works:

```
>>> class ExampleMeta(type):
...     def method(cls):
...         return cls
...
>>> class Example(metaclass=ExampleMeta):
...     pass
...
>>> Example.method
<bound method ExampleMeta.method of <class '__main__.Example'>>
>>> Example.method()
<class __main__.Example at 0x...>
```

The actual behavior of a method constructed this way is identical to a regular class method in most respects because they're built the same way internally. They can be called from the class itself, rather than requiring an instance, and they always receive the class object as an implicit first argument. The difference, however, is that class methods can still be called from instances, whereas a bound class method can only be called from the class itself.

The reason for this behavior is that the method is defined in the metaclass namespace, which only puts it in the MRO of instances of that metaclass. All classes that reference the metaclass will have access to the method, but it's not actually in their definitions. Methods decorated with @classmethod are placed directly in the namespace of the class where they're defined, which makes them available to instances of that class as well.

Even though this difference in visibility seems like metaclass-based class methods are just an inferior version of standard decorated class methods, there are two reasons why they may be beneficial to an application. First, class methods are generally expected to be called as attributes of the class, and are rarely called from instance objects. That's not a universal rule, and it's certainly not enough to justify the use of a metaclass on its own, but it's worth noting.

Perhaps more importantly, many applications that already use a metaclass also need to add class methods to any class that uses that metaclass. In this case, it makes sense to just define the methods on the existing metaclass, rather than using a separate class to hold the class methods. This is especially useful when that extra class wouldn't have anything valuable to add on its own; if the metaclass is the important part, it's best to keep everything there.

Static Methods

Occasionally, even the class is more information than is necessary for a method to do its job. This is the case for static methods, which are often implemented for the sake of establishing a namespace for functions that could otherwise be implemented at the module level. Using the staticmethod decorator, the method won't receive any implicit arguments at any time:

```
>>> class Example:
...     @staticmethod
...     def method():
...         print('static!')
...
>>> Example.method
<function method at 0x...>
>>> Example.method()
static!
```

As you can see, static methods don't really look like methods at all. They're just standard functions that happen to sit in a class. The next section shows how a similar effect can be achieved on instances by taking advantage of Python's dynamic nature.

Assigning Functions to Classes and Instances

Python allows most attributes to be overwritten simply by assigning a new value, which presents an interesting opportunity for methods:

```
>>> def dynamic(obj):
...     return obj
...
>>> Example.method = dynamic
>>> Example.method()
Traceback (most recent call last):
  ...
TypeError: dynamic() takes exactly 1 positional argument (0 given)
>>> ex = Example()
>>> ex.method()
<__main__.Example object at 0x...>
```

Notice here that the function assigned to the class still needs to be written to accept an instance as its first argument. Once assigned, it works just like a regular instance method, so the argument requirement doesn't change at all. Assigning to instances works similarly in syntax, but because the function never gets assigned to a class, there's no binding involved at all. A function assigned directly to an instance attribute works just like a static method that was attached to the class:

```
>>> def dynamic():
...     print('dynamic!')
...
>>> ex.method = dynamic
>>> ex.method()
dynamic!
>>> ex.method
<function dynamic at 0x...>
```

210

Magic Methods

Objects in Python can be created, manipulated, and destroyed in a number of different ways, and most of the available behaviors can be modified by implementing some extra methods on your own custom classes. Some of the more specialized customizations can be found in Chapter 5, but there are several of these special methods that are common to all types of classes. These methods can be categorized according to what aspect of classes they deal with, so the following sections each cover a few different methods.

Creating Instances

The transition from a class to an object is called instantiation. An instance is little more than a reference to the class that provides behavior and a namespace dictionary that's unique to the instance being created. When creating a new object without overriding any special methods, the instance namespace is just an empty dictionary, waiting for data.

Therefore, the first method most classes implement is __init__(), with the purpose of initializing the namespace with some useful values. Sometimes these are just placeholders until more interesting data arrives, while at other times the interesting data comes into the method directly, in the form of arguments. This happens because any arguments passed in to the class instantiation get passed right along to __init__() along the way:

```
>>> class Example:
...     def __init__(self):
...         self.initialized = True
...
>>> e = Example()
>>> e.initialized = True
>>> class Example2:
...     def __init__(self, name, value="):
...         self.name = name
...         self.value = value
...
```

```
>>> e = Example2()
Traceback (most recent call last):
  ...
TypeError: __init__() takes at least 2 positional arguments (1 given)
>>> e = Example2('testing')
>>> e.name
'testing'
>>> e.value
"
```

Like any Python function, you're free to do whatever you like inside of __init__(), but keep in mind that's intended to initialize the object, nothing more. Once __init__() has finished executing the object should be ready to be used for more practical purposes, but anything beyond basic setup should be deferred to other more explicit methods.

Of course, the real definition of initialization could mean different things to different objects. For most objects, you'll only need to set a few attributes to either some default values or to the values passed in to __init__(), as shown in the previous example. Other times, those initial values may require calculations, such as converting different units of time into seconds, so everything's normalized.

In some less common cases initialization may include more complicated tasks, such as data validation, file retrieval, or even network traffic. For example, a class for working with a web service might take an API token as its only argument to __init__(). It might then make a call to the web service to convert that token into an authenticated session, which would allow other operations to take place. All of the other operations require separate method calls, but the authentication that underlies all of them could happen in __init__().

The main concern with doing too much in __init__() is that there's no indication that anything's going on, short of documentation. Unfortunately, some users just won't read your documentation no matter how hard you try; they may still expect initialization to be a simple operation, and they might be surprised to see errors if they don't have a valid network connection, for example. See the example in the next section for one way to address this.

Even though __init__() is probably the most well-known magic method of all, it's not the first that gets executed when creating a new object. After all, remember that __init__() is about initialization an object, not creating it. For the latter, Python provides the __new__() method, which gets most of the same arguments but is responsible for actually creating the new object prior to initializing it.

Rather than working with the typical instance object self, the first argument to __new__() is actually the class of the object being created. This makes it look a lot like a class method, but you don't need to use any decorators to make it work this way—it's a special case in Python. Technically, however, it's a static method, so if you try to call it directly you'll always need to supply the class; it will never be sent implicitly, like it would be if it were a true class method.

After the class parameter—typically named cls, like a regular class method—the __new__() method receives all the same arguments that __init__() would receive. Whatever you pass in to the class when trying to create the object will be passed along to __new__() to help define it. These arguments are often useful when customizing the new object for the needs at hand.

This is often different from initialization, because __new__() is typically used to change the very nature of the object being created, rather than just setting up some initial values. To illustrate, consider an example in which the class of an object can change depending on what values are passed in when creating it.

Example: Automatic Subclasses

Some libraries consist of a large variety of classes, most of which share a common set of data, but with perhaps different behaviors or other data customizations. This often requires users of the library to keep track of all the different classes and determine which features of their data correspond to the appropriate classes.

Instead, it can be much more helpful to provide a single class the user can instantiate which actually returns an object that can be of different classes depending on arguments. Using __new__() to customize the creation of new objects, this can be achieved rather simply. The exact behavior will depend on the application at hand, but the basic technique is easy to illustrate with a generic example.

Consider a class that picks a subclass randomly whenever it's instantiated into an object. This isn't the most practical use, of course, but it illustrates how the process could work. Using random.choice() to pick from the values available from using __subclasses__(), it then instantiates the subclass it finds, rather than the one defined:

```
>>> import random
>>> class Example:
...     def __new__(cls, *args, **kwargs):
...         cls = random.choice(cls.__subclasses__())
...         return super(Example, cls).__new__(cls, *args, **kwargs)
...
>>> class Spam(Example):
...     pass
...
>>> class Eggs(Example):
...     pass
...
>>> Example()
<__main__.Eggs object at 0x...>
>>> Example()
<__main__.Eggs object at 0x...>
>>> Example()
<__main__.Spam object at 0x...>
>>> Example()
<__main__.Eggs object at 0x...>
>>> Example()
<__main__.Spam object at 0x...>
>>> Example()
<__main__.Spam object at 0x...>
```

In another real-world example, you could pass in the contents of a file to a single File class and have it automatically instantiate a subclass whose attributes and methods are built for the format of the file provided. This can be especially useful for large classes of files, such as music or images, that behave similarly in most respects on the surface but have underlying differences that can be abstracted away.

Dealing with Attributes

With an object in use, one of the more common needs is to interact with its attributes. Ordinarily this is as simple as just assigning and accessing attributes directly, given their name, such as `instance.attribute`. There are a few cases in which this type of access isn't sufficient on its own, so you need more control.

If you don't know the name of the attribute at the time you write the application, you can supply a variable for the name if you use the built-in `getattr()` function instead. For example, `instance.attribute` would become `getattr(instance, attribute_name)`, where the value for `attribute_name` can be provided from anywhere, as long as it's a string.

That approach only handles the case in which you're given a name as a string and you need to look up the instance attribute referenced by that name. On the other side of the equation, you can also tell a class how to deal with attributes it doesn't explicitly manage. This behavior is controlled by the `__getattr__()` method.

If you define this method, Python will call it whenever you request an attribute that hasn't already been defined. It receives the name of the attribute that was requested, so your class can decide what should be done with it. One common example is a dictionary that allows you to retrieve values by attribute instead of just using the standard dictionary syntax:

```
>>> class AttributeDict(dict):
...     def __getattr__(self, name):
...         return self[name]
...
>>> d = AttributeDict(spam='eggs')
>>> d['spam']
'eggs'
>>> d.spam
'eggs'
```

> **Note**   A not-so-obvious feature of __getattr__() is that it only gets called
> for attributes that don't actually exist. If you set the attribute directly, referencing
> that attribute will retrieve it without calling __getattr__(). If you need to catch
> every attribute regardless, use __getattribute__() instead. It takes the same
> arguments and functions just like __getattr__(), except that it gets called even
> if the attribute is already on the instance.

Of course, a dictionary that allows attribute access isn't terribly useful if attributes are read-only. In order to complete the picture, we should support storing values in attributes as well. Even beyond this simple dictionary example, there are a variety of needs for customizing what happens when you set a value to an attribute. As expected, Python provides a parallel in the form of the __setattr__() method.

This new method takes an extra argument because there's also a value that needs to be managed. By defining __setattr__(), you can intercept these value assignments and handle them however your application needs. Applying this to `AttributeDict` is just as simple as the previous example:

```
>>> class AttributeDict(dict):
...     def __getattr__(self, name):
...         return self[name]
...     def __setattr__(self, name, value):
...         self[name] = value
...
>>> d = AttributeDict(spam='eggs')
>>> d['spam']
'eggs'
>>> d.spam
'eggs'
>>> d.spam = 'ham'
>>> d.spam
'ham'
```

Tip   Just like getattr() provides for accessing attributes with a variable in place of a hardcoded name, Python provides setattr() for setting attributes. Its arguments match those of __setattr__(), as it takes the object, the attribute name, and the value.

Even though that might look like a complete picture of attribute access, there's still one component missing. When you no longer have use for an attribute and would like to remove it from the object altogether, Python provides the del statement. When you're working with fake attributes managed by these special methods, however, del on its own doesn't work.

For dealing with this situation, Python hooks into the __delattr__() method if one is present. Because the value is no longer relevant, this method only accepts the name of the attribute along with the standard self. Adding this to the existing AttributeDict is easy:

```
>>> class AttributeDict(dict):
...     def __getattr__(self, name):
...         return self[name]
...     def __setattr__(self, name, value):
...         self[name] = value
...     def __delattr__(self, name):
...         del self[name]
...
>>> d = AttributeDict(spam='eggs')
>>> d['spam']
'eggs'
>>> d.spam
'eggs'
>>> d.spam = 'ham'
>>> d.spam
'ham'
>>> del d.spam
>>> d.spam
```

```
Traceback (most recent call last):
  ...
KeyError: 'spam'
```

WARNING: RAISE THE RIGHT EXCEPTION

This error message brings up an important point about working with these types of overridden attributes. It's very easy to overlook how exceptions are handled inside your function, so you may end up raising an exception that doesn't make any sense; if an attribute doesn't exist, you would reasonably expect to see an `AttributeError`, rather than a `KeyError`.

This may seem like an arbitrary detail, but remember that most code explicitly catches specific types of exceptions, so if you raise the wrong type, you could cause other code to take the wrong path. Therefore, always make sure to raise `AttributeError` explicitly when encountering something that's the equivalent of a missing attribute. Depending on what the fake attribute does, it might be a `KeyError`, `IOError,` or perhaps even a `UnicodeDecodeError`, for example.

This will come up at various points throughout this book and elsewhere in the real world. Chapter 5 covers a variety of protocols in which it's just as important to get the exceptions right as the arguments.

String Representations

Of all the different object types that are possible in Python, easily the most common is the string. From reading and writing files to interacting with web services and printing documents, strings dominate many aspects of software execution. Even though most of our data exists in other forms along the way, sooner or later most of it gets converted to a string.

In order to make that process as simple as possible, Python provides an extra hook to convert an object to its string representation. The `__str__()` method, when implemented on a class, allows its instances to be converted to a string using the built-in `str() function`, which is also used when using `print()` or string formatting. Details on those features and more can be found in Chapter 7, but for now, look at how `__str__()` works in a simple class:

```
# First, without __str__()

>>> class Book:
...     def __init__(self, title):
...         self.title = title
...
>>> Book('Pro Python')
<__main__.Book object at 0x...>
>>> str(Book('Pro Python'))
'<__main__.Book object at 0x...>'

# And again, this time with __str__()

>>> class Book:
...     def __init__(self, title):
...         self.title = title
...     def __str__(self):
...         return self.title
...
>>> Book('Pro Python')
<__main__.Book object at 0x...>
>>> str(Book('Pro Python'))
'Pro Python'
```

The addition of __str__() allows the class to specify what aspects of the object should be displayed when representing the object as a string. In this example it was the title of a book, but it could also be the name of a person, the latitude and longitude of a geographic location, or anything else that succinctly identifies the object among a group of its peers. It doesn't have to contain everything about the object, but there needs to be enough to distinguish one from another.

Notice also that when the expression in the interactive interpreter doesn't include the call to str(), it doesn't use the value returned by __str__(). Instead, the interpreter uses a different representation of the object, which is intended to more accurately represent the code nature of the object. For custom classes this representation is fairly unhelpful, only showing the name and module of the object's class and its address in memory.

219

For other types, however, you'll notice that the representations can be quite useful in determining what the object is all about. In fact, the ideal goal for this representation is to present a string that, if typed back into the console, would recreate the object. This is extremely useful for getting a feel for the objects in the interactive console:

```
>>> dict(spam='eggs')
{'spam': 'eggs'}
>>> list(range(5))
[0, 1, 2, 3, 4]
>>> set(range(5))
{0, 1, 2, 3, 4}

>>> import datetime
>>> datetime.date.today()
datetime.date(2009, 10, 31)
>>> datetime.time(12 + 6, 30)
datetime.time(18, 30)
```

This alternate representation is controlled by the __repr__() method, and is used primarily in cases just like this, to describe an object inside the interactive console. It's automatically triggered when referencing an object on its own in the interpreter and is sometimes used in logging applications where __str__() often doesn't provide enough detail.

For the built-ins such as lists and dictionaries, the representation is a literal expression that can reproduce the object easily. For other simple objects that don't contain very much data, the date and time examples show that simply providing an instantiation call will do the trick. Of course, datetime would have to be imported first, but it gets the job done.

In cases in which the data represented by the object is too numerous to condense into a simple representation like this, the next best thing is to provide a string, surrounded in angle brackets, which describes the object in a more reasonable amount of detail. This is often a matter of showing the class name and a few pieces of data that would identify it. For the Book example, which in the real world would have many more attributes, it could look like this:

```
>>> class Book:
...     def __init__(self, title, author=None):
...         self.title = title
...         self.author = author
...     def __str__(self):
...         return self.title
...     def __repr__(self):
...         return '<%s by %s>' % (self.title, self.author or '<Unknown
            Author>')
...
>>> Book('Pro Python', author='Marty Alchin')
<Book: Pro Python by Marty Alchin>
>>> str(Book('Pro Python', author='Marty Alchin'))
'Pro Python'
```

Exciting Python Extensions: Iterators

An iterator is an object that can be iterated over; in other terms, you could say it is an "iterable" or "loopable" item. A list, tuple, and string are iterable; they hold more than one item, and thus are iterable containers. There are two iterator objects in Python. The first, a sequence iterator, works on an arbitrary sequence. The second object iterates over callable objects items with a sentinel value ending the process. Let's see them in action to understand this a bit more.

A very simple example is an enhanced *for loop* which iterates over all of the items (you must have more than one) in the container. Consider the following:

```
my_string=('Hello Python!')
for item in my_string:
        print(item)
my_list=[1,2,3,4]
for item in my_list:
        print (item, end=' ')
#Note newline after printing is replaced with space
```

```
print()
my_tuple='Fred','Wilma', 1, 3
for item in my_tuple:
            print (item)
```

Now, if you had a text file in the same folder as the Python script, such as perhaps a CSV file with data, you could do something like the following:

```
for the_line in open("file.csv"):
                  print (the_line)
```

With Python iterators you can also combine structures for enhanced functionality. Do keep it readable. Note that we are looping through a string and counting the instances of the letter "b."

```
#Combine control structures
my_string=('ababaaabbbbaaaabb')
counter=0
for character in [char for char in my_string if char == 'b']:
            counter +=1
print('There were ', counter, ' letter b')
```

Another example might be Caesar cipher encryption:

```
#Secret message Ceasar cipher!
my_string = input('Type secret message:  ')
print (my_string)
new_string = ' '
z=input('How much to Ceasar shift by?  ')
for letter in my_string:
            x=ord(letter)
            t=x+int(z)
            print (chr(t),)
```

Now let's look at the **iteration protocol**. The ***next*** function iterates with the first item and continues to the last, but it returns a *StopIteration* error when it tries to print item four, which is not present in the list:

```
# Simple iteration over a list
simple_list = [1, 3, 2]
simple_iter = iter(simple_list)
counter = 1
while counter <=4:
        print(next(simple_iter))
        counter +=1
```

Now, you could add try and except to keep this running, but this shows how things work at a general level. Time spent working with iterators will pay off well.

Taking It With You

A thorough understanding of classes unlocks a world of possibilities for your applications, whether they're simple personal projects or large frameworks built for mass distribution. In addition to all this freedom, there is a set of established protocols that can allow your classes to work just like some of Python's most well-known types.

CHAPTER 5

Common Protocols

Most of the time, you'll want to define objects that are highly customized to the needs of your application. This often means coming up with your own interfaces and APIs that are unique to your own code. The flexibility to do this is essential to the expansion capabilities of any system, but there is a price. Everything new that you invent must be documented and understood by those who need to use it.

Understanding how to use the various classes made available by a framework can be quite a chore for users of that framework, even with proper documentation. A good way to ease the burden on users is to mimic interfaces they're already familiar with. There are many existing types that are standard issue in Python programming, and most of them have interfaces that can be implemented in custom classes.

Methods are the most obvious way to implement an existing interface, but with many of the built-in types, most of the operations are performed with native Python syntax rather than explicit method calls. Naturally, these syntactic features are backed by actual methods behind the scenes, so they can be overridden to provide custom behaviors.

The following sections show how the interfaces for some of the most common types used in Python can be imitated in custom code. This is by no means an exhaustive list of all the types that ship with Python, nor is every method represented. Instead, this chapter is a reference for those methods that aren't so obvious because they're masked by syntactic sugar.

© J. Burton Browning and Marty Alchin 2019
J. B. Browning and M. Alchin, *Pro Python 3*, https://doi.org/10.1007/978-1-4842-4385-5_5

Basic Operations

Even though there are a wide variety of object types available in Python, most of them share a common set of operations. These are considered to be something of a core feature set, representing some of the most common high-level aspects of object manipulation, many of which are just as applicable to simple numbers as they are to many other objects.

One of the simplest and most common needs in all of programming, Python included, is to evaluate an expression to a Boolean value so that it can be used to make simple decisions. Typically this is used in if blocks, but these decisions also come into play when using while, and Boolean operations such as and and or. When Python encounters one of these situations, it relies on the behavior of the __bool__() method to determine the Boolean equivalent of an object.

The __bool__() method, if implemented, accepts just the usual self and must return either True or False. This allows any object to determine whether it should be considered to be true or false in a given expression, using whatever methods or attributes are appropriate:

```
>>> bool(0)
False
>>> bool(1)
True
>>> bool(5)
True
```

As another example, consider that a class representing a rectangle might use its area to determine whether the rectangle is considered true or false. Therefore, __bool__() only has to check whether there exists a nonzero width and a nonzero height, since with a bool 0 is false and any other positive value, typically 1, is true. Here we use the built-in bool(), which uses __bool__() to convert the value to a Boolean:

```
>>> class Rectangle:
...     def __init__(self, width, height):
...         self.width = width
...         self.height = height
...     def __bool__(self):
...         if self.width and self.height:
...             return True
...         return False
...
>>> bool(Rectangle(10, 15))
True
>>> bool(Rectangle(0, 0))
False
>>> bool(Rectangle(0, 15))
False
```

Tip   The __bool__() method isn't the only way to customize Python's Boolean behavior. If, instead, an object provides a __len__() method, which is described in the section on sequences later in this chapter, Python will fall back to that and consider any nonzero lengths to be true, while lengths of zero are false.

With the truthfulness of objects taken into account, you automatically get control over the behavior of such operators as and, or, and not. Therefore, there are no separate methods to override in order to customize those operators.

In addition to being able to determine the truthfulness of an object, Python offers a great deal of flexibility in other operations as well. In particular, the standard mathematical operations can be overridden because many of them can apply to a variety of objects beyond just numbers.

Mathematical Operations

Some of the earliest forms of math stemmed from observations about the world around us. Therefore, most of the math we learned in elementary school applies just as easily to other types of objects as it does to numbers. For example, addition could be seen as simply putting two things together (concatenation), such as tying two strings together to make a single longer string.

If you only look at it mathematically, you could say that you're really just adding two lengths together, resulting in a single, greater length. But when you look at what really just happened, you now have a brand-new string, which is different from the two strings that went into it originally.

This analogy extends easily into Python strings as well, which can be concatenated using standard addition, rather than requiring a separate, named method. Similarly, if you need to write the same string out multiple times, you can simply multiply it the same way you would a regular number. These types of operations are very common in Python because they can be a simple way to implement common tasks:

```
>>> 2 + 2
4
>>> 'two' + 'two'
'twotwo'
>>> 2 * 2
4
>>> 'two' * 2
'twotwo'
```

Like __bool__(), these behaviors are controlled by special methods of their own. Most of them are fairly straightforward, accepting the usual self as well as an other argument. These methods are bound to the object on the left side of the operator, with the additional other being the object on the right side.

The four basic arithmetic operations—addition, subtraction, multiplication, and division—are represented in Python using the standard operators +, -, *, and /. Behind the scenes, the first three are powered by implementations of the __add__(), __sub__(), and __mul__() methods. Division is a bit more complicated, and we'll get to that shortly, but for now, let's take a look at how this operator overloading works.

Consider a class that acts as a simple proxy around a value. There's not much use for something like this in the real world, but it's a good starting point to explain a few things:

```
>>> class Example:
...     def __init__(self, value):
...         self.value = value
...     def __add__(self, other):
...         return self.value + other
...
>>> Example(10) + 20
30
```

This is just one example of a few basic arithmetic operations that are available for your code to customize. You'll find more advanced operations detailed throughout the remainder of this chapter; Table 5-1 lists these basic arithmetic operators.

Table 5-1. *Basic Arithmetic Operators*

Operation	Operator	Custom Method
Addition	+	__add__()
Subtraction	-	__sub__()
Multiplication	*	__mul__()
Division	/	__truediv__()

Here's where things get interesting, because you'll notice that the method for division isn't __div__(), as you might expect. The reason for this is that division comes in two different flavors. The kind of division you get when you use a calculator is called *true division* in Python, which uses the __truediv__() method, which works as you'd expect.

However, *true division* is the only arithmetic operation that can take two integers and return a noninteger. In some applications, it's useful to always get an integer back instead. If you're displaying an application's progress as a percentage, for instance, you don't really need to display the full floating point number.

Instead an alternative operation is available called *floor division*; you may also have heard it referred to as *integer division*. If the result of true division would land between two integers, floor division will simply return the lower of the two, so that it always returns an integer. Floor division, as you might expect, is implemented with a separate __floordiv__() and is accessed using the // operator:

```
>>> 5 / 4
1.25
>>> 5 // 4
1
```

There's also a modulo operation, which is related to division. In the event that a division operation would result in a remainder, using modulo would return that remainder, so *modulo returns only the remainder of division*. This uses the % operator, implemented using __mod__(). This is used by strings to perform standard variable interpretation, even though that has nothing to do with division:

```
>>> 20 // 6
3
>>> 20 % 6
2
>>> 'test%s' % 'ing'
'testing'
```

In effect, you can use floor division and a modulo operation to obtain the integer result of a division operation as well as its remainder, which retains all the information about the result. This is sometimes preferable to true division, which would simply produce a floating point number. For example, consider a function that takes a number of minutes and has to return a string containing the number of hours and minutes:

```
>>> def hours_and_minutes(minutes):
...     return minutes // 60, minutes % 60
...
>>> hours_and_minutes(60)
(1, 0)
>>> hours_and_minutes(137)
(2, 17)
>>> hours_and_minutes(42)
(0, 42)
```

In fact, this basic task is common enough that Python has its own function for it: divmod(). By passing in a base value and a value to divide it by, you can get the results of floor division and a modulo operation at the same time. Rather than simply delegating to those two methods independently, however, Python will try to call a __divmod__() method, which allows a custom implementation to be more efficient.

In lieu of a more efficient implementation, the __divmod__() method can be illustrated using the same technique as the hours_and_minutes() function. All we have to do is accept a second argument in order to take the hard-coded 60 out of the method:

```
>>> class Example:
...     def __init__(self, value):
...         self.value = value
...     def __divmod__(self, divisor):
...         return self.value // divisor, self.value % divisor
...
>>> divmod(Example(20), 6)
(3, 2)
```

There's also an extension of multiplication called exponentiation, where a value is multiplied by itself a number of times. Given its relationship to multiplication, Python

uses a double-asterisk ** notation to perform the operation. It's implemented using a
__pow__() method, because real-world math typically calls it raising a value to a power
of some other value:

```
>>> class Example:
...     def __init__(self, value):
...         self.value = value
...     def __pow__(self, power):
...         val = 1
...         for x in range(power):
...             val *= self.value
...         return val
...
>>> Example(5) ** 3
125
```

Unlike the other operations, exponentiation can be performed in one other way as
well, by way of the built-in pow() function. The reason there's a different operator is that
it allows for an extra argument to be passed in. This extra argument is a value that should
be used to perform a modulo operation after the exponentiation has been performed.
This extra behavior allows for a more efficient way to perform such tasks as finding prime
numbers, which is commonly used in cryptography:

```
>>> 5 ** 3
125
>>> 125 % 50
25
>>> 5 ** 3 % 50
25
>>> pow(5, 3, 50)
25
```

In order to support this behavior with the __pow__() method, you can optionally accept an extra argument, which will be used to perform the modulo operation. This new argument must be optional in order to support the normal ** operator. There's no reasonable default value that can be used blindly without causing problems with standard exponentiation, so it should default to None to determine whether the modulo operation should be performed:

```
>>> class Example:
...     def __init__(self, value):
...         self.value = value
...     def __pow__(self, power, modulo=None):
...         val = 1
...         for x in range(power):
...             val *= self.value
...         if modulo is not None:
...             val %= modulo
...         return val
...
>>> Example(5) ** 3
125
>>> Example(5) ** 3 % 50
25
>>> pow(Example(5), 3, 50)
25
```

Caution As with the __divmod__() implementation shown previously, this example is not a very efficient approach at solving the problem. It does produce the correct values, but it should be used only for illustration.

Bitwise Operations

Bitwise operations are used in situations in which you are working on binary files, cryptography, encoding, hardware drivers, and networking protocols. As such, they are often associated with low-level programming; however, they are certainly not exclusively reserved for that domain. With *bitwise operations*, a scparate group of operations act on values not as numbers directly, but rather as a sequence of individual bits. At that level, there are a few different ways of manipulating values that are applicable to not only numbers but some other types of sequences as well. The simplest bitwise manipulation is a shift, where the bits within a value are moved to the right or to the left, resulting in a new value.

In binary arithmetic, shifting bits one place to the left multiplies the value by two. This is just like in decimal math: if you move all the digits in a number one place to the left and fill in the gap on the right with a zero, you've essentially multiplied the value by ten. This behavior exists for any numbered base, but computers work in binary, so the shifting operations do as well.

Shifting is achieved using the << and >> operators for left and right, respectively. The right-hand side of the operator indicates how many positions the bits should be shifted. Internally, these operations are supported by the __lshift__() and __rshift__() methods, each of which accepts the number of positions to shift as its only additional argument:

```
>>> 10 << 1
20
>>> 10 >> 1
5
```

In addition to shuffling the bits around, there are a few operations that compare the bits in each value to each other, resulting in a new value that represents some combination of the two individual values. The four bitwise comparison operations are &, |, ^, and ~, referred to AND, OR, XOR (exclusive OR), and inversion, respectively.

An AND comparison returns 1 only if both of the individual bits being compared are 1. If it's any other combination, the result is 0. This behavior is often used to create a bitmask, where you can reset all irrelevant values to 0 by applying AND to a value that has 1 for each of the useful bits and 0 for the rest. This will clear out any bits you aren't interested in, allowing for easy comparisons with sets of binary flags. Supporting this behavior in your code requires the presence of an __and__() method.

OR comparisons return 1 if either of the individual bits being compared is 1. It doesn't matter if both of them are 1; as long as at least one of them is 1, the result will be 1. This is often used to join sets of binary flags together, so that all the flags from both sides of the operator are set in the result. The method required to support this functionality is __or__().

The standard OR operator is sometimes called an inclusive OR, to contrast it with its cousin, the exclusive OR, which is typically abbreviated as XOR. In an XOR operation, the result is 1 only if one of the individual bits was 1 but not the other. If both bits are 1 or both bits are 0, the result will be 0. XOR is supported by the __xor__() method.

Finally, Python also offers bitwise inversion, where each of the bits gets flipped to the opposite value from what it is currently; 1 becomes 0, and vice versa. Numerically, this swaps between negative and positive values, but it doesn't simply change the sign. Here's an example of how numbers react when inverted using the ~ operator:

```
>>> ~42
-43
>>> ~-256
255
```

This behavior is based on the way computers work with signed values. The most significant bit is used to determine whether the value is positive or negative, so flipping that bit changes the sign. The change in the absolute value after inversion is due to a lack of –0. When 0 is inverted it becomes –1 rather than –0, so all other values follow suit after that.

In custom code, inversion is typically most useful when you have a known set of all possible values, along with individual subsets of those values. Inverting these subsets would remove any existing values and replace them with any values from the master set that weren't previous in the subset.

This behavior can be provided by supplying an __invert__() method on your object. Unlike the other bitwise methods, however, __invert__() is unary, so it doesn't accept any additional arguments beyond the standard self.

Note   The inversion behavior described here is valid for numbers that are encoded using the two's-complement method for working with signed numbers. There are other options[1] available that can behave differently than what's shown here if a custom number class provides the __invert__() method to do so. By default, Python works only with the two's-complemented encoding method.

Variations

In addition to the normal behavior of operations, there are a couple different ways they can also be accessed. The most obvious issue is that the methods are typically bound to the value on the left-hand side of the operator. If your custom object gets placed on the right-hand side instead, there's a good chance that the value on the left won't know how to work with it, so you'll end up with a TypeError instead of a usable value.

This behavior is understandable but unfortunate, because if the custom object knows how to interact with the other value, it should be able to do so regardless of their positions. To allow for this, Python gives the value on the right-hand side of the operator a chance to return a valid value.

When the left-hand side of the expression fails to yield a value, Python then checks to see if the value on the right is of the same type. If it is, there's no reason to expect that it would be able to do any better than the first time around, so Python simply raises the TypeError. If it's a different type, however, Python will call a method on the right-hand value, passing in the left-hand value as its argument.

This process swaps the arguments around, binding the method to the value on the right-hand side. For some operations, such as subtraction and division, the order of the values is important, so Python uses a different method to indicate the change in ordering. The names of these separate methods are mostly the same as the left-hand methods, but with an r added after the first two underscores:

---

[1]http://en.wikipedia.org/wiki/Signed_number_representations.

```
>>> class Example:
...     def __init__(self, value):
...         self.value = value
...     def __add__(self, other):
...         return self.value + other
...
>>> Example(20) + 10
30
>>> 10 + Example(20)
Traceback (most recent call last):
  ...
TypeError: unsupported operand type(s) for +: 'int' and 'Example'
>>> class Example:
...     def __init__(self, value):
...         self.value = value
...     def __add__(self, other):
...         return self.value + other
...     def __radd__(self, other):
...         return self.value + other
...
>>> Example(20) + 10
30
>>> 10 + Example(20)
30
```

Tip   In cases like this in which the order of the values doesn't affect the result, you can actually just assign the left-hand method to the name of the right-hand method. Just remember that not all operations work that way, so you can't blindly copy the method to both sides without ensuring that it makes sense.

Another common way to use these operators is to modify an existing value and assign the result right back to the original value. As has been demonstrated without explanation earlier in this chapter, an alternative form of assignment is catered to these modifications. By simply appending = to the operator you need, you can assign the result of the operation to the value on the left-hand side:

```
>>> value = 5
>>> value *= 3
>>> value
15
```

By default, this form of augmented assignment uses the standard operator methods in the same way as was described previously in this chapter. However, that requires creating a new value after the operation, which is then used to rebind an existing value. Instead, it can sometimes be advantageous to modify the value in place, as long as you can identify when this assignment is taking place.

Like the right-hand side methods, in-place operators use essentially the same method names as standard operators, but this time with an i after the underscores. There's no right-hand side equivalent of this operation, however, because the assignment is always done with the variable on the left-hand side. With everything taken into account, Table 5-2 lists the available operators, along with the methods required to customize their behavior.

Table 5-2. *Available Operators*

Operation	Operator	Left-hand	Right-hand	In-line
Addition	+	__add__()	__radd__()	__iadd__()
Subtraction	-	__sub__()	__rsub__()	__isub__()
Multiplication	*	__mul__()	__rmul__()	__imul__()
True division	/	__truediv__()	__rtruediv__()	__itruediv__()
Floor division	//	__floordiv__()	__rfloordiv__()	__ifloordiv__()
Modulo	%	__mod__()	__rmod__()	__imod__()
Division & modulo	divmod()	__divmod__()	__rdivmod__()	N/A
Exponentiation	**	__pow__()	__rpow__()	__ipow__()
Left binary shift	<<	__lshift__()	__rlshift__()	__ilshift__()
Right binary shift	>>	__rshift__()	__rrshift__()	__irshift__()
Bitwise AND	&	__and__()	__rand__()	__iand__()
Bitwise OR	|	__or__()	__ror__()	__ior__()
Bitwise XOR	^	__xor__()	__rxor__()	__ixor__()
Bitwise inversion	~	__invert__()	N/A	N/A

> **Note**   There's no in-line method for the division and modulo operation because it's not available as an operator that supports assignment. It's only called as the `divmod()` method, which has no in-line capabilities. Also, bitwise inversion is a unary operation, so there's no right-side or in-line method available.

Even though these operations are primarily focused on numbers, many of them also make sense for other types of objects. There is another set of behaviors, however, that really only makes sense for numbers and objects that can act like numbers.

Numbers

Underneath it all computers are all about numbers, so it's only natural that they play an important role in most applications. Beyond the operations outlined in the previous section, there are many various behaviors exhibited by numbers that may not be as obvious.

The most basic behavior a custom number can have is to convince Python that it is in fact a number. This is necessary when trying to use an object as an index in a sequence. Python requires that all indexes be integers, so there needs to be a way to coerce an object into an integer for the sake of being used as an index. For this Python uses an __index__() method, raising a TypeError if it doesn't exist or it returns something other than an integer:

```
>>> sequence = [1, 2, 3, 4, 5]
>>> sequence[3.14]
Traceback (most recent call last):
  ...
TypeError: list indices must be integers, not float
>>> class FloatIndex(float):
...     def __index__(self):
...         # For the sake of example, return just the integer portion
...         return int(self)
...
>>> sequence[FloatIndex(3.14)]
4
>>> sequence[3]
4
```

In addition to simple index access, __index__() is used to coerce an integer for the sake of slicing and to generate a starting value for conversion using the built-in bin(), hex(), and oct() functions. When looking to explicitly force an integer in other situations, you can use the __int__() method, which is used by the built-in int() function. Other type conversions can be performed using __float__() to support float() and __complex__() for complex().

One of the most commonly required operations when converting one number to another is rounding. Unlike int(), which blindly truncates any part of the value that's not an integer, rounding affords more control over what type of value you end up with and how much precision is retained.

When you pass a decimal or a floating point number into int(), the effect is essentially just a floor operation. Like floor division mentioned previously, a floor operation takes a number between two integers and returns the lower of the two. The math module contains a floor() function to perform this operation.

As you might expect, this relies on a __floor__() method on a custom object to perform the floor operation. It doesn't require any arguments beyond the usual self and should always return an integer. Python doesn't actually enforce any requirements on the return value, however, so if you're working with some subclass of integers, you can return one of those instead.

By contrast, you may need to go with the higher of the two, which would be a ceiling operation. This is done using math.ceil() and implemented with the __ceil__() method. Like __floor__(), it doesn't take any additional arguments and returns an integer.

More likely, you'll need to round a value to a specific number of digits. This is achieved using the round() function, which is a built-in function, rather than being located in the math module. It takes up to two arguments and is implemented using the __round__() method on a custom object.

The first argument to round() is the object that __round__() will be bound to, so it comes through as the standard self. The second argument is a bit more nuanced, however. It's the number of digits to the right of the decimal point that should be considered significant, and thus retained in the result. If it's not provided, round() should assume that none of those digits are significant and return an integer:

```
>>> round(3.14, 1)
3.1
>>> round(3.14)
3
>>> round(3.14, 0)
3.0
```

```
>>> import decimal
>>> round(decimal.Decimal('3.14'), 1)
Decimal('3.1')
>>> round(decimal.Decimal('3.14'))
3
```

As you can see, there's actually a difference between passing a second argument of 0 and not passing one at all. The return value is essentially the same, but when not passing it in, you should always get an integer. When passing in a 0 instead, you'll get whatever type you pass in, but with only the significant digits included.

In addition to rounding digits to the right of the decimal point, round() can act on the other side as well. By passing in a negative number, you can specify the number of digits to the left of the decimal point that should be rounded away, leaving the other digits remaining:

```
>>> round(256, -1)
260
>>> round(512, -2)
500
```

Sign Operations

There is also a selection of unary operations that can be used to adjust the sign of a value. The first, -, negates the sign, swapping between positive and negative values. Customization of this behavior is made available by providing a __neg__() method, which accepts no extra arguments beyond self.

To complement the negative sign, Python also supports a positive sign, using +. Because numbers are ordinarily assumed to be positive, this operator actually doesn't do anything on its own; it simply returns the number unchanged. In the event that a custom object needs an actual behavior attached to this, however, a __pos__() method can provide it.

Finally, a number can also have an absolute value, which is generally defined as its distance from zero. The sign is irrelevant, and all values become positive. Therefore, applying abs() to a number removes the negative sign if present but leaves positive values unchanged. This behavior is modified by an __abs__() method.

Comparison Operations

The operations shown thus far have been concerned with returning a modified value, based at least in part on one or more existing values. Comparison operators, by contrast, return either True or False, based on the relationship between two values.

The most basic comparison operators, is and is not, operate directly on the internal identity of each object. Because the identity is typically implemented as the object's address in memory, which can't be changed by Python code, there's no way to override this behavior. Its use is generally reserved for comparison with known constants, such as None.

The operators that are available represent the standard numerical comparisons, which detect if one value is higher, lower, or exactly equal to another. The most versatile is testing for equality, using ==. Its versatility comes from the fact that it's not limited to numerical values because many other types can have objects that are considered equal to each other. This behavior is controlled by an __eq__() method.

Inequality is represented in Python by the != operator, which behaves just as you would expect. What you might not expect, however, is that this functionality is not tied to == in any way. Rather than simply calling __eq__() and inverting its result, Python relies on a separate __ne__() method to handle inequality testing. Therefore, if you implement __eq__(), always remember to supply __ne__() as well to ensure that everything works as expected.

In addition, you can compare one value as less than or greater than another, using < and >, which are implemented using __lt__() and __gt__(), respectively. Equality can also be combined with these, so that one value can be greater than or equal to another, for instance. These operations use <= and >= and are supported by __lte__() and __gte__().

These comparisons are often used for objects that are predominantly represented by a number, even if the object itself is much more than that. Dates and times are notable examples of objects that are easily comparable because they're each essentially a series of numbers that can each be compared individually if needed:

```
>>> import datetime
>>> a = datetime.date(2019, 10, 31)
>>> b = datetime.date(2017, 1, 1)
>>> a == b
False
>>> a < b
True
```

Strings are an interesting case with regard to comparisons. Even though a string isn't numeric in an obvious sense, each character in a string is simply another representation of a number, so string comparisons also work. These comparisons drive the sorting features of strings.

Iterables

It may seem like sequences are the obvious next choice, but there's a more generic form to consider first. An object is considered iterable if it can yield objects one at a time, typically within a for loop. This definition is intentionally simple, because at a high level, iterables really don't go beyond that. Python does have a more specific definition of iterables, however.

In particular, an object is iterable if passing it into the built-in iter() function returns an iterator. Internally, iter() inspects the object passed in, looking first for an __iter__() method. If such a method is found, it's called without any arguments and is expected to return an iterator. There's another step that will take place if __iter__() wasn't available, but for now, let's focus on iterators.

Even though the object is considered iterable, it's the iterator that does all the real work, but there's really not that much to it. There's no requirement for what the __init__() method should look like, because it gets instantiated within the __iter__() method of its master object. The required interface consists of just two methods.

The first method, perhaps surprisingly, is __iter__(). Iterators should always be iterable on their own as well, so they must provide an __iter__() method. There's usually no reason to do anything special in this method, though, so it's typically implemented to just return self. If you don't supply __iter__() on the iterator the main object will still be iterable in most cases, but some code will expect its iterator to be usable on its own as well.

More importantly, an iterator must always provide a __next__() method, where all the real work happens. Python will call __next__() to retrieve the next value from the iterator, with that value being used in the body of whatever code called the iterator. When that code needs a new value, typically for the next pass in a loop, it calls __next__() again to get a new value. This process continues until one of a few things happens.

If Python encounters anything that causes the loop to complete while the iterator still has items it could produce, the iterator just stands by, waiting for some other code to ask for another item. If that never happens, eventually there will be no more code that knows about the iterator at all, so Python will remove it from memory. Chapter 6 covers this garbage collection process in greater detail.

There are a few different cases where an iterator might not be given a chance to finish. The most obvious is a break statement, which would stop the loop and continue on afterward. Additionally, a return or a raise statement would implicitly break out of any loop it's part of, so the iterator is left in the same state as when a break occurs.

More commonly, however, the loop will just let the iterator run until it doesn't have any more items to produce. When using a generator, this case is handled automatically when the function returns without yielding a new value. With an iterator, this behavior must be provided explicitly.

Because None is a perfectly valid object that could reasonably be yielded from an iterator, Python can't just react to __next__() failing to return a value. Instead, the StopIteration exception provides a way for __next__() to indicate that there are no more items. When this is raised the loop is considered complete, and execution resumes on the next line after the end of the loop.

To illustrate how all of this fits together, let's take a look at the behavior of the built-in range() function. It's not a generator because you can iterate over it multiple times. To provide similar functionality we need to return an iterable object instead, which can then be iterated as many times as necessary:

```
class Range:
    def __init__(self, count):
        self.count = count
    def __iter__(self):
        return RangeIter(self.count)

class RangeIter:
    def __init__(self, count):
        self.count = count
        self.current = 0

    def __iter__(self):
        return self

    def __next__(self):
        value = self.current
        self.current += 1
        if self.current > self.count:
            raise StopIteration
        return value
>>> def range_gen(count):
...     for x in range(count):
...         yield x
...
>>> r = range_gen(5)
>>> list(r)
[0, 1, 2, 3, 4]
>>> list(r)
[]
>>> r = Range(5)
>>> list(r)
[0, 1, 2, 3, 4]
>>> list(r)
[0, 1, 2, 3, 4]
```

Iterators are the most powerful and flexible way to implement an iterable, so they're generally preferred, but there's also another way to achieve a similar effect. What makes an object iterable is the fact that iter() returns an iterator, so it's worth noting that iter() supports a certain kind of special case.

If an object doesn't have an __iter__() method, but contains a __getitem__() method instead, Python can use that in a special iterator that exists just to handle that case. We'll get to more details in the next section on sequences, but the basic idea is that __getitem__() accepts an index and is expected to return the item in that position.

If Python finds __getitem__() instead of __iter__(), it will automatically create an iterator designed to work with it. This new iterator calls __getitem__() several times, each with a value from a series of numbers, beginning with zero, until __getitem__() raises an IndexError. Therefore, our custom Range iterable can be rewritten quite simply:

```python
class Range:
    def __init__(self, count):
        self.count = count

    def __getitem__(self, index):
        if index < self.count:
            return index
        raise IndexError

>>> r = Range(5)
>>> list(r)
[0, 1, 2, 3, 4]
>>> list(r)
[0, 1, 2, 3, 4]
```

Note   Python will only use this __getitem__() behavior if __iter__() is not present. If both are provided on a class, the __iter__() method will be used to control the iteration behavior.

Example: Repeatable Generators

The ability to iterate over an object multiple times is very common among explicitly iterable object types, but generators are often more convenient to work with. If you need to have a generator that can restart itself each different time the iterator is accessed, it may seem like you're stuck either losing out on that functionality or adding a bunch of otherwise unnecessary code that exists solely to allow for proper iteration.

Instead, like many other behaviors, we can rely on Python's standard way to augment a function and factor it out into a decorator. When applied to a generator function, this new decorator can handle everything necessary to create an iterable that triggers the generator from the beginning each time a new iterator is requested:

```python
def repeatable(generator):
    """
    A decorator to turn a generator into an object that can be
    iterated multiple times, restarting the generator each time.
    """
    class RepeatableGenerator:
        def __init__(self, *args, **kwargs):
            self.args = args
            self.kwargs = kwargs
        def __iter__(self):
            return iter(generator(*self.args, **self.kwargs))

    return RepeatableGenerator

>>> @repeatable
... def generator(max):
...     for x in range(max):
...         yield x
...
```

```
>>> g = generator(5)
>>> list(g)
[0, 1, 2, 3, 4]
>>> list(g)
[0, 1, 2, 3, 4]
```

By creating a new class that can be instantiated when the generator function is called, its __iter__() method will get called instead of the generator's. This way, the generator can be called from scratch each time a new loop begins, yielding a new sequence rather than trying to pick up where it left off, which would often mean returning an empty sequence.

Caution   Even though most generators return a similar sequence each time through and can be restarted without worry, not all of them behave that way. If a generator changes its output based on when it's called, picks up where it left off on subsequent calls or produces side effects, this decorator is not recommended. By changing the behavior to explicitly restart the decorator each time, the new generator could yield unpredictable results.

There's one problem with the code as it stands, however. The @repeatable decorator receives a function but returns a class, which works fine in the example provided but has some very troubling implications. To start, remember from Chapter 3 that wrapper functions have new properties, a problem that can be fixed using the @functools.wraps decorator.

Before we can even consider using another decorator, however, we have to solve the bigger problem: we're returning a completely different type than the original function. By returning a class instead of a function, we'll cause problems with any code that expects it to be a function, including other decorators. Worse yet, the class returned can't be used as a method because it doesn't have a __get__() method to bind it to its owner class or an instance of it.

To solve these issues, we have to introduce a wrapper function around the class, which will instantiate the object and return it. This way, we can use @functools.wraps to retain as much of the original decorator as possible. Better yet, we can then also return a function, which can be bound to classes and instances without any trouble:

```
import functools

def repeatable(generator):
    """
    A decorator to turn a generator into an object that can be
    iterated multiple times, restarting the generator each time.
    """
    class RepeatableGenerator:
        def __init__(self, *args, **kwargs):
            self.args = args
            self.kwargs = kwargs

        def __iter__(self):
            return iter(generator(*self.args, **self.kwargs))

    @functools.wraps(generator)
    def wrapper(*args, **kwargs):
        return RepeatableGenerator(*args, **kwargs)
    return wrapper
```

Sequences

After numbers, sequences are perhaps some of most commonly used data structures in all of programming, including Python. Lists, tuples, and even strings are sequences that share a common set of features, which are actually a specialized type of iterator. In addition to being able to yield a series of items individually, sequences have additional attributes and behaviors supporting the fact that they know about the entire set of items all at once.

These extra behaviors don't necessarily require that all the items be loaded into memory at the same time. The efficiency gains achieved through iteration are just as valid with sequences as with any other iterable, so that behavior doesn't change. Instead, the added options simply refer to collection as a whole, including its length and the ability to get a subset of it, as well as accessing individual items without getting the whole sequence.

The most obvious feature of a sequence is the ability to determine its length. For objects that can contain any arbitrary items, this requires knowing—or perhaps counting—all those items. For others, the object can use some other information to reach the same result. Customization of this behavior is achieved by providing a __len__() method, which is called internally when the object is passed into the built-in len() function.

To continue along the same lines as previous examples, here's how a simple replacement Range class could use knowledge of its configuration to return the length without having to yield a single value:

```python
class Range:
    def __init__(self, max):
        self.max = max

    def __iter__(self):
        for x in range(self.max):
            yield x

    def __len__(self):
        return self.max
```

Because sequences contain a fixed collection of items, they can be iterated not only from start to finish but also in reverse. Python provides the reversed() function, which takes a sequence as its only argument and returns an iterable that yields items from the sequence in reverse. There may be particular efficiency gains to be had, so a custom sequence object can provide a __reversed__() method to customize the internal behavior of reversed().

Taking this notion to the Range class again, it's possible to provide a reversed range using an alternative form of the built-in range():

```python
class Range:
    def __init__(self, max):
        self.max = max
```

```
    def __iter__(self):
        for x in range(self.max):
            yield x

    def __reversed__(self):
        for x in range(self.max - 1, -1, -1):
            yield x
```

Now that we have the ability to iterate over a sequence both forward and backward as well as report its length, the next step is to provide access to individual items. In a plain iterable, you can only access items by retrieving them one at a time as part of a loop. With all the values in the sequence known in advance, a custom class can provide access to any item at any time.

The most obvious task is to retrieve an item given an index that's known in advance. For example, if a custom object contained the arguments passed in on the command line, the application would know the specific meaning of each argument and would typically access them by index rather than simply iterating over the whole sequence. This uses the standard sequence[index] syntax, with its behavior controlled by the __getitem__() method.

With __getitem__(), individual items can be picked out of the sequence or retrieved from some other data structure if necessary. Continuing on the Range theme again, __getitem__() can calculate what the appropriate value should be without cycling through the sequence. In fact, it can even support the full range of arguments that are available to the built-in range():

```
class Range:
    def __init__(self, a, b=None, step=1):
        """
        Define a range according to a starting value, an end value and a step.
        If only one argument is provided, it's taken to be the end value. If
        two arguments are passed in, the first becomes a start value, while the
        second is the end value. An optional step can be provided to control
        how far apart each value is from the next.
        """
```

```
        if b is not None:
            self.start = a
            self.end = b
        else:
            self.start = 0
            self.end = a
        self.step = step

    def __getitem__(self, key):
        value = self.step * key + self.start
        if value < self.end:
            return value
        else:
            raise IndexError("key outside of the given range")
>>> r = Range(5)
>>> list(r)
[0, 1, 2, 3, 4]
>>> r[3]
3
>>> r = Range(3, 17, step=4)
>>> list(r)
[3, 7, 11, 15]
>>> r[2]
11
>>> r[4]
Traceback (most recent call last):
  ...
IndexError: indexed value outside of the given range
```

In the event that the index passed in is beyond the range of available items, __getitem__() should raise an IndexError. Highly specialized applications could define a more specific subclass and raise that instead, but most use cases will simply catch IndexError on its own.

In addition to matching the expectations of most Python programmers, properly raising IndexError is essential to allow a sequence to be used as an iterable without implementing __iter__(). Python will simply pass in integer indexes until the __getitem__() method raises an IndexError, at which point it will stop iterating over the sequence.

Beyond just accessing a single item at a time, a sequence can provide access to subsets of its contents by way of slicing. When using the slicing syntax, __getitem__() receives a special slice object instead of an integer index. A slice object has dedicated attributes for the start, stop, and step portions of the slice, which can be used to determine which items to return. Here's how this affects the Range object we've been examining:

```python
class Range:
    def __init__(self, a, b=None, step=1):
        """
        Define a range according to a starting value, an end value and a step.
        If only one argument is provided, it's taken to be the end value. If
        two arguments are passed in, the first becomes a start value, while the
        second is the end value. An optional step can be provided to control
        how far apart each value is from the next.
        """
        if b is not None:
            self.start = a
            self.end = b
        else:
            self.start = 0
            self.end = a
        self.step = step

    def __getitem__(self, key):
        if isinstance(key, slice):
            r = range(key.start or 0, key.stop, key.step or 1)
            return [self.step * val + self.start for val in r]
        value = self.step * key + self.start
        if value < self.end:
            return value
        else:
            raise IndexError("key outside of the given range")
```

The next logical step is to allow an individual item in the sequence to be set according to its index. This in-place assignment uses essentially the same sequence[index] syntax but as the target of an assignment operation. It's supported by a custom object in its __setitem__() method, which accepts both the index to access and the value to store at that index.

Like __getitem__(), however, __setitem__() can also accept a slice object as its index, rather than an integer. Because a slice defines a subset of the sequence, however, the value that's passed is expected to be another sequence. The values in this new sequence will then take the place of those in the subset referenced by the slice.

Things aren't exactly as they seem, however, because the sequence being assigned to the slice doesn't actually need to have the same number of items as the slice itself. In fact, it can be of any size, whether larger or smaller than the slice it's being assigned to. The expected behavior of __setitem__() is simply to remove the items referenced by the slice, then place the new items in that gap, expanding or contracting the size of the total list as necessary to accommodate the new values.

Note   The __setitem__() method is only intended for replacing existing values in the sequence, not for strictly adding new items. To do that you'll need to also implement append() and insert(), using the same interfaces as standard lists.

Removing an item from a list can be achieved in one of two different ways. The explicit method for this is remove() (e.g., my_list(range(10, 20)).remove(5)), which takes the index of the item that should be removed. The remaining items that were positioned after the removed item are then shifted to the left to fill in the gap. This same behavior is also available using a del sequence[index] statement.

Implementing remove() is straightforward enough, given that it's an explicit method call. The simple case for del works just like remove(), but using a __delitem__() method instead. In fact, if deleting a single item was all that mattered, you could simply assign an existing remove() method to the __delitem__ attribute, and it would work as expected. Unfortunately, slicing complicates matters slightly.

Deleting items from a slice works just like the first portion of the slicing behavior of __setitem__(). Instead of replacing the items in the slice with a new sequence, however, the sequence should simply shift its items to close up the gap.

With all the different ways to make changes to the contents of a sequence, the last—but not least—important feature is to test whether an item is a part of the given sequence. By default, Python will simply iterate over the sequence—using the techniques listed previously in the section on iterables—until it either finds the item being tested or exhausts all the values provided by the iterator. This allows a membership test to be performed on iterables of any type, without being limited to full sequences.

In order to be more efficient, sequences can override this behavior as well, by providing a __contains__() method. Its signature looks like __getitem__(), but rather than accepting an index, it accepts an object and returns True if the given object is present in the sequence or False otherwise. In the Range example examined previously, the result of __contains__() can be calculated on the fly, based on the configuration of the object:

```python
class Range:
    def __init__(self, a, b=None, step=1):
        """
        Define a range according to a starting value, an end value and a step.
        If only one argument is provided, it's taken to be the end value. If
        two arguments are passed in, the first becomes a start value, while the
        second is the end value. An optional step can be provided to control
        how far apart each value is from the next.
        """

        if b is not None:
            self.start = a
            self.end = b
        else:
            self.start = 0
            self.end = a
        self.step = step

    def __contains__(self, num):
        return self.start <= num < self.end and \
                not (num - self.start) % self.step
```

```
>>> list(range(5, 30, 7))
[5, 12, 19, 26]
>>> 5 in Range(5, 30, 7)
True
>>> 10 in Range(5, 30, 7)
False
>>> 33 in Range(5, 30, 7)
False
```

Many of the methods presented here for sequences are also valid for the next container type, which maps a collection of keys to associated values.

Mappings

Whereas sequences are contiguous collections of objects, mappings work a bit differently. In a mapping the individual items are actually a pair, consisting of both a key and a value. Keys don't have to be ordered because iterating over them isn't generally the point. Instead, the goal is to provide fast access to the value referenced by a given key. The key is typically known in advance, and most common usage expects it.

Accessing a value by its key uses the same syntax as using indexes in sequences. In fact, Python doesn't know or care if you're implementing a sequence, a mapping or something completely different. The same methods, __getitem__(), __setitem__(), and __delitem__(), are reused to support the obj[key] syntax regardless of which type of object is used. That doesn't mean the implementations of these methods can be identical, however.

For a mapping, a key is used as the index. Even though there's no difference in syntax between the two, keys support a wider range of allowed objects. In addition to plain integers, a key may be any hashable Python object such as dates, times, or strings; of these, strings are by far the most common. It's up to your application, however, to decide whether there should be any limitations on what keys to accept.

Python supports so much flexibility, in fact, that you can even use the standard slicing syntax without regard to what values are involved in the slice. Python simply passes along whatever objects were referenced in the slice, so it's up to the mapping to decide how to deal with them. By default, lists handle slices by explicitly looking for integers, using __index__() if necessary to coerce objects into integers. For dictionaries, by contrast, slice objects aren't hashable, so dictionaries don't allow them to be used as keys.

257

Tip   For the most part you can accept anything in a custom dictionary, even if you intend to use only a specific type, such as strings, as your keys. As long as it only gets used in your own code, it won't make any difference because you're in control of all its uses. If you make modifications that prove to be useful outside of your application, other developers will make use of it for their own needs. Therefore, you should restrict the available keys and values only if you really need to; otherwise, it's best to leave options open, even for yourself.

Even though this chapter hasn't generally covered any methods that are called directly as part of the public interface, mappings have three methods that provide particularly useful access to internal components, which should always be implemented. These methods are necessary because mappings essentially contain two separate collections—keys and values—which are then joined together by association, whereas sequences only contain a single collection.

The first of these extra methods, keys(), iterates over all the keys in the mapping without regard to their values. By default, the keys can be returned in any order, but some more specialized classes could choose to provide an explicit order for these keys. This same behavior is provided by iteration over the mapping object itself, so be sure to always supply an __iter__() method that does the same thing as keys().

The next method, values(), is complementary, iterating over the values side of the mapping instead. Like the keys, these values generally aren't assumed to be in any sort of order. In practice, the C implementation of Python uses the same order as it does for the keys, but order is never guaranteed, even between the keys and values of the same object.

In order to reliably get all the keys and values in their associated pairs, mappings provide an items() method. This iterates over the entire collection, yielding each pair as a tuple in the form of (key, value). Because this is often more efficient than iterating over the keys and using mapping[key] to get the associated value, all mappings should provide an items() method and make it as efficient as possible.

Callables

In Python, both functions and classes can be called to execute code at any time, but those aren't the only objects that can do so. In fact, any Python class can be made callable by simply attaching a single extra method to the class definition. This method, appropriately named __call__(), accepts the usual self along with any arguments that should be passed along in the method call.

There are no special requirements for what arguments __call__() can accept because it works like any other method when it's being called. The only difference is that it also receives the object it's attached to as the first argument:

```
>>> class CallCounter:
...     def __init__(self):
...         self.count = 0
...     def __call__(self, *args, **kwargs):
...         self.count += 1
...         return 'Number of calls so far: %s' % self.count
...     def reset(self):
...         self.count = 0
...
>>> counter = CallCounter()
>>> counter()
'Number of calls so far: 1'
>>> counter()
'Number of calls so far: 2'
>>> counter()
'Number of calls so far: 3'
>>> counter.reset()
>>> counter()
'Number of calls so far: 1'
```

Caution   As a method itself, __call__() can also be decorated any number of times, but remember that it's still a method, even though it is invoked by calling the object directly. As a method, any decorators applied to it must be able to deal with the first argument being an instance of the object.

As for what __call__() can do, the sky is the limit. Its purpose is solely to allow an object to be callable; what happens during that call depends entirely on the needs at hand. This example shows that it can also take any additional arguments you may need, like any other method or function. Its greatest strength, however, is that it allows you to essentially provide a function that can be customized on its own, without the need for any decorators.

Context Managers

As mentioned briefly in Chapter 2, objects can also be used as context managers for use in a with statement. This allows an object to define what it means to work within the context of that object, setting things up prior to executing the contained code and cleaning up after execution has finished.

One common example is file handling, because a file must be opened for a specific type of access before it can be used. Then it also needs to be closed when it's no longer in use, to flush any pending changes to disk. This makes sure other code can open the same file later on, without conflicting with any open references. What happens between those two operations is said to be executed within the context of the open file.

As mentioned, there are two distinct steps to be performed by a context manager. First, the context needs to be initialized, so that the code that executes inside the with block can make use of the features provided by the context. Just prior to execution of the interior code block, Python will call the __enter__() method on the object. This method doesn't receive any additional arguments, just the instance object itself. Its responsibility is then to provide the necessary initialization for the code block, whether that means modifying the object itself or making global changes.

If the with statement includes an as clause, the return value of the __enter__() method will be used to populate the variable referenced in that clause. It's important to realize that the object itself won't necessarily be that value, even though it may seem that way looking at the syntax for the with statement. Using the return value of __enter__() allows the context object to be more flexible, although that behavior can be achieved by simply returning self.

Once the code inside the with block finishes executing, Python will call the __exit__()
method on the object. This method is then responsible for cleaning up any changes
that were made during __enter__(), returning the context to whatever it was prior to
processing the with statement. In the case of files, this would mean closing the file, but it
could be virtually anything.

Of course, there are a few ways that execution within the with block can complete.
The most obvious is if the code simply finishes on its own, without any problems or
other flow control. Statements such as return, yield, continue, and break can also stop
execution of the code block, in which case __exit__() will still be called because the
cleanup is still necessary. In fact, even if an exception is raised, __exit__() is still given a
chance to reverse any changes that were applied during __enter__().

In order to identify whether the code finished normally or stopped early by way of an
exception, the __exit__() method will be given three additional arguments. The first is
the class object for the exception that was raised, followed by the instance of that class,
which is what was actually raised in the code. Finally, __exit__() will also receive a
traceback object, representing the state of execution as of when the exception was raised.

All three of those arguments are always passed in, so any implementations of __
exit__() must accept them all. If execution completed without raising any exceptions,
the arguments will still be provided, but their values will simply be None. Having access
to both the exception and a traceback allows your implementation of __exit__() to
intelligently react to whatever went wrong and what led to the problem.

Tip The __exit__() method doesn't suppress any exceptions on its own. If __
exit__() completes without a return value, the original exception, if any, will be
reraised automatically. If you need to explicitly catch any errors that occur within
the with block, simply return True from __exit__() instead of letting it fall off
the end, which would return an implicit None.

To show one simple example, consider a class that uses the context management
protocol to silence any exceptions that are raised within the with block. In this case,
__enter__() doesn't need to do anything because the exception handling will be done
in __exit__():

```
>>> class SuppressErrors:
...     def __init__(self, *exceptions):
...         if not exceptions:
...             exceptions = (Exception,)
...         self.exceptions = exceptions
...     def __enter__(self):
...         pass
...     def __exit__(self, exc_class, exc_instance, traceback):
...         if isinstance(exc_instance, self.exceptions):
...          return True
...         return False
...
>>> with SuppressErrors():
...     1 / 0  # Raises a ZeroDivisionError
...
>>> with SuppressErrors(IndexError):
...     a = [1, 2, 3]
...     print(a[4])
...
>>> with SuppressErrors(KeyError):
...     a = [1, 2, 3]
...     print(a[4])
...
Traceback (most recent call last):
  ...
IndexError: list index out of range
```

Exciting Python Extensions: Scrapy

If you ever have the need to extract data from the Internet, most specifically making sense of data on web sites, then a web-scraping tool will be of great benefit. Scrapy is an open source and full featured tool for web scraping. If you have heard of "spiders" or "web crawling," then you already are familiar with other terms for web scraping, but they are all the same. In the big scope of things, a web-scraping tool is one part of working with big data. Web scraping allows you to data mine information from the Internet while other tools would allow you to clean it up and others to categorize the raw and cleaned data you obtained. Python makes it easy to build a scaper. Read on to see how to get your raw data with Scrapy.

Installation

First you will need to install the libraries for the web-scraping tool Scrapy. To do this, get to an escalated command prompt (Windows) and type:

pip install scrapy (Enter)

MacOS and Linux will be similar; just check the scrapy.org site for details.

Running Scrapy

You can run a spider directly via the run spider command or you can create a project directory that can hold one or more spiders. For quick work, such as just running one spider, it is just one simple command: *scrapy runspider my_spider.py*. However, sometimes you may want a project directory so that you can store configuration information and multiple spiders in an orderly manner. For our purposes, one spider will more than suffice.

Project Setup

The initial process will be to find and download web pages and then extract information, based on given criteria, from the pages. To do this you will want your spider in a folder of your choice to organize everything into one area. Make a folder on your system you can easily navigate to from a command prompt for this example. For example, if on the root of your C: drive is on MS Windows:

md firstspider (Enter)

It really does not matter where you make the folder, but do make sure you are able to navigate to it. Next, using your Python IDLE IDE, write the following very basic spider code and save the file as *scraper.py* to the folder you just created:

```python
import scrapy
# filename scraper.py
class QuotesSpider(scrapy.Spider):
        name = "quotes"

        def start_requests(self):
            urls = [ 'http://quotes.toscrape.com/page/1/' ]
            for url in urls:
                    yield scrapy.Request(url=url, callback=self.parse)

        def parse(self, response):
            print('\nURL we went to: ', response, '\n')
```

Now, running the aforementioned code is not very exciting. For our purposes, Scrapy will run better via the command line using the Scrapy command interface. It is very similar to how you would run a Python script from the command line. With Python it would be **python *name_of_file.py*** and with Scrapy it will be similar, from within the folder you just created and where you saved your file to: **scrapy runspider *scraper.py*** (Enter). If everything runs properly, you should see something similar to the following:

```
2018-07-20 09:50:55 [scrapy.core.engine] DEBUG: Crawled (200) <GET http://quotes
.toscrape.com/page/1/> (referer: None)

URL we went to:  <200 http://quotes.toscrape.com/page/1/>

2018-07-20 09:50:55 [scrapy.core.engine] INFO: Closing spider (finished)
2018-07-20 09:50:55 [scrapy.statscollectors] INFO: Dumping Scrapy stats:
{'downloader/request_bytes': 225,
 'downloader/request_count': 1,
 'downloader/request_method_count/GET': 1,
 'downloader/response_bytes': 2333,
 'downloader/response_count': 1,
 'downloader/response_status_count/200': 1,
 'finish_reason': 'finished',
 'finish_time': datetime.datetime(2018, 7, 20, 13, 50, 55, 719471),
 'log_count/DEBUG': 2,
 'log_count/INFO': 7,
 'response_received_count': 1,
 'scheduler/dequeued': 1,
 'scheduler/dequeued/memory': 1,
 'scheduler/enqueued': 1,
 'scheduler/enqueued/memory': 1,
 'start_time': datetime.datetime(2018, 7, 20, 13, 50, 55, 255135)}
2018-07-20 09:50:55 [scrapy.core.engine] INFO: Spider closed (finished)
```

Figure 5-1. *Screen capture running the sample scraper via the terminal*

If you received any errors, it could be that your path or search drive to find Scrapy is not set. If on Windows and you receive a win32api error, you will need to most likely install pypiwin32. Complete this if needed by typing from an escalated command prompt:

```
pip install pypiwin32api (Enter)
```

By itself, this was only exciting in that there were (hopefully) no errors and we showed the URL we went to. That being said, let's now perform a bit more productive work.

Retrieve Web Data with Scrapy

Scrapy has a command line interface that is quite handy. Of course you will write your spider(s) in Python, but the Scrapy shell can help you with what to write in your spider code. Consider how to view a web page with Scrapy.

View a Web Page via Scrapy

From an escalated command prompt, *scrapy view http://quotes.toscrape.com/page/1/* will cause Scrapy to load the URL you specify, in a browser. This is handy because you may want to check a site before having Scrapy extract data from it. Note the title of the page; we will extract only that next.

Shell Options

You will, of course, what to know what Scrapy shell options are available. To see them, use the interactive shell and enter from the command line*scrapy shell http://quotes. toscrape.com/page/1/*. You now see options. Try from the command prompt: *response. css('title')*. Note that you are still in the Scrapy interactive shell, and note that the title, from the HTML markup tags, is returned. Use CTRL Z to exit the shell.

To perform the same thing programmatically with Python, consider the following:

```python
import scrapy

class QuotesSpider(scrapy.Spider):
    name = "quotes"
    def start_requests(self):
```

```
    urls = [
        'http://quotes.toscrape.com/page/1/'   ]
    for url in urls:
        yield scrapy.Request(url=url, callback=self.parse)

def parse(self, response):
    print()
    print("Title will follow: \n")
    print(response.css("title"))
    print()
```

This will give use the extracted title from the page, with markup tags.

```
2018-07-20 09:04:43 [scrapy.extensions.telnet] DEBUG: Telnet console listening o
n 127.0.0.1:6023
2018-07-20 09:04:44 [scrapy.core.engine] DEBUG: Crawled (200) <GET http://quotes
.toscrape.com/page/1/> (referer: None)

Title will follow:

[<Selector xpath='descendant-or-self::title' data='<title>Quotes to Scrape</titl
e>'>]

2018-07-20 09:04:44 [scrapy.core.engine] INFO: Closing spider (finished)
2018-07-20 09:04:44 [scrapy.statscollectors] INFO: Dumping Scrapy stats:
```

Figure 5-2. *CLI output of title*

Now, to clean it up a bit, change the line:

print(response.css("title"))

to:

print(response.css("title").extract_first(),)

Then save and rerun the spider, and you will note a much cleaner and usable output of the HTML tags and the title. The extract_first() method returns a string of the first occurrence found.

Of course, this is just a bit to get you started with Scrapy. You can do much more with it; use what you have learned to expand your web-scraping skills. The best place to find more information would be at the docs.scrapy.org site for more information on methods and features of Scrapy. In fact, the *Quotes* URL used in this example is the same used in the Scrapy sites tutorials.

Taking It With You

There is perhaps one thing that is most important to understand about all the protocols listed in this chapter: they aren't mutually exclusive. It is possible—and sometimes very advantageous—to implement multiple protocols on a single object. For example, a sequence can also be used as a callable and a context manager if both of those behaviors make sense for a given class.

This chapter has dealt primarily with the behaviors of objects, as provided by their classes; the next chapter will cover how you can manage those objects and their data once they have been instantiated in working code.

CHAPTER 6

Object Management

Creating an instance of a class is only the beginning; once you have an object, there are a number of things you can do with it. This is obvious, of course, because objects have methods and attributes that are intended to control their behavior, but those are defined by each class. Objects, as a whole, have an additional set of features that allow you to manage them in a number of different ways.

In order to understand these features, it's first necessary to understand what actually constitutes an object. At a high level, an object is simply the product of data and behavior, but internally, Python considers an object to be a combination of three specific things (five if you add base cclasses and attributes):

- *Identity*: Each object is unique, with an identity that can be used to compare objects to each other without having to look at any other details. This comparison, using the is operator, is very strict, however, without access to any of the subtleties outlined in Chapter 5. In actual implementations, an object's identity is simply its address in memory, so no two objects can ever have the same identity.

- *Type*: The subject of the previous two chapters, an object's type is defined by its class and any base classes that support it. Unlike identity, a type is shared among all of its instances; each object simply contains a reference to its class.

- *Value*: With a shared type to provide behavior, each object also has a value that makes it distinct among its peers. This value is provided by a namespace dictionary that is specific to a given object, where any aspect of its individuality can be stored and retrieved. This is different from the identity, however, because the value is designed to work with the type to do useful things; identity is unrelated to the type at all, so it doesn't have anything to do with the behaviors specified for the class.

269

© J. Burton Browning and Marty Alchin 2019
J. B. Browning and M. Alchin, *Pro Python 3*, https://doi.org/10.1007/978-1-4842-4385-5_6

These three things can be referenced and, in some cases, changed to suit the needs of an application. An object's identity can't be modified at any time, so its value is constant for the life of the object. But once the object is destroyed, its identity can—and often will—be reused for a future object, which then retains that identity until the object is destroyed.

If you want to retrieve an identity at any time, you can pass the object into the built-in id() function because the object itself doesn't know anything about its identity (ID method). In fact, the identity isn't related to anything specific to the object; none of its attributes have any bearing on its identity. Therefore, you won't get the same identity if you instantiate what would otherwise be an identical object. It also varies based on available memory, so in one session the location (returned as an integer) will most likely be different during another session. Types have been covered thoroughly in the previous two chapters, so the next obvious component is the value, which is implemented by way of a namespace dictionary.

Namespace Dictionary

As hinted at previously, an object's namespace is implemented as a dictionary that is created for each new object as it's being instantiated. This is then used to store values for all the attributes on the object, thus comprising the value for the object as a whole.

Unlike the identity, however, this namespace dictionary can be accessed and modified at runtime, as it's available as the __dict__ attribute on an object. In fact, because it's an attribute, it can even be replaced with a new dictionary altogether. This is the basis of what's commonly referred to as the Borg pattern, named after the collective consciousness from the Star Trek universe.

Example: Borg Pattern

Like its namesake, the Borg pattern allows a large number of instances to share a single namespace. In this way the identity for each object remains distinct, but its attributes—and thus its behaviors—are always the same as all of its peers. This primarily allows a class to be used in applications in which it could be instantiated several times, with potential modifications made to it each time. By using the Borg pattern these changes can be accumulated in a single namespace, so each instance reflects all the changes that have been made to each object.

This is achieved by attaching a dictionary to the class and then assigning that dictionary to the namespace of each object as it is being instantiated. As Chapter 4 demonstrated, this can be achieved like this: __init__() and __new__(). Because both methods execute during instantiation of the object, they seem to be equally viable options. However, let's take a look at how they would each work individually.

The __init__() method is the usual place to start because it's much better understood and more widely adopted. This method typically initializes instance attributes, so the dictionary assignment would need to take place prior to any other initialization. That's easy enough to do, however, by simply placing it at the beginning of the method. Here's how this would work:

```
>>> class Borg:
...     _namespace = {}
...     def __init__(self):
...         self.__dict__ = Borg._namespace
...         # Do more interesting stuff here.
...
>>> a = Borg()
>>> b = Borg()
>>> hasattr(a, 'attribute')
False
>>> b.attribute = 'value'
>>> hasattr(a, 'attribute')
True
>>> a.attribute
'value'
>>> Borg._namespace
{'attribute': 'value'}
```

This certainly does the job, but there are a few pitfalls with the approach, particularly when you start working with inheritance. All subclasses would need to make sure they use super() in order to call the initialization procedures from the Borg class. If any subclass fails to do so, it won't use the shared namespace; nor will any of its subclasses, even if they do use super(). Furthermore, subclasses should use super() before

271

doing any attribute assignments of their own. Otherwise, those assignments will get overwritten by the shared namespace.

That only applies when Borg is applied to other classes that know about it, however. The problem is even more pronounced when working with Borg as a mixin, because it would get applied alongside classes that don't know about it—and they shouldn't have to. But because they can get combined anyway, it's worth examining what would happen:

```
>>> class Base:
...     def __init__(self):
...         print('Base')
...
>>> class Borg:
...     _namespace = {}
...     def __init__(self, *args, **kwargs):
...         self.__dict__ = Borg._namespace
...         print('Borg')
...
>>> class Testing(Borg, Base):
...     pass
...
>>> Testing()
Borg
<__main__.Testing object at 0x...>
>>> class Testing(Base, Borg):
...     pass
...
>>> Testing()
Base
<__main__.Testing object at 0x...>
```

As you can see, this exhibits the typical problem when not using super(), where the order of base classes can completely exclude the behaviors of one or more of them. The solution, of course, is to just use super(), but in the case of mixins, you typically don't have control over both the classes involved. Adding super() would suffice in the case of

Borg coming before its peer, but mixins are usually applied after their peers, so it doesn't really help much.

With all this in mind, it's worth considering the alternative __new__() method. All methods are vulnerable to the same types of problems that were shown for __init__(), but at least we can reduce the chance of collisions that would cause those problems. Because the __new__() method is less commonly implemented, the odds of running into conflicting implementations are much smaller.

When implementing the Borg pattern with __new__(), the object must be created along the way, usually by calling __new__() on the base object. In order to play nicely with other classes as a mixin, however, it's still better to use super() here as well. Once the object is created, we can replace its namespace dictionary with one for the entire class:

```
>>> class Base:
...     def __init__(self):
...         print('Base')
...
>>> class Borg:
...     _namespace = {}
...     def __new__(cls, *args, **kwargs):
...         print('Borg')
...         obj = super(Borg, cls).__new__(cls, *args, **kwargs)
...         obj.__dict__ = cls._namespace
...         return obj
...
>>> class Testing(Borg, Base):
...     pass
...
>>> Testing()
Borg
Base
<__main__.Testing object at 0x...>
>>> class Testing(Base, Borg):
...     pass
...
```

```
>>> Testing()
Borg
Base
<__main__.Testing object at 0x...>
>>> a = Testing()
Borg
Base
>>> b = Testing()
Borg
Base
>>> a.attribute = 'value'
>>> b.attribute
'value'
```

Now, Borg comes first in the most common situations, without any unusual requirements on any classes that operate alongside them. There's still one problem with this implementation, however, and it's not very obvious from this example. As a mixin, Borg could be applied in any class definition, and you might expect that its namespace behavior would be limited to that defined class and its subclasses.

Unfortunately, that's not what would happen. Because the _namespace dictionary is on Borg itself, it'll be shared among all the classes that inherit from Borg at all. In order to break that out and apply it only to those classes where Borg is applied, a slightly different technique is necessary.

Because the __new__() method receives the class as its first positional argument, the Borg mixin can use that object as a namespace on its own, thereby splitting up the managed dictionary into individual namespaces, with one for each class that is used. In a nutshell, Borg.__new__() must create a new dictionary for each new class it encounters, assigning it to a value in the existing _namespace dictionary, using the class object as its key:

```
>>> class Borg:
...     _namespace = {}
...     def __new__(cls, *args, **kwargs):
...         obj = super(Borg, cls).__new__(cls, *args, **kwargs)
...         obj.__dict__ = cls._namespace.setdefault(cls, {})
```

```
...             return obj
...
>>> class TestOne(Borg):
...     pass
...
>>> class TestTwo(Borg):
...     pass
...
>>> a = TestOne()
>>> b = TestOne()
>>> a.spam = 'eggs'
>>> b.spam
'eggs'
>>> c = TestTwo()
>>> c.spam
Traceback (most recent call last):
  ...
AttributeError: 'TestTwo' object has no attribute 'spam'
>>> c.spam = 'burger'
>>> d = TestTwo()
>>> d.spam
'burger'
>>> a.spam
'eggs'
```

As you can see, by using cls as a kind of namespace of its own, we can
compartmentalize the managed values on a per-class basis. All instances of TestOne
share the same namespace, whereas all instances of TestTwo share a separate
namespace, so there's never any overlap between the two.

Example: Self-Caching Properties

Even though attributes are the primary means of accessing an object's namespace
dictionary, remember from Chapter 4 that attribute access can be customized using
special methods, such as __getattr__() and __setattr__(). Those methods are what
Python actually uses when accessing an attribute, and it's up to those methods to look

things up in the namespace dictionary internally. If you were to define them in pure Python, they'd look a lot like this:

```
class object:
    def __getattr__(self, name):
        try:
            return self.__dict__[name]
        except KeyError:
            raise AttributeError('%s object has no attribute named %s'
                % (self.__class__.__module__, name))

    def __setattr__(self, name, value):
        self.__dict__[name] = value

    def __delattr__(self, name):
        try:
            del self.__dict__[name]
        except KeyError:
            raise AttributeError('%s object has no attribute named %s'
                % (self.__class__.__module__, name))
```

As you can see, every access to the attribute performs a lookup in the namespace, raising an error if it wasn't there. This means that in order to retrieve an attribute, its value must have been created and stored previously. For most cases this behavior is appropriate, but in some cases the attribute's value can be a complex object that's expensive to create, and it might not get used very often, so it's not very advantageous to create it along with its host object.

One common example of this situation is an Object-Relational Mapping (ORM) sitting between application code and a relational database. When retrieving information about a person, for instance, you'd get a Person object in Python. That person might also have a spouse, children, a house, an employer, or even a wardrobe filled with clothing, all of which could also be represented in the database as related to the person you've retrieved.

If we were to access all of that information as attributes, the simple approach described previously would require all of that data to be pulled out of the database every time a person is retrieved. Then, all of that data must be collected into separate objects for each of the types of data: Person, House, Company, Clothing, and probably a host of others. Worse yet, each of those related objects has other relationships that would be accessible as attributes, which can quickly seem like you need to load up the entire database every time a query is made.

Instead, the obvious solution is to load that information only when requested. By keeping track of a unique identifier for the person, along with a set of queries that know how to retrieve the related information, methods can be added that will be able to retrieve that information when necessary.

Unfortunately, methods are expected to perform their task every time they're called. If you need the person's employer, for example, you'd have to call a `Person.get_employer()` method, which would make a query in the database and return the result. If you call the method again another query is made, even though it's often unnecessary. This could be avoided by storing the employer as a separate variable, which could be reused instead of calling the method again, but that doesn't hold up once you start passing the `Person` object around to different functions that might have different needs.

Instead, a more preferable solution would be to make an attribute that starts out with as little information as possible—perhaps even none at all. Then, when that attribute is accessed, the database query is made, returning the appropriate object. This related object can then be stored in the main object's namespace dictionary, where it can be accessed directly later on, without having to hit the database again.

Querying a database when accessing an attribute is a fairly easy task, actually. Applying the `@property` decorator to a method will produce the desired effect, calling the function whenever the attribute is accessed. Caching its return value requires a bit more finesse, however, but it's really fairly simple: simply overwrite the existing value if there's already one in the object's namespace or create a new one otherwise.

This could be simply added into the behavior of an existing property, as it only requires a few extra lines of code to support. Here's all it would take:

```
class Example:
    @property
    def attribute(self):
        if 'attribute' not in self.__dict__:
            # Do the real work of retrieving the value
            self.__dict__['attribute'] = value
        return self.__dict__['attribute']
```

> **Caution**   When caching property values like this, be careful to check that
> the computed value shouldn't change based on the value of other attributes.
> Computing a full name based on first and last names, for example, is a poor
> candidate for caching because changing the first name or last name should change
> the value of the full name as well; caching would prevent incorrect behavior.

Notice, however, that this really just performs a little work before the real code and a little bit afterward, making it an ideal task for a decorator. Here's what that decorator could look like:

```python
import functools

def cachedproperty(name):
    def decorator(func):
        @property
        @functools.wraps(func)
        def wrapper(self):
            if name not in self.__dict__:
                self.__dict__[name] = func(self)
            return self.__dict__[name]
        return wrapper
    return decorator
```

Once applied to a function, cachedproperty() will work like a standard property, but with the caching behavior applied automatically. The one difference you'll notice, however, is that you must supply the name of the attribute as an argument to cachedproperty() in addition to naming the function that you're decorating. Assuming you typed in the previous function, here's how it would look:

```python
>>> class Example:
...     @cachedproperty('attr')
...     def attr(self):
```

```
...          print('Getting the value!')
...          return 42
...
>>> e = Example()
>>> e.attr
Getting the value!
42
>>> e.attr
42
```

Why must the name be supplied twice? The problem, as mentioned in previous chapters, is that descriptors, including properties, don't get access to the names they're given. Because the cached value is stored in the object namespace according to the name of the attribute, we need a way to pass that name into the property itself. This is a clear violation of DRY, however, so let's see what other techniques are available and what their pitfalls would be.

One option would be to store a dictionary on the cached property descriptor directly, using object instances as keys. Each descriptor would get a unique dictionary, and each key would be a unique object, so you'd be able to store as many values as you have objects that have the attribute attached:

```
def cachedproperty(func):
    values = {}

    @property
    @functools.wraps(func)
    def wrapper(self):
        if self not in values:
            values[self] = func(self)
        return values[self]
    return wrapper
```

This new decorator allows you to cache an attribute without having to specify the name. If you're skeptical about it, however, you might wonder about storing those values in a single dictionary for all objects, without referencing the name of the attribute. After all, that would seem to mean that if you had more than one cached property on a single object, their values would overwrite each other and you'd have all sorts of confusion.

That's not a problem in this situation, however, because the dictionary is created inside of the `cachedproperty()` function, which means each property gets its own dictionary name values. This way there's no chance of collision, no matter how many cached properties you place on an object. The dictionary will be shared only if you assign an existing property to a new name without redefining it. In that case, the second name should always behave exactly like the first, and the cache described here will still maintain that behavior.

However, there is one other problem with this property that may not be so obvious. Believe it or not, this contains a memory leak, which could be severely harmful if it gets used in a large part of an application without being fixed (this will be discussed shortly in more detail).

In some cases the best fix will be to simply go back to the first form described in this chapter, where the attribute's name is provided explicitly. Because the name isn't provided to a descriptor, this approach would require the use of a metaclass. Of course, metaclasses are overkill for simple situations like this, but in cases in which a metaclass is used for other reasons anyway, having the name available can be quite useful. Chapter 11 showcases a framework that uses the metaclass approach to great effect.

In order to avoid using a metaclass, it's first necessary to understand what the memory leak is, why it's happening, and how we can avoid it. It all has to do with how Python removes objects from memory when they're no longer in use, a process called garbage collection.

Garbage Collection

Unlike lower-level languages like C, Python doesn't require you to manage your own memory usage. You don't have to allocate a certain amount of memory for an object or remove your claim on that memory when the object is no longer needed. In fact, you often don't even need to worry about how much memory an object will take up or how to determine when it's no longer needed. Python handles those gritty details behind the scenes.

Garbage collection is easy to understand: Python deletes any objects that are identified as garbage, clearing whatever memory they were using so that memory is available for other objects. Without this process every object created would stay in memory forever, and you'd slowly—or quickly—run out of memory, at which point everything comes to a grinding halt.

As you probably noticed, effective garbage collection first requires the ability to reliably identify an object as garbage. Even with the ability to remove garbage from memory, failing to recognize garbage will cause memory leaks to creep into an application. The last example in the previous section contains a simple situation that can cause Python to not notice when an object becomes garbage, so we need to examine how that gets determined. It is important to note that because Python is not a *strongly typed* language (you do not explicitly declare a variables type), variables that are changed during a command session are rereferenced if you redeclare the variable with a previously used value during that session. The next terminal prompt example shows this by showing the location of the variable in memory, and as you will note it changes back with the original value:

```
>>> x=10
>>> type(x)
<class 'int'>
>>> id(x)  #location of x
1368047320
>>> x="foobar"
>>> type(x)
<class 'str'>
>>> id(x)  #location of x as a string instead of int
62523328
>>> x=10
>>> id(x)  #back to the original location of x as an int at 10
1368047320
```

Reference Counting

At a high level, an object is considered garbage when it's no longer accessible by any code. In order to determine whether an object is accessible, Python counts how many data structures refer to the object at any given time.

The most obvious way to reference an object is to assign it in any namespace, including modules, classes, objects, and even dictionaries. Other types of references include any kind of container object, such as a list, tuple, or set. Even less obvious is that every function has its own namespace, which can contain references to objects, even in the case of closures. Essentially, anything that provides access to an object increases its reference count. In turn, removing an object from such a container decreases its reference count.

To illustrate, here are a few examples of situations that would create new references:

```
>>> a = [1, 2, 3]
>>> b = {'example': a}
>>> c = a
```

After executing these three lines of code, there are now three references to the list [1, 2, 3]. Two of them are fairly obvious, when it was assigned to a and later reassigned to c. The dictionary at b also has a reference to that list, however, as the value of its 'example' key. That dictionary, in turn, has just one reference, having been assigned as the value of b.

The del statement is perhaps the most obvious way to remove a reference to an object, but it's not the only option. If you replace a reference to one object with a reference to another (rebind it), you'll also implicitly remove the reference to the first object. For example, if we were to run these two lines of code, we end with just one reference to the list shown as a:

```
>>> del c
>>> a = None
```

Even though it's no longer available in the root namespace, that list is still available as part of the dictionary, which itself is still accessible as b. Therefore, they each have just one reference, and neither will be garbage collected. If you were to del b right now, the reference count for the dictionary becomes zero and will be eligible for garbage collection. Once that's been collected, the reference count for the list is reduced to zero and is collected as garbage.

Tip   By default, Python simply clears out the memory that was occupied by the object. You don't need to do anything in order to support that behavior, and it works just fine for most cases. In the rare event that an object has some special needs to address when it's deleted, the __del__() method can provide this customization.

Instead of deleting objects, there are a number of other things you can do with them as well. Here's a look at a very different situation that can alter the way reference counting works.

Cyclical References

Consider the scenario in which you have a dictionary that refers to a list as one of its values. Because lists are containers as well, you could actually append the dictionary as a value to the list. What you end up with is a cyclical reference, where each object refers to the other. To extend the previous examples, let's examine what would happen with this line of code:

```
>>> b['example'].append(b)
```

Prior to this the dictionary and the list had one reference each, but now the dictionary gains another reference by being included as a member of the inner list. This situation will work just fine in normal operation, but it does present an interesting problem when it comes to garbage collection.

Remember that using del b would decrease the reference count of the dictionary by one, but now that the list also contains a reference to that same dictionary, its reference count goes from two to one, rather than dropping to zero. With a reference count above zero, the dictionary wouldn't be considered garbage and it would stay in memory, along with its reference to the list. Therefore, the list also has a reference count of one, keeping it in memory.

What's the problem here? Well, after you delete the reference at the variable b, the references those two objects have to each other are now the only references they have in the entire Python interpreter. They're completely cut off from any code that will continue executing, but because garbage collection uses reference counts, they'll stay in memory forever unless something else is done.

To address this, Python's garbage collection comes with code designed to spot these structures when they occur, so they can be removed from memory as well. Any time a set of objects is referenced only by other objects in that set—and not from anywhere else in memory—it's flagged as a reference cycle. This allows the garbage collection system to reclaim the memory it was using.

Things start to get really tricky when you implement __del__(), however. Ordinarily, __del__() works just fine because Python can intelligently figure out when to delete the object. Therefore, __del__() can be executed in a predictable manner, even when multiple objects are deleted within a short span.

When Python encounters a reference cycle that's inaccessible from any other code, it doesn't know the order to delete the objects in that cycle. This becomes a problem with the custom __del__() method, because it could act on related objects as well. If one object is part of an orphaned reference cycle, any related objects are all also scheduled for deletion, so which one should fire first?

After all, each object in the cycle could reference one or more of the other objects in that same cycle. Without an object to be considered first, Python would have to simply guess which one it should be. Unfortunately, that leads to behavior that is not only unpredictable but also unreliable across the many times it could occur.

Therefore, Python has to take one of only two predictable, reliable courses of action. One option would be to simply ignore the __del__() method and delete the object just as it would if the __del__() method wasn't found. Unfortunately, that changes the behavior of the object based on things outside that object's control.

The other option, which Python does take, is to leave the object in memory. This avoids the problem of trying to order a variety of __del__() methods while maintaining the behavior of the object itself. The problem, however, is that this is in fact a memory leak, and it's only there because Python can't make a reliable assumption about your intentions.

IN THE FACE OF AMBIGUITY, REFUSE THE TEMPTATION TO GUESS

This situation with __del__() in a cyclical reference is a perfect example of ambiguity because there's no clear way to handle the situation. Rather than guess, Python sidesteps it by simply leaving the objects in memory. It's not the most memory-efficient way to address the problem, but consistency is far more important in situations like this. Even though it potentially means more work for the programmer, that extra work results in much more explicit, reliable behavior.

There are three ways you can avoid this problem. First, you can avoid having any objects with __del__() methods involved in any cyclical references. The easiest way to accomplish that is to avoid the __del__() method entirely. Most of the common reasons to customize an object's teardown are more appropriately handled using a context manager.

In those rare cases in which __del__() proves necessary, the second option is to simply avoid having the objects appear in reference cycles. That's not always easy to do, however, because it requires you to have complete control over all the ways the object might be used. That might work for some highly internalized implementation details, but if it's part of a public interface, it's probably not an option.

Finally, if you can't prevent the cycles from being orphaned, Python does provide a way that you can still detect them and have a chance to clean them up on a regular basis. Once all other references are removed and the garbage collection cycle runs, Python keeps the entire cycle alive by placing each object involved into a special list, available in the gc module.

The gc module provides a few options that are useful for getting into the guts of the garbage collection system, but the factor at hand here is the garbage attribute. This attribute contains objects that are otherwise unreachable but are part of a cycle that includes __del__() somewhere along the line. Accessing them as part of gc.garbage allows you to try to break the cycle after the fact, which will allow their memory to be relinquished.

Consider the following example, which also shows the usage of gc.collect(), a module-level function that manually runs the garbage collector so that cyclical references are detected and placed in gc.garbage accordingly:

```
>>> import gc
>>> class Example:
...     def __init__(self, value):
...         self.value = value
...     def __repr__(self):
...         return 'Example %s' % self.value
...     def __del__(self):
...         print('Deleting %r' % self)
...
```

```
>>> e = Example(1)
>>> e
Example 1
>>> del e
>>> gc.collect()
Deleting Example 1
0

# Now let's try it with a cyclical reference

>>> e = Example(2)
>>> e.attr = e
>>> del e
>>> gc.collect()
2
>>> gc.garbage

# From here, we can break the cycle and remove it from memory

>>> e = gc.garbage[0]
>>> del e.attr
>>> del e
>>> gc.collect()
0
>>> gc.garbage

# Don't forget to clear out gc.garbage as well

>>> gc.garbage[:] = []
Deleting Example 2
>>> gc.garbage
[]
```

In the real world, however, __del__() is rarely needed, and it's even more rare to run into very severe problems with cyclical references. Far more common, however, is the need to adjust how references themselves are created and what to do when you don't really need a reference all your own.

Weak References

As we've seen, assigning an object creates a reference to it, and those references keep that object alive in memory. But what happens when you need to access an object but you don't care to keep it alive? For this, Python provides the concept of a weak reference: you get a reference to the object without increasing its reference count.

By getting a reference without increasing the object's reference count, you can perform operations on that object without getting in the way of how it would ordinarily be deleted. This can be very important for applications that register objects for use later. The registry itself keeps references to all the registered objects, which ordinarily wouldn't get deleted, because the application that knows about the object typically doesn't know anything about the registration system.

Creating a weak reference is fairly simple, thanks to the weakref module in the standard library. The ref() class within that module creates a weak reference to whatever object is passed into it, allowing that reference to be used later. To provide access to the original object, a weak reference is a callable object that takes no arguments and returns the object.

In order to see what was supposed to happen, we have to first store a reference to that object outside the weak reference. That way we cannot only create a weak reference that has access to the object, but we can then delete the additional reference to see how the weak reference behaves:

```
>>> import weakref
>>> class Example:
...     pass
...
>>> e = Example()
>>> e
<__main__.Example object at 0x...>
>>> ref = weakref.ref(e)
>>> ref
<weakref at ...; to 'Example' at ...>
>>> ref()
<__main__.Example object at 0x...>
```

```
>>> del e
>>> ref
<weakref at ...; dead>
>>> ref()
>>>
```

As you can see, as long as there's at least one other reference keeping the object alive, the weak reference has easy access to it. Once the object is deleted elsewhere, the weak reference object itself is still available, but it simply returns None when called. We could make the example even simpler as well, by passing a new object directly into the weak reference:

```
>>> ref = weakref.ref(Example())
>>> ref
<weakref at ...; dead>
>>> ref()
>>>
```

Wait, what just happened? Where did the Example object go? This simple example illustrates one of the most common problems you're likely to encounter with weak references. Because you're instantiating the object as part of the call to ref(), the only reference that gets created for that object is inside of ref().

Ordinarily that would be fine, but that particular reference doesn't help keep the object alive, so the object is immediately marked for garbage collection. The weak reference provides access to the object only if there's something else to keep it alive, so in this case, the reference simply returns None when called. That situation may seem obvious, but there are a few others that may come up when you least expect them.

One such situation that can come up involves creating a weak reference inside of a function:

```
>>> def example():
...     e = Example()
...     ref = weakref.ref(e)
```

```
...       return ref
...
>>> e = example()
>>> e
<weakref at ...; dead>
>>> e()
>>>
```

As you can see, even though the `example()` function stores a strong reference inside itself, the weak reference goes dead immediately. The problem here is that every function gets a brand-new namespace every time it executes, and it's deleted when the function finishes, because execution is the only thing keeping it alive.

By default, all assignments in the function take place in that namespace, so once it's destroyed any objects assigned are destroyed as well unless they have references stored elsewhere. In this case the only other reference to the `Example` object is weak, so the object gets destroyed once the `example()` function returns.

The recurring theme here is that weak references can cause problems when used along with any kind of implicit reference removal. We've discussed two already, but there are other similar situations as well. For example, a `for` loop automatically assigns at least one variable each time the loop begins, overwriting any values that were previously assigned to the same name. Because that also destroys the reference to whatever object was used in the previous iteration, a weak reference created inside the loop isn't enough to keep that object alive.

Pickling

So far we've only discussed how objects are handled inside of Python, but it's often necessary to exchange data with external processes such as files, databases, and network protocols. Most of the time the structure of that data outside of Python is already established, so your application will need to adhere to that structure. Other times, however, the only reason to send the data into something else is to store it for a while and read it back into Python later. The *Pickle* command is used to convert a Python object such as a list or dictionary into a persistent character stream that can be reloaded later to recreate the object for use in a different Python application. It is used for serializing and deserializing a Python object to and from a file.

In this case, the external system really doesn't care what your data is or how it's structured. As long as it's a data type that system can understand, it should be usable. You should note that def functions and classes cannot be pickled. Because the most flexible and widely supported data type is a string, it's necessary to export Python's data structures to strings. For this, Python provides the pickle module. PEP 3137 has some very interesting details on byte types and strings by Guido.

In the real world, pickling is a way of preserving food so it can be stored for long periods of time and consumed much later. Without preservation techniques like pickling, food would have to be consumed almost immediately after it's produced. The same is true for data: it's easy to consume shortly after it's produced, but saving it for later requires some extra work.

The action of pickling is performed by using the pickle module's dump() or dumps() functions. Both of these functions can take any object as the first argument, but they differ in where they output the string representing that object. In the case of dump(), a second required argument specifies a writable file-like object that the function will use as the destination for the pickled value. The dumps() function, by contrast, simply returns the string directly, allowing the code that called the function to decide where to put it. Beyond that the two functions are identical, and the examples throughout the rest of this section will use dumps(), as it shows the output much more easily:

```
>>> import pickle
>>> pickle.dumps(1)
b'\x80\x03K\x01.'
>>> pickle.dumps(42)
b'\x80\x03K*.'
>>> pickle.dumps('42')
b'\x80\x03X\x02\x00\x00\x0042q\x00.'
```

As you can see, the pickled output can contain more information than the original objects value because it also needs to store the type, so the object can be reconstituted later.

Once a value has been pickled, the resulting string can be stored or passed around however your application requires. Once it's time to retrieve the object back into Python, the pickle module provides two addition functions, load() and loads(). The difference between the two is similar to the dump functions: load() accepts a readable file-like object, while loads() accepts a string:

```
>>> pickled = pickle.dumps(42)
>>> pickled
b'\x80\x03K*.'
>>> pickle.loads(pickled)
42
```

Dumping objects into pickled strings and loading them back again are just the external tasks, however. Like in the many protocols described previously, Python allows individual objects to control how they're pickled and restored. Because pickling represents a sort of snapshot of the object at the time it was pickled, these functions are named to refer to the state of the object at a given time.

The first method to consider is __getstate__(), which controls what gets included in the pickled value. It doesn't take any additional arguments and returns whatever value Python should include in the pickled output. For complex objects the value will typically be a dictionary or perhaps a tuple, but it's completely up to each class to define what values are pertinent to the object.

For example, a currency conversion class might contain a number to use as the current amount as well as a string to indicate the currency being represented. In addition, it would likely have access to a dictionary of current exchange rates, so that it can convert the amount to a different currency. If a reference to that dictionary were placed on the object itself, Python would pickle it all together:

```
>>> class Money:
...     def __init__(self, amount, currency):
...         self.amount = amount
...         self.currency = currency
...         self.conversion = {'USD': 1, 'CAD': .95}
...     def __str__(self):
...         return '%.2f %s' % (self.amount, self.currency)
```

```
...     def __repr__(self):
...         return 'Money(%r, %r)' % (self.amount, self.currency)
...     def in_currency(self, currency):
...         ratio = self.conversion[currency] / self.conversion[self.
            currency]
...         return Money(self.amount * ratio, currency)
...
>>> us_dollar = Money(250, 'USD')
>>> us_dollar
Money(250, 'USD')
>>> us_dollar.in_currency('CAD')
Money(237.5, 'CAD')
>>> pickled = pickle.dumps(us_dollar)
>>> pickled
b'\x80\x03c__main__\nMoney\nq\x00)\x81q\x01}q\x02(X\x08\x00\x00\
x00currencyq\x03
X\x03\x00\x00\x00USDq\x04X\x06\x00\x00\x00amountq\x05K\xfaX\n\x00\x00\
x00convers
ionq\x06}q]\x07(h\x04Kx01X\x03\x00\x00\x00CADq\x08G?\xeeffffffuub.'
```

As you can see, this is already quite an expansive pickled value, and that's with just having two currencies stored in the dictionary. Because the currency conversion values aren't specific to the instance at hand—and they'll change over time anyway—there's no reason to store them in the pickled string, so we can use __getstate__() to provide just those values that are actually important.

If you look closely at the pickled output of the existing Money object, you'll notice that the attribute names are also included because Python doesn't know if they're important. In lieu of any explicit instructions from __getstate__(), it includes as much information as possible, to be sure the object can be recreated later. Because we already know that there are just two values that are necessary, we can return just those two values as a tuple:

```
>>> class Money:
...     def __init__(self, amount, currency):
...         self.amount = amount
```

```
...            self.currency = currency
...            self.conversion = {'USD': 1, 'CAD': .95}
...        def __str__(self):
...            return '%.2f %s' % (self.amount, self.currency)
...        def __repr__(self):
...            return 'Money(%r, %r)' % (self.amount, self.currency)
...        def __getstate__(self):
...            return self.amount, self.currency
...        def in_currency(self, currency):
...            ratio = self.conversion[currency] / self.conversion[self.
               currency]
...            return Money(self.amount * ratio, currency)
...
>>> us_dollar = Money(250, 'USD')
>>> us_dollar
Money(250, 'USD')
>>> us_dollar.in_currency('CAD')
Money(237.5, 'CAD')
>>> pickled = pickle.dumps(us_dollar)
>>> pickled
b'\x80\x03c__main__\nMoney\nq\x00)\x81q\x01K\xfaX\x03\x00\x00\x00USDq\x02\
x86q\x
03b.'
```

As you can see, this cuts the size of the pickled output to just over a third of what it was before. In addition to being more efficient, it's more practical because it doesn't contain unnecessary information. Other attributes that should avoid being pickled are initialization values, system-specific details, and other transient information that are simply related to the object's value rather than being part of that value directly.

That's only half of the equation, however. Once you have customized the pickled output of an object, it can't be retrieved back into a Python object without also customizing that side of things. After all, by storing the value as a tuple, we've removed some of the hints Python used to rebuild the object, so we have to provide an alternative.

As you might have guessed, the complement to __getstate__() is __setstate__(). The __setstate__() method accepts just one additional argument: the state of the object to restore. Because __getstate__() can return any object to represent state, there's no specific type that will also be passed into __setstate__(). It's not at all random, however; the value passed into __setstate__() will be exactly the same value that was returned from __getstate__().

In the case of our currency converter, the state is represented by a 2-tuple containing the amount and currency:

```
>>> class Money:
...     def __init__(self, amount, currency):
...         self.amount = amount
...         self.currency = currency
...         self.conversion = {'USD': 1, 'CAD': .95}
...     def __str__(self):
...         return '%.2f %s' % (self.amount, self.currency)
...     def __repr__(self):
...         return 'Money(%r, %r)' % (self.amount, self.currency)
...     def __getstate__(self):
...         return self.amount, self.currency
...     def __setstate__(self, state):
...         self.amount = state[0]
...         self.currency = state[1]
...     def in_currency(self, currency):
...         ratio = self.conversion[currency] / self.conversion[self.
            currency]
...         return Money(self.amount * ratio, currency)
...
>>> us_dollar = Money(250, 'USD')
>>> pickled = pickle.dumps(us_dollar)
>>> pickle.loads(pickled)
Money(250, 'USD')
```

And with that, the Money class now fully controls how its value gets pickled and unpickled. That should be the end of it, right? Well, just to be sure, let's test that in_currency() method again, because that's an important aspect of its behavior:

```
>>> us_dollar = pickle.loads(pickled)
>>> us_dollar
Money(250, 'USD')
>>> us_dollar.in_currency('CAD')
Traceback (most recent call last):
  ...
AttributeError: 'Money' object has no attribute 'conversion'
```

So why didn't this work? When unpickling an object, Python doesn't call __init__()
along the way because that step is only supposed to take place when setting up new
objects. Because the pickled object was already initialized once before the state was
saved, it would usually be wrong to try to initialize it again. Instead, you can include
initialization behaviors like that inside of __setstate__() to ensure that everything is
still properly in place:

```
>>> class Money:
...     def __init__(self, amount, currency):
...         self.amount = amount
...         self.currency = currency
...         self.conversion = self.get_conversions()
...     def __str__(self):
...         return '%.2f %s' % (self.amount, self.currency)
...     def __repr__(self):
...         return 'Money(%r, %r)' % (self.amount, self.currency)
...     def __getstate__(self):
...         return self.amount, self.currency
...     def __setstate__(self, state):
...         self.amount = state[0]
...         self.currency = state[1]
...         self.conversion = self.get_conversions()
...     def get_conversions(self):
...         return {'USD': 1, 'CAD': .95}
```

```
...     def in_currency(self, currency):
...         ratio = self.conversion[currency] / self.conversion[self.
            currency]
...         return Money(self.amount * ratio, currency)
...
>>> us_dollar = Money(250, 'USD')
>>> pickled = pickle.dumps(us_dollar)
>>> pickle.loads(pickled)
Money(250, 'USD')
>>> us_dollar.in_currency('CAD')
Money(237.5, 'CAD')
```

Of course, all of this is only useful if you're copying an object to be stored or sent to a non-Python consumer outside. If all you'll need to do is work with it inside of Python itself, you can simply copy the object internally.

Copying

Mutable objects come with one potentially prominent drawback: changes made to an object are visible from every reference to that object. All mutable objects work this way because of how Python references objects, but that behavior isn't always the most useful. In particular, when working with objects passed in as arguments to a function, the code that called the function will often expect the object to be left unchanged. If the function needs to make modifications in the course of its work, you'll need to take some extra care.

In order to make changes to an object without those changes showing up elsewhere, you'll need to copy the object first. Some objects provide a mechanism for this right out of the box. Lists, for instance, support slicing to retrieve items from the list into a new list. That behavior can be used to get all the items at once, creating a new list with those same items. Simply leave out the start and end values, and the slice will copy the list automatically:

```
>>> a = [1, 2, 3]
>>> b = a[:]
>>> b
[1, 2, 3]
```

```
>>> b.append(4)
>>> b
[1, 2, 3, 4]
>>> a
[1, 2, 3]
```

Similarly, dictionaries have their own way to copy their contents, although not using a syntax like lists use. Instead, dictionaries provide a copy() method, which returns a new dictionary with all the same keys and values:

```
>>> a = {1: 2, 3: 4}
>>> b = a.copy()
>>> b[5] = 6
>>> b
{1: 2, 3: 4, 5: 6}
>>> a
{1: 2, 3: 4}
```

Not all objects include this type of copying behavior internally, but Python allows you to copy any object, even if it doesn't have its own copying mechanism.

Shallow Copies

To get a copy of any arbitrary object, Python provides a copy module. The simplest function available in that module is also named copy(), and it provides the same basic behavior as the techniques shown in the previous section. The difference is that rather than being a method on the object you want to copy, copy.copy() allows you to pass in any object and get a shallow copy of it. Not only can you copy a wider variety of objects, you can do so without needing to know anything about the objects themselves:

```
>>> import copy
>>> class Example:
...     def __init__(self, value):
```

```
...          self.value = value
...
>>> a = Example('spam')
>>> b = copy.copy(a)
>>> b.value = 'eggs'
>>> a.value
'spam'
>>> b.value
'eggs'
```

Of course, this is just a shallow copy. Remember from the beginning of this chapter that an object is really the combination of three components: an identity, a type, and a value. When you make a copy of an object, what you're really doing is creating a new object with the same type, but with a new identity and a new—but identical—value.

For mutable objects, that value typically contains references to other objects, such as the items in a list or the keys and values in a dictionary. The value for the copied object may have a new namespace, but it contains all the same references. Therefore, when you make changes to a member of the copied object, those changes get reflected in all other references to that same object, just like any other namespace. To illustrate, consider a dictionary that contains lists as its values:

```
>>> a = {'a': [1, 2, 3], 'b': [4, 5, 6]}
>>> b = a.copy()
>>> a['a'].append(4)  #Copy to a and b
>>> b['b'].append(7)  #Copy to a and b
>>> a
{'a': [1, 2, 3, 4], 'b': [4, 5, 6, 7]}
>>> b
{'a': [1, 2, 3, 4], 'b': [4, 5, 6, 7]}
```

As you can see, the copy only goes one level deep, so it's considered to be "shallow." Beyond the object's own namespace only references get copied, not the objects themselves. This is true for all types of objects, not just the lists and dictionaries shown here. In fact, custom objects can even customize this behavior by providing a __copy__() method.

The copy() function will call __copy__() with no arguments if it exists, so that method can determine which values get copied and how they're handled.

Typically, shallow copies are useful when the first layer is the only part of a value you need to change, particularly when it makes more sense to specifically keep the rest of the objects intact. The basic example case for this is sorting a list, where a new list must be created in order to sort the items, but those items themselves should remain as they were.

To illustrate, consider a custom implementation of Python's built-in sorted() method, which sorts the items into a new list while keeping the original unchanged:

```
>>> def sorted(original_list, key=None):
...     copied_list = copy.copy(original_list)
...     copied_list.sort(key=key)
...     return copied_list
...
>>> a = [3, 2, 1]
>>> b = sorted(a)
>>> a
[3, 2, 1]
>>> b
[1, 2, 3]
```

Of course, this still relies on the object passed in being a list, but it illustrates how shallow copies can be useful. In other situations you may need to modify the whole structure as deep as you can get.

Deep Copies

It's often necessary for algorithms to need to reorganize data in large structures in order to solve a particular problem. Sorting, indexing, aggregating, and rearranging data are all common tasks to perform in these more complex operations. Because the goal is simply to return some analysis of that data, the original structure needs to remain intact. We need a deeper copy than what we've examined so far.

For these situations Python's copy module also contains a deepcopy() method, which copies not only the original structure but also the objects that are referenced by it. In fact, it looks recursively through all those objects for any other objects, copying each in turn. This way you're free to modify the copy however you like, without fear of modifying the original or any modifications to the original being reflected in the copy:

```
>>> original = [[1, 2, 3], [1, 2, 3]]
>>> shallow_copy = copy.copy(original)
>>> deep_copy = copy.deepcopy(original)
>>> original[0].append(4)
>>> shallow_copy
[[1, 2, 3, 4], [1, 2, 3]]
>>> deep_copy
[[1, 2, 3], [1, 2, 3]]
```

It's not truly recursive, however, because full recursion would sometimes make for infinite loops if the data structure had a reference to itself at any time. Once a particular object is copied Python makes a note of it, so that any future references to that same object can simply be changed to refer to the new object rather than create a brand-new one every time (deepcopy function).

Not only does that avoid recursively copying the same object if it's somehow a member of itself; it also means that any time the same object is found more than once in the structure, it will only be copied once and referenced as many times as necessary. That means the copied structure will have the same behavior as the original with regard to how changes are reflected in referenced objects:

```
>>> a = [1, 2, 3]
>>> b = [a, a]
>>> b
[[1, 2, 3], [1, 2, 3]]
>>> b[0].append(4)
>>> b
[[1, 2, 3, 4], [1, 2, 3, 4]]
>>> c = copy.deepcopy(b)
>>> c
```

```
[[1, 2, 3, 4], [1, 2, 3, 4]]
>>> c[0].append(5)
>>> c
[[1, 2, 3, 4, 5], [1, 2, 3, 4, 5]]
```

This is a must for algorithms that rely on objects being present in multiple places of a structure. Each copy will behave the same as the original in that regard, so there's no worry about how many times it gets copied before an algorithm starts working with it.

One other problem that can come up with deep copies is that Python doesn't know what might or might not be important, so it copies everything, which might end up being far more than you need. In order to control that behavior, custom objects can specify the deep copying behavior separately from shallow copies.

By supplying a __deepcopy__() method, an object can specify which values are pertinent to the copy, much like how __getstate__() works for pickling. The biggest difference from __getstate__(), and from __copy__() as well, is that __deepcopy__() also accepts a second argument, which will be a dictionary used to manage the identity of objects during copies. Because the deep copy should only copy each object once and use references any other time that object is used, this identity namespace provides a way to keep track of which objects are indeed the same because it maps their identities to the objects themselves.

Exciting Python Extensions: Beautiful Soup

Beautiful Soup is a de facto standard library for working with HTML and XML documents. It is a file parser or screen-scraper that gives you great control in shaping files to meet your data extraction needs. In Chapter 5 you used Scrapy for web scraping. The documents you obtained can be easily cleaned to remove markup language with Beautiful Soup. This is a great library to use in conjunction with other Python extensions such as Scrapy. Consider that you would obtain the data with a tool like Scrapy and then clean it with Beautiful Soup. Beautiful Soup has some powerful searching capabilities as well, but let's just focus on the parsing ability.

Installing Beautiful Soup

Documentation for the extension is available at `https://www.crummy.com/software/BeautifulSoup`:

`pip install beautifulsoup4 (Enter)`

Of course, with other operating systems you would use the appropriate install tool; with Elementary or Ubuntu, for example, it would be **sudo apt-get *name-of-package***.

Using Beautiful Soup

Make sure your install is working first by running from a Python interactive prompt:

`from bs4 import BeautifulSoup (Enter)`

If no errors result, then your libraries are installed. If you receive errors check that you do not have another Python installation, such as Anaconda, or path issues.

As an example of the power of Beautiful Soup, we will take the HTML file harvested in Chapter 5 with Scrapy and clean it up so that it is a text file only, with the markup tags removed. This will create a file that is much better suited to data analysis such as searching for key words or occurrences. Key in and run the following code, with the quotes.html file we created in the previous chapter in the same folder, and you will see raw HTML output and prettified Beautiful Soup output:

```
from bs4 import BeautifulSoup

path='quotes-1.html'

filedata=open(path,'r',errors='ignore')
page=filedata.read()

soup = BeautifulSoup(page, 'lxml')
print(soup.prettify()) # show raw HTML markup

print('\n\nAnd a cleaner version:\n')
print(soup.get_text()) # return plain text only
```

What you should see is the raw HTML text, then the cleaned-up version via Beautiful Soup. Note that some extraneous data was left (but not much) that we could not clean up via a looping structure. Next let's only search for items that have a HTML 'span' tag, count the occurrences, and print a cleaner output of only those selected items:

```
from bs4 import BeautifulSoup

path='quotes-1.html'

filedata=open(path,'r',errors='ignore')
page=filedata.read()

soup = BeautifulSoup(page, 'lxml')

print('\nWe found this many span tags:  ',len(soup.find_all('span')))

print('\n\nShow only span tag items\n\n')

print(soup.find_all('span'))
print('------------------')
print('\nNow clean up the span tags\n\n')
for item in soup.find_all('span'):
    print(item.text)
```

In this last example we searched for a tag, then used an enhanced *for* to print the individual items, with the tags removed via item.text. Is there more you could do with Beautiful Soup? Certainly, but this should serve as a good stepping-off point to experiment more.

Taking It With You

Every application knows how to deal with objects at a basic level, but with the techniques shown in this chapter you'll be able to move on to managing large collections of objects, spanning a wide variety of different types. In the next chapter, we'll shift from a macro-level view of objects to a micro-level examination of one specific type of object: the humble string.

CHAPTER 7

Strings

Given the fundamental nature of strings in all forms of programming, it should come as no surprise that Python's string features can fill an entire chapter. Whether it's interacting with users by way of keyboard input, sending content over the Web, analyzing big data, or participating in a Turing test,[1] strings can and are used for many applications.

With all this emphasis on strings, Python makes sure to include a wide variety of features to support them. Some of these features are built right into the string objects themselves, while others are provided by modules in the standard library and many third-party libraries, such as Boost, offer even more options. This chapter, however, will focus on Python built-in string functions rather than investigating third-party applications.

The first thing to understand about Python strings is that there are actually two different formats to consider: bytes and Unicode strings. Let's examine bytes first.

Bytes

At a very basic level, a string is really just a sequence of individual bytes. In this general sense, bytes are used for every piece of data a computer processes. Numbers, strings, and more complex objects are all stored as bytes at some point, and anything more structured is built on top of a sequence of bytes. In a byte string, represented in Python by a `bytes` object, each character represents exactly one byte, so it's easy to interact with files and other interfaces to the outside world.

While standard strings—described later in the section on text—are identified as literals simply with a pair of straight single quotes (`'example'`), byte string literals include a b before the first quote. This is used in the source code as well as the `repr()` output for these values:

---

[1]See "xx," `http://propython.com/turing_test/`.

J. B. Browning and M. Alchin, *Pro Python 3*, https://doi.org/10.1007/978-1-4842-4385-5_7

```
>>> b'example' #the keyword print is assumed since it is a command prompt
statement versus a script.
b'example'
```

The primary use of bytes is to convey nontextual information such as numbers, dates, sets of flags, and a number of other things. Even though Python doesn't directly know how to deal with those particular values, a bytes object *will make sure that they pass through unchanged*, so that your own code can handle each situation appropriately. Without any assumptions about the intentions of the data, bytes offer you maximum flexibility, but that means you'll need some way to convert data back and forth between bytes and something with more meaning to your application.

Simple Conversion: chr( ) and ord( )

At a basic level a byte is really just a number, which happens to be represented by a character of some kind. Python considers numbers and characters to be two different things, but their values are equivalent, so it's fairly easy to convert between them. Given a single byte, you can pass it into the built-in ord(#) function, which will return its equivalent integer value:

```
>>> ord(b'A')
65
>>> ord(b'!')
33
>>> list(b'Example')
[69, 120, 97, 109, 112, 108, 101]
```

Notice what happens when iterating over a sequence of bytes. Rather than one-character byte strings, you actually get the raw integers immediately, removing the need for ord() at all. This works well when converting single-byte values from bytes to numbers, but going in the other direction requires the built-in chr() function. As an inverse to ord(), it returns a single character based on the integer value you pass in:

```
>>> chr(65)
'A'
>>> chr(33)
'!'
>>> [chr(o) for o in [69, 120, 97, 109, 112, 108, 101]]
['E', 'x', 'a', 'm', 'p', 'l', 'e']
>>> ".join(chr(o) for o in [69, 120, 97, 109, 112, 108, 101])
'Example'
```

There's one important thing to notice here: the string returned by chr() is a regular string, rather than a byte string, as evidenced by the lack of a b prefix. As you'll see in the section on text later in this chapter, standard strings work a bit differently from byte strings. The biggest problem for our purposes here, however, is that a standard string doesn't always equate directly to a single byte, so it's possible to get things wrong. In order to get things to work more reliably and get some extra features on top of it, we can use the struct module.

Complex Conversion: The Struct Module

In addition to the problem with chr() returning standard strings, a big problem with the ord()/chr() combination is that it can only be reliably used when working with individual bytes. When converting numbers to bytes, that limits it to values from 0 to 255. In order to support a wider range of values and some other interesting features, Python provides the struct module.

Similarly to how chr() and ord() represent a pair to convert values between byte strings and native Python values, struct.pack() writes out byte strings, while struct. unpack() reads those values back into Python. Unlike those simpler functions, however, the struct module uses a format string to specify how values should get converted. This format has its own sort of simple syntax to control what types of values to use and how they work.

Because we came by struct to overcome some difficulties with chr(), we'll start by looking at how struct.pack() can provide the intended functionality. The format to use for a single, unsigned byte is B, and here's how you'd use it in practice:

```
>>> import struct
>>> struct.pack(b'B', 65)
b'A'
>>> struct.pack(b'B', 33)
b'!'
>>> struct.pack(b'BBBBBBB', 69, 120, 97, 109, 112, 108, 101)
b'Example'
```

As you can see, the first argument is the format string itself, with one character for each argument that should get converted into the byte string. All additional arguments are used to provide the values that should be converted. Therefore, for each format specifier, you'll need to include an argument at the equivalent position.

As mentioned, B specifies an unsigned value, which means there can be no negative values. With this you could provide values from 0 to 255, but nothing below 0. A signed value, by contrast, allows negative values by using one of the eight bits in the byte to identify whether the value is positive or negative. There are still 256 unique values, but the range is shifted a bit so that half the values are on each side of the sign. With 0 being considered a positive value, a signed byte can contain values from –128 to 127. To complement unsigned bytes, the format specifier for signed bytes is b:

```
>>> struct.pack(b'b', 65)
b'A'
>>> struct.pack(b'Bb', 65, -23)
b'A\xe9'
>>> struct.pack(b'B', 130)
b'\x82'
>>> struct.pack(b'b', 130)
Traceback (most recent call last):
  ...
struct.error: byte format requires -128 <= number <= 127
```

Of course, B and b are only valid for single byte values, limited to 256 total values. To support larger numbers you can use H and h for two-byte numbers, allowing up to 65,536 values. Just like the single-byte option, the uppercase format assumes an unsigned value, whereas the lowercase format assumes a signed value:

```
>>> struct.pack(b'Hh', 42, -137)
b'*\x00w\xff'
```

Now that a single value can span multiple bytes, there comes the question of which byte comes first. One of the two bytes contains the 256 smallest values, while the other contains the values 0 to 256 but multiplied by 256. Therefore, getting the two mixed up can greatly affect the value that gets stored or retrieved. This is easy enough to see by taking a quick look at the inverse function, struct.unpack():

```
>>> struct.unpack(b'H', b'*\x00')
(42,)
>>> struct.unpack(b'H', b'\x00*')
(10752,)
```

As you can see, the function call for struct.unpack() looks very similar to struct.pack(), but there are a couple notable differences. First, there are always only two arguments to unpack(), because the second argument is the raw byte string. This string can contain multiple values to be pulled out, but it's still passed as just one argument, unlike pack().

Instead the return value is a tuple, which could contain multiple values. Therefore, struct.unpack() is a true inverse of struct.pack(); that is, you can pass the result from one into the call to the other and get the same value you passed in the first time. All you need is to ensure that you use the same format string in each of the individual function calls:

```
>>> struct.unpack(b'Hh', struct.pack(b'Hh', 42, -42))
(42, -42)
>>> struct.pack(b'Hh', *struct.unpack(b'Hh', b'*\x00\x00*'))
b'*\x00\x00*'
```

So what's the problem with values spanning multiple bytes? After all, these examples show that values can be converted to a string and back without worrying about how those strings are created or parsed. Unfortunately, it's only easy because we're currently working only within Python, which has an implementation that is consistent with itself. If you have to work with strings, such as file contents, that need to be used with other applications, you'll need to make sure you match up with what those applications expect.

Therefore, struct formats also allow you to explicitly specify the *endianness* of a value. Endianness is the term for how the bytes of a value are ordered; in a *big-endian* value, the most significant byte—the byte that provides the largest part of the number—gets stored first. For *little-endian* values, the least significant byte is stored first.

To distinguish between the two, the format specification can take a prefix. If you place a < before the format, you can explicitly declare it to be little-endian. Conversely, using > will mark it as big-endian. If neither option is supplied, as in the previous examples, the default behavior is to use the same endianness as the system in which Python is executing, which is typically little-endian on modern systems. This allows you to control the way values are treated for both pack() and unpack(), covering both sides of the conversion process:

```
>>> struct.pack(b'<H', 42)
b'*\x00'
>>> struct.pack(b'>H', 42)
b'\x00*'
>>> struct.unpack(b'<H', b'*\x00')
(42,)
>>> struct.unpack(b'>H', b'*\x00')
(10752,)
```

Now that it's possible to control the ordering of multiple-byte numbers, it's easier to work with larger values. In addition to the one- and two-byte integers discussed previously, struct supports four-byte values using I and i, whereas eight-byte values can be specified using Q and q. Like the others, uppercase letters indicate unsigned values, whereas lowercase letters indicate signed values.

The struct module goes beyond just conversion of integers, however. You can also convert floating-point values using the f format, or perhaps even the b format for greater precision. In fact, you can use struct to work with strings inside strings as well, giving you some extra flexibility. Use the s format code, combined with a numeric prefix, to indicate the size of the string to read or write:

```
>>> struct.pack(b'7s', b'example')
b'example'
>>> struct.unpack(b'7s', b'example')
(b'example',)
>>> struct.pack(b'10s', b'example')
b'example\x00\x00\x00'
```

As you can see, pack() will add in null bytes to fill in as many bytes as necessary to match the prefix supplied in the format. But why would you want to use struct to turn a string into a string? The benefit is that you can pack and unpack multiple values at a time, so the string might just be part of the structure. Consider a simple byte string that contains a person's contact information:

```
>>>import struct
>>>first_name = 'Marty'
>>> last_name = 'Alchin'
>>> age = 28
>>> struct.pack(b'10s10sB', bytes(first_name, 'utf8'), bytes(last_name,
    'utf8'), age)
>>> data
b'Alchin\x00\x00\x00\x00Marty\x00\x00\x00\x00\x00\x1c'
```

If you're looking to work with strings in this manner, however, you're more likely working with text, in which the string has meaning as a whole rather than its characters being conversions of some other types of values. The format of how you do this changed a bit in Python 3.2, so now you must encode string (str) text to byte strings, normally utf8 encoding.

Text

Conceptually, text is a collection of written words. It's a linguistic concept that existed long before computing, but once it became clear that computers would need to work with text, it was necessary to determine how to represent text in a system designed for numbers. When programming was still young, text was limited to a set of characters known as the American Standard Code for Information Interchange (ASCII), or EBCDIC, or others.

Notice the reference to "American"; this set of 127 characters—only 95 of them printable—is designed to address only the needs of the English language. ASCII only covered seven bits of each byte, so there was some room for potential future expansion, but even another 128 values weren't enough. Some applications employed special tricks to convey additional letters by adding accents and other marks, but the standard was still very limited in scope.

Unicode

To resolve this limitation, the Unicode standard emerged as an alternative that could contain most of the characters used in the vast majority of the world's languages. In order for Unicode to support as many code points as it needs, each code point takes up more than one byte, unlike in ASCII. When loaded in memory, this isn't a problem because it's only used within Python, which only has one way of managing those multiple-byte values.

Note   The Unicode standard is actually made up of more than a million individual "code points" rather than characters. A code point is a number that represents some facet of written text, which can be a regular character, a symbol, or a modifier, such as an accented character. Some characters are even present at multiple code points for compatibility with systems in use prior to the introduction of Unicode.

By default, all standard strings in Python are Unicode, supporting a wide array of languages in the process. The byte strings shown in the previous section all required the use of a b prefix to distinguish them as different from standard Unicode strings.

The trouble comes when writing those values out to strings that can be read by other systems because not all systems use the same internal representation of Unicode strings. Instead, there are several different encodings that can be used to collapse a Unicode string into a series of bytes for storage or distribution.

Encodings

Much like how multiple bytes can be used to store a number larger than one byte would allow, Unicode text can be stored in a multiple-byte format. Unlike numbers, though, text generally contains a large number of individual characters, so storing each as up to four bytes would mean a long passage of text could end up much larger than it may seem.

To support text as efficiently as possible, it quickly became clear that not all text requires the full range of available characters. This book, for example, is written in English, which means the vast majority of its content lies within the ASCII range. As such, most of it could go from four bytes per character down to just one.

ASCII is one example of a text encoding. In this particular case, a small set of available characters is mapped to specific values from 0 to 127. The characters chosen are intended to support English, so it contains all the available letters in uppercase and lowercase variants, all 10 numerals and a variety of punctuation options. Any text that contains just these values can be converted to bytes using the ASCII encoding.

The encoding process itself is managed using a string's encode() method. Simply pass in the name of an encoding and it will return a byte string representing the text in the given encoding. In the case of ASCII, the representation of the byte string looks just like the input text, because each byte maps to exactly one character:

```
>>> 'This is an example, with punctuation and UPPERCASE.'.encode('ascii')
b'This is an example, with punctuation and UPPERCASE.'
```

By mapping each byte to a single character, ASCII is very efficient, but it only works if the source text contains those characters specified in the encoding. Certain assumptions had to be made about what characters were important enough to include in such a small range. Other languages will have their own characters that take priority, so they use different encodings in order to be as efficient as ASCII is for English (UTF-8 is the most popular).

Some languages, including Chinese and Japanese, have so many characters that there's no way a single byte could hope to represent them. Some encodings for these languages use two bytes for every character, further highlighting how different the various text encodings can be. Because of this, an encoding designed for a particular language often can't be used for text outside of that language.

To address this, there are some more generic Unicode-focused encodings. Because of the sheer number of available characters, these encodings use a variable-length approach. In UTF-8, the most common of these, characters within a certain range can be represented in a single byte. Other characters require two bytes, while still others can use three or even four bytes. UTF-8 is desirable because of a few particular traits it exhibits:

- It can support any available Unicode code point, even if it isn't commonly in actual text. That feature isn't unique to UTF-8, but it definitely sets it apart from other language-specific encodings, such as ASCII.

- The more common the character is in actual use, the less space its code point takes. In a collection of mostly English documents, for example, UTF-8 can be nearly as efficient as ASCII. Even when encoding non-English text most languages share certain common characters, such as spaces and punctuation, which can be encoded with a single byte. When it has to use two bytes, it's still more efficient than an in-memory Unicode object.

- The single-byte range precisely coincides with the ASCII standard, making UTF-8 completely backward compatible with ASCII text. All ASCII text can be read as UTF-8, without modification. Likewise, text that only contains characters that are also available in ASCII can be encoded using UTF-8 and still be accessed by applications that only understand ASCII.

For these reasons, among others, UTF-8 has emerged as a very common encoding (since 2008) for applications that need to support multiple languages or where the language of the application isn't known at the time it's being designed. That may seem like an odd situation to be in, but it comes up fairly frequently when looking at frameworks, libraries, and other large-scale applications. They could be deployed in any environment on the planet, so they should do as much as possible to support other languages. Chapter 8 will describe, in more detail, the steps an application can take to support multiple languages.

The consequences of using the wrong encoding or decoding can vary depending on the needs of the application, the encoding used, and the text passed in. For example, ASCII text can be decoded using UTF-8 without a problem, yielding a perfectly valid Unicode string. Reversing that process is not always as forgiving, because a Unicode string can contain code points outside the valid ASCII range:

```
>>> ascii = 'This is a test'.encode('ascii')
>>> ascii
b'This is a test'
>>> ascii.decode('utf-8')
'This is a test'
>>> unicode = 'This is a test: \u20ac'  # A manually encoded Euro symbol
>>> unicode.encode('utf-8')
b'This is a test: \xe2\x82\xac'
>>> unicode.encode('ascii')
Traceback (most recent call last):
  ...
UnicodeEncodeError: 'ascii' codec can't encode character '\u20ac' in
position 16
: ordinal not in range(128)
```

At other times text can seem to be encoded or decoded properly, only to have the resulting text be gibberish. Typically, however, problems like that arise when upgrading an application to include proper Unicode support, but existing data wasn't encoded consistently. Building an application for Unicode from the ground up doesn't completely eliminate the possibility of these problems, but it greatly helps avoid them.

Simple Substitution

There are different ways to produce a string with information that's only available at runtime. Perhaps the most obvious is to concatenate multiple strings together using the + operator, but that only works if all the values are strings. Python won't implicitly convert other values to strings to be concatenated, so you'd have to convert them explicitly, by first passing them into the str() function, for example.

As an alternative, Python strings also support a way to inject objects into a string. This uses placeholders inside a string to denote where objects should go, along with a collection of objects that should fill them in. This is called string substitution, and is performed using the % operator, using a custom __mod__() method, as described in Chapter 5.

Placeholders consist of a percent sign and a conversion format, optionally with some modifiers between them to specify how the conversion should take place. This scheme allows the string to specify how objects should get converted, rather than having to call separate function explicitly. The most common of these formats is %s, which is equivalent to using the str() function directly:

```
>>> 'This object is %s' % 1
'This object is 1'
>>> 'This object is %s' % object()
'This object is <object object at 0x...>'
```

Because this is equivalent to calling str() directly, the value placed into the string is the result of calling the object's __str__() method. Similarly, if you use the %r placeholder inside the substitution string, Python will call the object's __repr__() method instead. This can be useful for logging arguments to a function, for example. Try the next example as a script:

```
def func(*args):
    for i, arg in enumerate(args):
        print('Argument %s: %r' % (i, arg))
```

```
func('example', {}, [1, 2, 3], object())
Your output will look like the following:
Argument 0: 'example'
Argument 1: {}
Argument 2: [1, 2, 3]
Argument 3: <object object at 0x...>
```

This example also illustrates how multiple values can be placed in the string at once, by wrapping them in a tuple. They're matched up with their counterparts in the string according to their position, so the first object goes in the first placeholder and so on. Unfortunately, this feature can also be a stumbling block at times, if you're not careful. The most common error occurs when attempting to inject a tuple into the substitution string:

```
>>> def log(*args):
...     print('Logging arguments: %r' % args)
...
>>> log('test')
"Logging arguments: 'test'"
>>> log('test', 'ing')
Traceback (most recent call last):
  ...
TypeError: not all arguments converted during string formatting
```

What's going on here is that Python makes no distinction between a tuple that was written as such in the source code and one that was merely passed from somewhere else. Therefore, string substitution has no way of knowing what your intention is. In this example, the substitution works fine as long as only one argument is passed in because there's exactly one placeholder in the string. As soon as you pass in more than one argument, it breaks.

In order to resolve this, you'll need to build a one-item tuple to contain the tuple you want to place in the string. This way the string substitution always gets a single tuple, which contains one tuple to be placed in a single placeholder:

```
>>> def log(*args):
...     print('Logging arguments: %r' % (args,))
...
>>> log('test')
"Logging arguments: ('test',)"
>>> log('test', 'ing')
"Logging arguments: ('test', 'ing')"
```

With the tuple situation sorted out, it's worth noting that objects can be inserted by keyword as well. Doing so requires the substitution string to contain the keywords in parentheses, immediately following the percent sign. Then, to pass in values to inject, simply pass in a dictionary of objects, rather than a tuple:

```
>>> def log(*args):
...     for i, arg in enumerate(args):
...         print('Argument %(i)s: %(arg)r' % {'i': i, 'arg': arg})
...
>>> log('test')
Argument 0: 'test'
>>> log('test', 'ing')
Argument 0: 'test'
Argument 1: 'ing'
```

In addition to being able to more easily rearrange placeholders in the substitution string, this feature allows you to include just those values that are important. If you have a dictionary with more values than you need in the string, you can reference only the ones you need. Python will simply ignore any values that aren't mentioned by name in the string. This is in contrast to the positional option, where supplying more values than you've marked in the string will result in a TypeError.

Formatting

For a more powerful alternative to the simple string substitution described in the previous section, Python also includes a robust formatting system for strings. Rather than relying on a less obvious operator, string formatting uses an explicit `format()` method on strings. In addition, the syntax used for the formatting string is considerably different from what was used in simple substitution previously.

Instead of using a percent sign and a format code, `format()` expects its placeholders to be surrounded by curly braces. What goes inside those braces depends on how you plan to pass in the values and how they should be formatted. The first portion of the placeholder determines whether it should look for a positional argument or a keyword argument. For positional arguments the content is a number, indicating the index of the value to work with, while for keyword arguments, you supply the key that references the appropriate value:

```
>>> 'This is argument 0: {0}'.format('test')
'This is argument 0: test'
>>> 'This is argument key: {key}'.format(key='value')
'This is argument key: value'
```

This may look a lot like the older substitution technique, but it has one major advantage already. Because formatting is initiated with a method call, rather than an operator, you can specify both positional and keyword arguments together. That way you can mix and match indexes and keys in the format string if necessary, referencing them in any order.

As an added bonus, that also means that not all positional arguments need to be referenced in the string in order to work properly. If you supply more than you need, `format()` will just ignore anything it doesn't have a placeholder for. This makes it much easier to pass a format string into an application that will call `format()` on it later, with arguments that may come from another source. One such example is a customizable validation function that accepts an error message during customization:

```
>>> def exact_match(expected, error):
...     def validator(value):
...         if value != expected:
...             raise ValueError(error.format(value, expected))
...     return validator
...
>>> validate_zero = exact_match(0, 'Expected {1}, got {0}')
>>> validate_zero(0)
>>> validate_zero(1)
Traceback (most recent call last):
  ...
ValueError: Expected 0, got 1
>>> validate_zero = exact_match(0, '{0} != {1}')
>>> validate_zero(1)
Traceback (most recent call last):
  ...
ValueError: 1 != 0
>>> validate_zero = exact_match(0, '{0} is not the right value')
>>> validate_zero(1)
Traceback (most recent call last):
  ...
ValueError: 1 is not the right value
```

As you can see, this feature lets the validator function call format() using all of the information it has available at the time, leaving it up to the format string to determine how to lay it out. With the other string substitution, you'd be forced to use keywords to achieve the same effect because positional arguments just didn't work the same way.

Looking Up Values Within Objects

In addition to being able to reference the objects being passed in, the format string syntax allows you to refer to portions of those objects specifically. The syntax for this looks much like it would in regular Python code. To reference an attribute, separate its name from the object reference with a period. To use an indexed or keyword value, supply the index or keyword inside square brackets; just don't use quotes around the keyword:

```
>>> import datetime
>>> def format_time(time):
...     return '{0.minute} past {0.hour}'.format(time)
...
>>> format_time(datetime.time(8, 10))
'10 past 8'
>>> '{0[spam]}'.format({'spam': 'eggs'})
'eggs'
```

Distinguishing Types of Strings

You may remember that simple substitution required you to specify either %s or %r to indicate whether the __str__() method or the __repr__() method should be used to convert an object to a string, while the examples given thus far haven't included such a hint. By default, format() will use __str__(), but that behavior can still be controlled as part of the format string. Immediately following the object reference, simply include an exclamation point, followed by either s or r:

```
>>> validate_test = exact_match('test', 'Expected {1!r}, got {0!r}')
>>> validate_test('invalid')
Traceback (most recent call last):
  ...
ValueError: Expected 'test', got 'invalid'
```

Standard Format Specification

Where this new string formatting really differs from the previous substitution feature is in the amount of flexibility available to format the output of objects. After the field reference and the string type mentioned in previous sections, you can include a colon, followed by a string that controls the formatting of the referenced object. There's a standard syntax for this format specification, which is generally applicable to most objects.

The first option controls the alignment of the output string, which is used when you need to specify a minimum number of characters to output. Supplying a left angle bracket (<) produces a left-aligned value; a right angle bracket (>) aligns to the right; and a caret (^) centers the value. The total width can be specified as a number afterward:

```
>>> import os.path
>>> '{0:>20}{1}'.format(*os.path.splitext('contents.txt'))
'            contents.txt'
>>> for filename in ['contents.txt', 'chapter.txt', 'index.txt']:
...     print('{0:<10}{1}'.format(*os.path.splitext(filename)))
...
contents  .txt
chapter   .txt
index     .txt
```

Notice here that the default behavior of the length specification is to pad the output with spaces to reach the necessary length. That, too, can be controlled by inserting a different character before the alignment specifier. For example, some plain-text document formats expect headings to be centered within a length of equal signs or hyphens. This is easy to accomplish using string formatting:

```
>>> def heading(text):
...     return '{0:=^40}'.format(text)
...
>>> heading('Standard Format Specification')
```

```
'=====Standard Format Specification======'
>>> heading('This is a longer heading, beyond 40 characters')
'This is a longer heading, beyond 40 characters'
```

The second call here demonstrates an important property of the length format; if the argument string is longer than the length specified, format() will lengthen the output to match, rather than truncating the text. That creates a bit of a problem with the heading example, however, because if the input was too long, the output doesn't contain any of the padding characters at all. This can be fixed by explicitly adding one character each at the beginning and end of the string and reducing the placeholder's length by two to compensate:

```
>>> def heading(text):
...     return '={0:=^38}='.format(text)
...
>>> heading('Standard Format Specification')
'=====Standard Format Specification======'
>>> heading('This is a longer heading, beyond 40 characters')
'=This is a longer heading, beyond 40 characters='
```

Now the heading will always be at least 40 characters wide but also always have at least one equals sign on each side of the text, even if it runs long. Unfortunately, doing so now requires writing the equal sign three times in the format string, which becomes a bit of a maintenance hassle once we consider that sometimes the padding character will be a hyphen.

Solving one part of this problem is simple: because we're explicitly numbering the placeholders, we can pass in the padding character as an argument and just reference that argument twice in the format string; once at the beginning and once at the end. That alone doesn't really solve the problem, however, because it leaves the core problem untouched: how to replace just part of the argument reference for the text.

To solve that problem, the format specification also allows argument references to be nested. Inside the placeholder for the text portion, we can add another placeholder at the position reserved for the padding character; Python will evaluate that one first, before trying to evaluate the other. While we're at it, this also allows us to control how many characters the output will fill up:

```
>>> def heading(text, padding='=', width=40):
...     return '{1}{0:{1}^{2}}{1}'.format(text, padding, width - 2)
...
>>> heading('Standard Format Specification')
'=====Standard Format Specification======'
>>> heading('This is a longer heading, beyond 40 characters')
'=This is a longer heading, beyond 40 characters='
>>> heading('Standard Format Specification', padding='-', width=60)
'---------------Standard Format Specification----------------'
```

Example: Plain Text Table of Contents

Although there are many forms of documentation, plain text is perhaps the most common, as it doesn't require any additional software to view. Navigating large chunks of documentation can be difficult, however, because of the lack of links or page numbers for a table of contents. Line numbers could be used instead of page numbers, but a properly formatted table of contents can still be tedious to maintain.

Consider a typical table of contents, in which the title of a section is left-aligned and the page or line number is right-aligned, and the two are joined by a line of periods to help guide the eye from one to the other. Adding or removing lines from such a format is simple, but every time you change the name or location of a section you not only have to change the relevant information; you also need to update the line of periods in-between, which is less than ideal.

String formatting can come in handy here because you can specify both alignment and padding options for multiple values within a string. With this, you can set up a simple script that formats the table of contents for you automatically. The key to doing this, however, is to realize what you're working with.

On the surface, it seems like the goal is just as mentioned: to left-align the section title, right-align the line number, and place a line of periods in between. Unfortunately, there's no option to do exactly that, so we'll need to look at it a bit differently. By having each part of the string be responsible for part of the padding, it's fairly easy to achieve the desired effect:

```
>>> '{0:.<50}'.format('Example')
'Example..........................................'
>>> '{0:.<50}'.format('Longer Example')
'Longer Example...................................'
>>> '{0:.>10}'.format(20)
'........20'
>>> '{0:.>10}'.format(1138)
'......1138'
```

With these two parts in place, they just need to be combined in order to create a full line in the table of contents. Many plain text documents are limited to 80 characters in a single line, so we can expand it a bit to give some breathing room for longer titles. In addition, 10 digits is a bit much to expect for line numbers even in extremely long documents, so that can be reduced in order to yield more space for the titles as well:

```
>>> def contents_line(title, line_number=1):
...     return '{0:.<70}{1:.>5}'.format(title, line_number)
...
>>> contents_line('Installation', 20)
'Installation..............................................................20'
>>> contents_line('Usage', 112)
'Usage.....................................................................112'
```

Calling this function one line at a time isn't a realistic solution in the long run, however, so we'll create a new function that can accept a more useful data structure to work with. It doesn't need to be complicated, so we'll just use a sequence of two-tuples, each consisting of a section title and its corresponding line number:

```
>>> contents = (('Installation', 20), ('Usage', 112))
```

```
>>> def format_contents(contents):
...     for title, line_number in contents:
...         yield '{0:.<70}{1:.>5}'.format(title, line_number)
...
>>> for line in format_contents(contents):
...     print(line)
...
```

Custom Format Specification

The true strength of the new formatting system, however, is that `format()` isn't actually in control of the formatting syntax described in the previous section. Like many of the features described in Chapter 4, it instead delegates that control to a method on the objects passed in as arguments.

This method, `__format__()`, accepts one argument, which is the format specification that was written into the format string where the object is being placed. It doesn't get the entire bracketed expression, however, just the bit after the colon. This is true for all objects, as you can see by calling it directly on a brand-new instance of `object`. As of Python 3.3 and higher the format for this changed, so make sure you are using Python 3.3 or higher before trying the next example:

```
>>> object().__format__("")
'=====<object object at 0x0209F158>======'
```

Because of this, the standard format specification options described in the previous section aren't the only way to do things. If you have a custom need, you can override that behavior by replacing that method on the class you're working with. You can either extend the existing behavior or write a completely new one.

For example, you could have a class to represent a verb, which can have a present or a past tense. This `Verb` class could be instantiated with a word to use for each tense, and then be used in expressions to form complete sentences:

```
>>> class Verb:
...     def __init__(self, present, past=None):
...         self.present = present
...         self.past = past
...     def __format__(self, tense):
...         if tense == 'past':
...             return self.past
...         else:
...             return self.present
...
>>> format = Verb('format', past='formatted')
>>> message = 'You can {0:present} strings with {0:past} objects.'
>>> message.format(format)
'You can format strings with formatted objects.'
>>> save = Verb('save', past='saved')
>>> message.format(save)
'You can save strings with saved objects.'
```

In this example there's no way for the placeholder string to know how to format a past tense verb, so it delegates that responsibility to the verb passed in. This way, the string can be written once and used many times with different verbs, without skipping a beat.

Exciting Python Extensions

Feedparser

RSS feeds (Rich Site Summary) are published feeds on information such as blogs, news, and media. Also known as feeds, web feeds, or channels, they could include summarized information or headlines. Suffice to say they are a first step in keeping up-to-date in an information-overloaded world. The Python *feedparser* library handles formats including Atom, RDF, and RSS. From what we have already learned, accessing this data will be handy, and if used in conjunction with Beautiful Soup or other libraries, can yield much information.

How to Install

Use pip to install the libraries:

```
pip install feedparser (Enter)
```

Make sure you are at an escalated Windows command prompt. Linux and Mac will be similar. With no errors during the install, you are now set to use Feedparser.

How to Use

For this example we will harvest data from the "Anytime Fitness blog." The sample code will extract the title, subtitle, number of RSS entries, and their names. Of course you could do more, and you could just write the data to a file for later use by another library to extract key data. Try it out to see how easy it is:

```
#feedparser example

import feedparser
# main site is:  http://blog.anytimefitness.com/
c = feedparser.parse('http://feeds.feedburner.com/anytimefitnessofficial')
#all elements of the channel are now in container c
#print the title and subtitle and list # of elements of the feed
print (c['feed']['title'])
print (c['feed']['subtitle'])
print ("There are this many entries: ", len(c['entries']))
print()
for item in c['entries']:
    title = item.title
    print (title)

# try others such as item.summary, item.description, item.link, etc.
# write the data to a file for use with BeautifulSoup, etc.
```

In this example *c* is a container of named entries such as ***title***, ***subtitle***, and so on. Also, this container has an integer number of times in it (len).

Taking It With You

Because strings are so common throughout all kinds of programming, you'll find yourself with a wide range of needs. The features shown in this chapter will help you make better use of your strings, but the proper combination of techniques is something that can't be written for you. As you go forward with your code, you'll need to keep an open mind about which techniques to use so that you can choose what's best for your needs.

So far, these chapters have focused on how to use various aspects of Python to perform complex and useful tasks so that your applications can be that much more powerful. The next chapter will show you how to verify whether those tasks are being performed properly.

CHAPTER 8

Documentation

Documentation is arguably the most difficult part of any project. Code tends to come fairly easy to programmers, but documentation requires a different set of skills because the audience is strictly human. The magnitude of the differences can vary greatly between projects and audiences. Sometimes all that's necessary is some example code, whereas other topics can fill entire books and still have plenty left to cover.

The language of documentation is very different from that of code, so it can be difficult to excel at both. This causes many programmers to take the path of least resistance, opting for tools that automatically generate some minimal form of documentation from the code itself, so that the extra work is kept to a minimum. Although that can seem sufficient, such tools can only do so much because they're limited by what the code alone can tell them. Javadoc for JAVA and Epydoc for Python are examples of such tools.

This chapter will show the tools available to help describe your code and its features for human understanding. There are several options available, some of which go alongside the code itself, while others accompany it on the outside. These can be used individually or in combination to form a full set of documentation for any project. How much of each is necessary will differ based on the needs of each application, but each has its place.

Each section in this chapter will highlight how to document your code with the available tools, along with the benefits and drawbacks of each approach. The most important thing to remember about documentation, however, is that it's all about presenting what people need to know about your application and how to use it. You must always consider how your code works and what your users will need to know to interact with it. Only then can you pick the approaches that are best for your needs.

© J. Burton Browning and Marty Alchin 2019
J. B. Browning and M. Alchin, *Pro Python 3*, https://doi.org/10.1007/978-1-4842-4385-5_8

Proper Naming

The simplest form of documentation is to properly name the various aspects of your code. With very few exceptions, every single class, function, and variable is given a name when it's defined. Because these names are already required, all it takes is a little extra thought to make sure they're accurate and easy to understand. To illustrate how valuable this can be, take a look at a function signature with vague, generic names and see if you can guess what it does:

```
def action(var1, var2):
```

Given some code inside the body of the function, you might be able to get a good idea of its purpose, but the signature itself does nothing to help. In fact, the only reason the code in the body would be more helpful is that it would typically use more standardized features available from elsewhere. For instance, loops and slicing are easily recognizable, as are methods from commonly used objects, such as a string's `format()` method. These are just clues to help make an educated guess, however; the naming should make it obvious:

```
def find_words(text, word):
```

Just picking some more descriptive names makes the purpose of the function and its arguments much clearer. As a rule of thumb, classes and variables should be named as singular nouns, such as `Book`, `Person`, `Restaurant`, `index`, and `first_name`. Functions, by contrast, should be given verbs as names, such as `find()`, `insert()`, and `process_user()`.

PEP 8,[1] also included as an appendix in this book, offers some more specific guidelines for naming various types of objects. See its "Naming Conventions" section for details. Once you get inside a block of code things aren't always as easy to follow, so comments can help clarify.

---

[1]See "PEP 8: Style Guide for Python Code," http://www.python.org/dev/peps/pep-0008.

Comments

In classes and functions that are very long or complex, the name alone is often not sufficient to convey all the things the code is doing. Variable names can certainly help, but that usually only explains *what* the code does; it's typically more useful to explain *why* the code does what it does. Both of these can be addressed by placing comments in your code.

Comments are one of the most basic forms of documentation a programmer can use, yet they're also among the most powerful. Comments are placed directly alongside the rest of your code, where it's easiest to write and is often most helpful. Comments offer a convenient way to make small notes where they're most relevant, which can help make complex code easier to understand later on.

Python's comments are separated from code by the # symbol. All of the text that follows that symbol is treated as a comment, all the way to the end of the line. This allows comments to either take up a whole line or attach to the end of a line of code. Unlike some other languages, Python doesn't have any true syntax for multiline comments unless you use a *docstring* triple quoted string, as tweeted by Guido van Rossum in 2011. (A more detailed discussion of docstrings follows shortly, so hold on for more details.) Formally for strings, each line of a longer comment must be preceded by a # symbol. Note both methods here:

```
def foo(): #example of a docstring comment
    """alkaj
    laksjf
    alkdfj"""
x=1
print (x) # shows value for x
foo() # does nothing
```

```
# This function doesn't really do anything useful. It's only here to show
# how multi-line comments work in Python. Notice how each line has to have
# a separate # to indicate that it's a comment.

def example():
    pass
```

Like naming conventions, the Python Style Guide has a lot to say on how comments should be formatted. See the "Comments" heading of PEP 8 for details.

Perhaps the biggest limitation of comments is that they're only available when viewing the source file directly. Because comments don't have any impact on the execution of the code, there are no introspection tools available to read them at runtime. For that, we turn to docstrings.

Docstrings

In the previous section, as well as in Chapters 3 and 4, we referred briefly to docstrings and how they're used in code. A docstring is placed at the beginning of a module, function, or class; rather than assigning it to a variable, however, you can just leave the string as its own statement. As long as it's the first thing in the code block, Python will interpret it as a docstring:

```
def find_words(text, word):
    """
    Locate all instances of a word in a given piece of text.
    Return a list of indexes where the words were found.
    If no instances of the word were found, return an empty list.

    text -- a block of text to search
    word -- an individual word to search for
    """
```

This information could be presented in a set of comments, but there's one major advantage of using docstrings instead: Python makes them available in code. In keeping with the spirit of transparency, docstrings can be accessed at runtime through the __doc__ attribute of modules, classes, and functions. Perhaps the most obvious benefit this brings is that the various automatic documentation generators get a lot more information to work with. Better yet, that information is written specifically for humans, which can greatly improve the quality of the final output.

Exactly how it's written, however, is entirely up to you. Aside from where docstrings can be placed in your code, Python makes no assumptions or requirements about the format or structure of their contents. PEP 257,[2] also provided as an appendix, provides a number of recommendations, but the final decision is left up to you. The goal is to help people understand how to use your code, however, so there are a few particulars that everyone should follow.

Describe What the Function Does

As simple as it sounds, it can sometimes be difficult to step back from how the code works and simply describe what it does. For most functions you should be able to describe it in one sentence, preferably on a single line. Common examples are "add an item to the collection" and "cache an object for later use." The details of how the code achieves that goal are best left out of the docstring.

Explain the Arguments

Argument names are limited to one or two words. This works well as a simple reminder of their purpose, but more information is usually needed to understand their purposes in the first place. This is particularly important for optional arguments, which often help control how the function works. Even if the argument names are self-explanatory, including a brief description helps maintain consistency across your documentation.

---

[2]See "PEP 257: Docstring Conventions," http://www.python.org/dev/peps/pep-0257.

Don't Forget the Return Value

Any time a function returns a value, the nature of that value should be documented. It should include the return value's type as well as any relevant details about how the object will be formed. For example, `find_words()` returns a list, but that list contains indexes where the words were found, rather than returning the words themselves, so that behavior is documented.

Also, make sure that if the return value differs slightly based on what input was given or what other conditions the function works with, the different forms of return values are given. For example, a function to retrieve an object by name might be given a name that doesn't match any existing objects. In that case, it's important to document whether the function will create a new object or raise an exception.

Include Any Expected Exceptions

Every piece of code contains opportunities for exceptions to be raised. Sometimes those exceptions are actually part of the code's expected functionality, such as when looking for an object by a name that doesn't match anything. In these cases, the exceptions should be documented right alongside the return values. These explicit exceptions are frequently caught by the code that calls your function, so it's necessary to indicate which ones will be raised, as well as the circumstances under which they'll be raised.

Documentation Outside the Code

One thing you'll notice about the recommendations in the previous section is that they aren't specific to docstrings. You should also document your application outside of the code, and that documentation needs to include all the same details. What makes this external documentation different is how the information is presented, and it will also include additional information not covered inside the code itself.

This general class of documentation can cover a wide variety of topics, many of which wouldn't make any sense inside the code. After all, someone who's reading your code is likely to have something already in mind to look for. They'll be looking for more information about a specific module, class, or function that they already know how to find. Other users will have a broader range of needs, from installation and tutorials to more topical references that show how to combine multiple features toward a certain goal.

Installation and Configuration

Before anyone can use your software, they will need to obtain it and get it working. This almost goes without saying, but not quite. There are a number of issues that users need to tackle before they can use your code, and you need to make sure that those issues are addressed as thoroughly as possible.

Obtaining the code is the first step. However you choose to distribute your code, you'll need to make sure your users know how to get it. Sometimes it will be a simple one-line command, but in other cases it may require first obtaining other applications such as version control software to get the latest code without waiting for a release. Chapter 10 will describe some of the more common ways to distribute your code, along with what your choices will mean for the users who need to retrieve it.

Tutorials

After getting an application, many users want to immediately get an idea of how to use it. Everybody appreciates immediate gratification, so you can use their first experience with your software as an opportunity to accomplish something quickly. Tutorials are a great way to walk your users through the most common features of your application.

A tutorial can often showcase the greatest strengths of an application, so it can also be your first chance to convince someone to try it out in the first place. This is particularly true with libraries and frameworks, which are designed to be integrated into other code rather than be used independently. If your audience can get a quick feel for how your approach can help them work with their own code, it will make a lasting impression.

Reference Documents

Once your users have a good idea of how your application can help them and have gotten a bit of experience under their belts, their needs change again. At this point they no longer need to be convinced to use your software, and they're ready to move beyond learning how to use it. Now they need reminders of how all the features work, how those features work together, and how they can integrate with the tasks they're really trying to perform.

Different readers will look for different forms of reference documentation. Some may prefer method-level arguments and return values, like those contained in docstrings, whereas others may get more out of a broader overview, written in plain language. Some readers, like you, even enjoy a physical book, easy to pick up and flip through at a moment's notice.

With all of these different preferences, it's unlikely that you'll be able to write reference documentation in a way that will suit all tastes. As the author, it's your job to determine what type of documentation best suits your application. Look to your own preferences for the type of documentation you like to read most, as that's likely to be in the same spirit of the software you create. Just write the way you'd like to read. The users who like your documentation are likely to be the very same ones who will like your software.

Note   One important thing to remember is that you may not need reference documentation at all. For very simple applications, a tutorial alone may be enough to illustrate and explain all the available features.

Documentation Utilities

Some of the most challenging aspects of documentation have nothing to do with your application or how you plan to write about it. Beyond those concerns, tasks such as formatting, referencing, and presenting documentation can consume quite a bit of time and energy. The more documents you need to write, the harder these tasks become. The third-party `docutils` package[3] provides a comprehensive set of tools to make this process more manageable.

The crown jewel of the `docutils` package is reStructuredText, more often referred to as ReST or simply RST. reStructuredText is a markup language designed for writing technical documents, taking what its developers call a What You See Is What You Mean (WYSIWYM) approach. This is in contrast with the more traditional What You See Is What You Get (WYSIWYG), where editing based on the visual layout and formatting of the document.

---

[3]See "Docutils: Documentation Utilities," `http://docutils.sourceforge.net`.

In WYSIWYM, the goal is to indicate the structure and intentions of the document, without regard to exactly how it will be presented. Much like HTML, separating content from its presentation allows you to focus on what's really important about your documentation and leave the details of visual style for later. reStructuredText uses a more text-friendly approach than HTML, however, so that even unformatted documents are easily readable.

READABILITY COUNTS

In keeping with Python philosophy, reStructuredText focuses on readability at all times, even before the document gets formatted into its final format. The structure of a document and the instructions are designed to be understandable and easy to remember and format.

Formatting

The most basic unit of any type of document is the paragraph, so reStructuredText makes them the easiest to work with. All you need to do is write a block of text with each line of text starting immediately below the one before it. The number of lines and the length of each line are irrelevant, as long as there are no completely blank lines between any lines of text in a given paragraph.

Blank lines are reserved for separating paragraphs from each other and from other types of content. This forms a simple way to distinguish one paragraph from another. You can use multiple blank lines if you'd like, but only one is required. Indenting a paragraph indicates a quoted passage from another document, which will typically also be indented in the output. To illustrate, here are a couple of simple paragraphs written for reStructuredText:

```
The reStructuredText format is very simple when it comes down to it. It's all
about readability and flexibility. Common needs, such as paragraphs and inline
formatting, are simple to write, read and maintain. More complex features are
possible, and they use a simple, standardized syntax.
After all, the Zen of Python says:

    Simple is better than complex.
    Complex is better than complicated.
```

Most application documentation will also include blocks of code along with regular text. This is particularly useful for tutorials, in which a block of code can be built up in pieces, with explanations in between. Distinguishing between a paragraph and a block of code is based on a double colon at the end of a normal paragraph, followed by an indented block of code. This will end the first paragraph with a colon and format the indented text as code:

```
The reStructuredText format is very simple when it comes down to it. It's all
about readability and flexibility. Common needs, such as paragraphs and inline
formatting, are simple to write, read and maintain. More complex features are
possible, and they use a simple, standardized syntax.
After all, the Zen of Python says::

    Simple is better than complex.
    Complex is better than complicated.
```

Note   You'll notice that the example shown here isn't actually code. The double-colon format technically distinguishes a block of text as preformatted. This prevents the reStructuredText parser from doing any additional processing on that block. Therefore, even though it's most useful for including code in your documentation, it can be used for anything that already has its own formatting that should remain intact.

Inside an individual paragraph, you can also format text in all the ways you'd expect. Rather than directly marking things for italics or bold, this formatting requires the use of additional punctuation before and after the text you'd like to format. Surrounding a word or phrase with asterisks marks it as emphasized, which will typically render in italics. Using an extra pair of asterisks beyond that will indicate strong emphasis, often rendering as bold.

Links

When working with large amounts of documentation, one of the most important features you can offer is linking multiple documents together. The reStructuredText format offers several different ways to link to additional information, whether footnotes, other sections in the same document, or completely different documents. The simplest form of link you can include is a URL, which will be converted into a link when rendering the document. Other types of links require a bit more formatting.

Links take the form of an underscore following the text that should be used as the link. The target of the link is specified differently, depending on where that target is located. In the most common case, in which a document links to some external web page, the link target is placed in what might appear to be its own paragraph, with a structure that tells the parser that it's a link instead of an actual paragraph:

This paragraph shows the basics of how a link is formed in reStructuredText.
You can find additional information in the official documentation_.

.. _documentation: http://docutils.sf.net/docs/

This will cause the word "documentation" to be used as the link itself, referencing the target given on the bottom line. You'll usually need to use more than one word for the text of a link, but this doesn't provide a way to specify how much text should be included. To do that, you'll need to enclose the text in backticks (`). The underscore then goes outside the enclosure, immediately following the second backtick:

This paragraph shows the basics of how a link is formed in reStructuredText.
You can find additional information in the `official documentation`_.

.. _official documentation: http://docutils.sf.net/docs/

In this case, the link target is specified immediately below the paragraph where the link should be placed. This particular case can be simplified a bit by creating an anonymous link, which no longer requires rewriting the link text underneath. In order to distinguish it from a regular link, you'll need to use two underscores after the link text instead of just one. Then, the link target is specified with only two underscores at the beginning of the line:

This paragraph shows the basics of how a link is formed in reStructuredText.
You can find additional information in the `official documentation`__.

__ http://docutils.sf.net/docs/

READABILITY COUNTS

There's also another way to specify external links that's even more space-efficient: place the link target directly alongside the link text, inside the paragraph itself. Links formatted this way still use backticks to set the link apart from the rest of the text, but the link target goes inside the backticks as well, after being enclosed in angle brackets. To distinguish it as a link, two underscores are still used, so it is parsed as an anonymous link—for example, `Pro Python <http://propython.com/>`__.

The problem with this approach is that having the URL inside the paragraph can be very distracting when reading the source code for the document, even though the target will be hidden from view from the final output. Furthermore, named link targets can all be placed at the end of the document, so they don't even have to interrupt the flow from one paragraph to another.

Rather than referencing external documents, you can also include footnotes to be placed at the end of the same document or in an attached bibliography. Defining this type of link works much like standard links except that the link text is set apart by square brackets. Between the brackets, the text can either be just a number or a small piece of text, which will be used to reference the related information elsewhere.

Then, at the end of the document, the referenced information can be included in a format similar to named link targets. Rather than using an underscore to signify it, the reference text from earlier in the document is enclosed in square brackets again. After that, simply write the related text in the paragraph. This can be used for references to traditional publications, such as books, as well as for minor additions to further clarify the main text:

The reStructuredText format isn't part of Python itself, but it's popular enough that even published books [1]_ reference it as an integral part of the Python development process.

.. [1] Alchin, Marty. *Pro Python*. Apress, 2010.

In addition to these options, `docutils` allows reStructuredText to be expanded to provide other features. One application that provides some additional features is Sphinx.

Sphinx

The base features provided by reStructuredText are designed to work with individual documents. Even though it's easy to reference other documents, those references must be explicitly included in each document. If you write a complex application that requires multiple documents, each one will need to know the full structure of all the documents in order to reference them.

Sphinx[4] is an application that attempts to address that problem by working with the documents as a whole collection. In this way it's somewhat similar to other, more popular automated systems such as Javadoc and Doxygen, but Sphinx is designed to get its content from dedicated files rather than directly from the code itself. It can also include content based on code, but the main goal is to write documentation on its own.

By managing references across documents more effectively, Sphinx can generate an entire documentation package at once. This can be a web site full of linked HTML documents or even a single PDF document that includes all the documents as individual sections. In addition, Sphinx offers a variety of styling options, with many already supplied by a growing community.

Exciting Python Extensions: NumPy

As noted on the main site for NumPy, it is "the fundamental package for scientific computing with Python." As such, it offers much power to a Python programmer.

---

[4]See "Sphinx: Python Documentation Generator," http://sphinx.pocoo.org.

NumPy is the most fundamental package for scientific computing and data manipulation with Python. If you need to work in Python with standard arrays, than Numpy is the ticket. Typically, it will be used in conjunction with *SciPy*, and is one of the core packages in SciPy. One thing about the base Python implementation is that it does not have standard array structures as other languages do. By "standard" we mean arrays that hold like data (e.g., all integer, all character, etc.). So, to the rescue is NumPy. However, it does much more. Let's try a few of the interesting features in NumPy. First you will need to install it.

Install NumPy

If using Windows, try this from an escalated command prompt type:

pip install numpy (enter)

It should respond that it installed correctly or that it was already installed.

Using NumPy

First, standard non-Python arrays are handy things. Python uses *Lists, Dictionary's*, and *Tuples*; they are powerful, yet sometimes an old-fashioned array is just the thing to solve a problem. A NumPy array is just like one you might use in C++ or other languages in that they contain the same type of data elements (each is an int, float, character, etc.). It also cannot be changed with regard to size, unless you delete it and recreate a larger one. It is also interesting to note that a NumPy array is smaller in terms of memory usage than the same structure stored as a list.

Python array-like structures and standard arrays each offer their own unique benefits. So if you need a standard array, you can create them with NumPy with ease:

Try the following:

```
#NumPy create a 1 dimensional numeric array from a list
import numpy as mynp
my_list = [1,2,3,4,5]
array1 = mynp.array(my_list)
```

```
#Print array and its type
print (array1)
print(type(array1))
```

In the preceding example, each item in the list is treated as a numeric value. However, if you change one value in the list to alphanumeric, the entire array becomes a character array:

```
#NumPy create a 1 dimensional character array from a list
import numpy as mynp
my_list = [1,2,3,'a',5]
array1 = mynp.array(my_list)
```

```
#Print array and its type
print (array1)
print(type(array1))
```

So in this conversion it would not work well if you were performing some math manipulations on the values in the array, as in the next example:

```
#Add one to each value
import numpy as mynp
my_list = [1,2,3,4,5]
array1 = mynp.array(my_list)
```

```
#Print array and its type
print (array1)
print('With one added two each: ')
for item in array1:
    print (item + 1)
```

Since each was a numeric value in the array, we could add one to it and display the result. If you wanted to specify the array type, as you would with another language such as C++, you might do the following:

```
#NumPy 1 dimensional array from a list as floating-point values
#and make it a float array
import numpy as mynp
my_list = [1.1,2.1,3.1,4.1,5.1]
array1 = mynp.array(my_list, dtype='float')

#Print the array
print (array1)
```

You can also convert from one type to another with *astype*, as in *array1.astype('int')* or other valid data types such *as bool, str,* or *float.* Or, you could convert the array back to a list with array1.tolist().

Working With NumPy Arrays

You can address an array in a similar fashion to other Python structures. In this next example we will extract one element and find truth to a question, based on each element in the array:

```
#NumPy create a 1 dimensional array from a list
#and make it a float array
import numpy as mynp
my_list = [1.1,2.1,3.1,4.1,5.1]
array1 = mynp.array(my_list, dtype='float')

#Print the array
print (array1)
print("Print second element of array")
print (array1[1])
print("Print if element is > 2")
print (array1 > 2)
```

Statistical Measures

NumPy has some statistical functions built in, such as the standards min, max, and mean. With regard to random numbers (such as for random participant selection in a study or cryptographic work), the random library built in to NumPy is very similar to the enhanced features of C++'s random library. Use a numeric array to try it out:

```
#NumPy stats functions
import numpy as mynp
my_list = [1,2,7,4,5]
array1 = mynp.array(my_list, dtype='int')
print ('Minimum:> ',array1.min())
print ('Max:> ',array1.max())
print ('Mean of all values:> ',array1.mean())
#if you want only pseudo-randoms set a seed value
#np.random.seed(100)  # uncomment for pseudo-randoms
print('Random int between 1 and 100):> ',mynp.random.randint(0, 100))
```

Taking It With You

The tools shown here serve only as a base for the real work of documenting your code. The real work of documentation requires taking a step back from the code itself so that you can see your application the way your users and other developers would see it. Keeping that in mind, it's often useful to read documentation for other similar applications. That will give you a good idea of what your users are used to seeing, the types of questions they need answered, and how to distinguish your application as a superior alternative to the existing options.

On the other end of the spectrum, you can also help your users by taking a very close look at your code. Putting your code under the tightest scrutiny will allow you to write tests. The next chapter will show how tests can verify that your application works the way it should and that your documentation stays as accurate as possible.

CHAPTER 9

Testing

Writing an application is only part of the process; it's also important to check that all of the code works as it should. You can visually inspect the code, but it's better to execute it in a variety of situations that may arise in the real world to make sure it behaves properly. This process is called unit testing, because the goal is to test the smallest available units of execution.

Typically, the smallest unit is a function or method, many of which combine to form a full application. By breaking it down into individual units, you can minimize how much each test is responsible for. This way a failure of any particular unit doesn't involve hundreds of lines of code, so it's easier to track down exactly what's going wrong.

Testing each individual unit can be a lengthy process for large applications, given how many scenarios you may need to take into account. Rather than try to get through all of it manually, you can automate the process by letting your code do the heavy lifting. Writing a test suite allows you to easily try all the different paths your code might take, verifying that each behaves as it should.

Test-Driven Development

One of the more extreme examples of automated testing is the practice of test-driven development, often referred to simply as TDD. As the name implies, this practice uses automated testing to drive the development process. Whenever a new feature is written, tests for that feature are written first—tests that will fail right away. Once the tests are in place, you would write code to make sure those tests pass.

One value of this approach is that it encourages you to understand the desired behavior more thoroughly before setting out to write the code. For example, a function that processes text might have a number of common input strings, each with a desired output. Writing the test first encourages you to think about the output string for each available input string, without regard to how the string is processed internally. By shifting

© J. Burton Browning and Marty Alchin 2019
J. B. Browning and M. Alchin, *Pro Python 3*, https://doi.org/10.1007/978-1-4842-4385-5_9

the focus away from code at the outset, it's easier to see the big picture. The benefit of a focus on the interface (names, functions, method signatures, etc.) early is not to be underrated, since changes here are harder than implementation changes later.

The more obvious advantage, however, is that it ensures that every piece of code in an application has a set of tests associated with it. When code comes first, it's all too easy to run a few basic scenarios manually and then move on to coding the next feature. Tests can get lost in the shuffle, even though they're essential to the long-term health of the project. Getting into the habit of writing tests first is a good way to make sure they do get written.

Unfortunately, many developers find test-driven development far too strict for practical work. As long as the tests get written as comprehensively as possible, however, your code will reap the benefits. One of the easiest ways to do this is to write doctests.

Doctests

The topic of documentation was covered in Chapter 8, but one particular aspect of it can be useful for testing. Because Python supports docstrings that can be processed by code instead of just by people, the content within those strings can be used to perform basic tests as well.

In order to play double duty alongside regular documentation, doctests must look like documentation while still being something that can be parsed, executed, and verified for correctness. One format fits that bill very conveniently, and it's been in use throughout this book. Doctests are formatted as interactive interpreter sessions, which already contain both input and output in an easily identifiable format.

Formatting Code

Even though the overall format of a doctest is identical to the interpreter sessions shown throughout this book, there are some specific details that are important to identify. Each line of code to execute begins with three right-angle brackets (>>>) and a single space, followed by the code itself:

```
>>> a = 2
```

Just like the interactive interpreter, any code that extends beyond one line is indicated by new lines beginning with three periods (...) rather than brackets. You can include as many of these as necessary to complete multiline structures, such as lists and dictionaries, as well as function and class definitions:

```
>>> b = ('example',
... 'value')
>>> def test():
...     return b * a
```

All of the lines that start with periods like this are combined with the last line that started with angle brackets, and they're all evaluated together. That means you can leave extra lines if necessary, anywhere in the structure or even after it. This is useful for mimicking the output of an actual interpreter session, which requires a blank line to indicate when indented structures, such as functions or classes, are completed:

```
>>> b = ('example',
...
... 'value')
>>> def test():
...     return b * a
...
```

Representing Output

With the code in place, we just need to verify that its output matches what is expected. In keeping with the interpreter format, output is presented beneath one or more lines of input code. The exact formatting of the output will depend on the code being executed, but it's the same as you'd see when typing the code into the interpreter directly:

```
>>> a
2
>>> b
('example', 'value')
>>> test()
('example', 'value', 'example', 'value')
```

In these examples, the output string is equivalent to passing the return value from the expression into the built-in repr() function. Therefore, strings will always be quoted, and many specific types will have a different format than if you print them directly. Testing the output of str() can be achieved simply by calling str() in the line of code. Alternatively, the print() function is also supported and works just as you'd expect:

```
>>> for value in test():
...     print(value)
example
value
example
value
```

In examples like this, all lines of the output are checked against what was actually returned or printed by the code provided. This provides a very readable way to deal with sequences, as shown here. For longer sequences, as well as situations in which output is allowed to change from one run to another, output may also include three periods as ellipses, indicating a place where additional content should be ignored:

```
>>> for value in test():
...     print(value)
example
...
value
```

This form is particularly useful when testing exceptions: the interpreter output includes file paths, which will nearly always change from one system to another, and aren't relevant to most tests. In these cases what's important to test is that the exception is raised, that it's the correct type, and that its value, if any, is correct:

```
>>> for value in test:
...     print(value)
Traceback (most recent call last):
  ...
TypeError: 'function' object is not iterable
```

As the output format here suggests, the doctest will verify the first and last lines of the exception output, while ignoring the entire traceback in between. Because the traceback details are typically irrelevant to the documentation as well, this format is also much more readable.

Integrating With Documentation

Because the tests are meant to be built into documentation, there needs to be a way to make sure that only the tests are executed. In order to distinguish between the two without interrupting the flow of documentation, tests are set aside by nothing more than an extra newline. You'd always have to use one newline to avoid them all running together on a single line, so adding an extra simply leaves one blank line between the two:

```
"""
This is an example of placing documentation alongside tests in a single string.
Additional documentation can be placed between snippets of code, and it won't
disturb the behavior or validity of the tests.
"""

print("Hello, world!")
```

Running Tests

The actual execution of doctests is provided by the doctest module. In the simplest form, you can run a single function to test an entire module. This is useful when writing a set of tests for a file that was already written, because you can easily test the file individually after writing new tests. Simply import doctest and run its testmod() function to test the module. Here's an example module that contains a couple types of doctests:

```
def times2(value):
    """

    Multiplies the provided value by two. Because input objects can override
    the behavior of multiplication, the result can be different depending on
    the type of object passed in.
    >>> times2(5)
    10
    >>> times2('test')
    'testtest'
    >>> times2(('a', 1))
    ('a', 1, 'a', 1)
    """
    return value * 2
if __name__ == '__main__':
    import doctest
    doctest.testmod()
```

The docstring in times2() function includes tests, and because it's available as a module-level function, the testmod() can see it and execute the tests. This simple construct allows you to call the module directly from the command line and see the results of all doctests in the module. For example, if this module was called times2.py, you could invoke it from the command line as follows:

```
$ python times2.py
$
```

By default, the output only contains errors and failures, so if all the tests pass, there won't be any output at all. Failures are reported on individual tests, with each input/output combination being considered a unique test. This provides fine-grained details about the nature of the tests that were attempted and how they failed. If the final line in the example doctest were to read just ('a', 1) instead, here's what would happen:

```
$ python times2.py
**********************************************************************
File "...", line 11, in __main__.times2
Failed example:
    times2((a, '1'))
Expected:
    (a, '1')
Got:
    (a, '1', a, '1')
**********************************************************************
1 items had failures:
   1 of   3 in __main__.times2
***Test Failed*** 1 failures.
$
```

When working with more complicated applications and frameworks, however, the simple input/output paradigm of doctests breaks down fairly quickly. In those situations, there are two good tests in Python: Pytest and the unittest module. As a matter of providing an alternative to doctests, we will examine unittest next.

The unittest Module

Unlike doctests, which require your tests be formatted in a very specific way, `unittest` offers much more flexibility by allowing you to write your tests in real Python code. As is often the case, this extra power requires more control over how your tests are defined. In the case of unit tests, this control is provided by way of an object-oriented API for defining individual tests, test suites, and data fixtures for use with tests.

After importing the `unittest` module, the first place to start is the `TestCase` class, which forms the base of most of the module's features. You should also examine pytest.org, but this class should be considered first. The unittest module doesn't do much on its own, but when subclassed, it offers a rich set of tools to help define and control your tests. These tools are a combination of existing methods that you can use to perform individual tests and new methods you can define to control how your tests work. It all starts by creating a subclass of the `TestCase` class:

```
import unittest

class MultiplicationTestCase(unittest.TestCase):
    pass
```

Setting Up

The starting point for most test cases is the `setUp()` method, which you can define to perform some tasks at the start of all the tests that will be defined on the class. Common setup tasks include defining static values that will be compared later, opening connections to databases, opening files, and loading data to analyze.

This method takes no arguments and doesn't return anything. If you need to control its behavior with any parameters, you'll need to define those in a way that `setUp()` can access without them being passed in as arguments. A common technique is to check `os.environ` for specific values that affect the behavior of the tests. Another option is to have customizable settings modules that can be imported in `setUp()`, which can then modify the test behavior.

Likewise, any values that setUp() defines for later use can't be returned using the standard value. Instead, they can be stored on the TestCase object itself, which will be instantiated prior to running setUp(). The next section will show that individual tests are defined as methods on that same object, so any attributes stored during setup will be available for use by the tests when they execute:

```python
import unittest

class MultiplicationTestCase(unittest.TestCase):
    def setUp(self):
        self.factor = 2
```

Note   If you look at PEP 8 (Style Guide for Python Code), you'll notice that the name setUp() doesn't follow standard Python naming conventions. The capitalization style here is based on the Java testing framework, JUnit. Python's unit testing system was ported from Java, and some of its style carried over as well. Be sure to examine this PEP, as it provides some very important information about readability of code.

Writing Tests

With the setup in place, you can write some tests to verify whatever behavior you're working with. Like setUp(), these are implemented as custom methods on your test case class. Unlike setUp(), however, there's no single specific method that must implement all the tests. Instead, the test framework will look at your test case class for any methods whose names begin with the word test.

For each method that it finds, the test framework executes setUp() before executing the test method. This helps ensure that each method can rely on a consistent environment regardless of how many methods there are, what they each do, or in what order they're executed. Completely ensuring consistency requires one other step, but that will be covered in the next section.

When writing the body of a test method, the `TestCase` class offers some utility methods to describe how your code is supposed to work. These are designed in such a way that each represents a condition that must be true in order to continue. There are several of these methods, with each covering a specific type of assertion. If the given assertion passes, the test will continue to the next line of code; otherwise, the test halts immediately and a failure message will be generated. Each method provides a default message to use in case of a failure but also accepts an argument to customize that message:

- `assertTrue(expr, msg=None)`: This method tests that the given expression evaluates to `True`. This is the simplest assertion available, mirroring the built-in `assert` keyword. Using this method ties failures into the test framework, however, so it should be used instead. If you prefer the `assert` keyword, this method is also available as `assert_()`.

- `assertFalse(expr, msg=None)`: The inverse of `assertTrue()`, this test will only pass if the provided expression evaluates to `False`.

- `fail(msg=None)`: This method generates a failure message explicitly. This is useful if the conditions of the failure are more complex than the built-in methods provide for on their own. Generating a failure is preferable to raising an exception because it indicates that the code failed in a way that the test understands, rather than being unknown.

These functions alone provide a basic palette for the rest of your tests. To start converting the earlier doctest to a unit test, we can start by providing a `testNumber()` method to simulate the first test that was performed previously. Like doctests, the `unittest` module also provides a simple function to run all the tests found in the given module; this time, it's called `main()`:

```
import unittest
import times2
class MultiplicationTestCase(unittest.TestCase):
    def setUp(self):
        self.factor = 2
    def testNumber(self):
```

```
        self.assertTrue(times2.times2(5) == 10)
if __name__ == '__main__':
    unittest.main()
```

Tests are typically stored in a module called tests.py. After saving this file, we can execute it just like the doctest example shown previously:

```
$ python tests.py

.

-------------------------------------------------------------------
Ran 1 test in 0.001s
```

Unlike doctests, unit testing does show some statistics by default. Each period represents a single test that was run, so complex applications with dozens, hundreds, or even thousands of tests can easily fill several screens with results. Failures and errors are also represented here, using E for errors and F for failures. In addition, each failure will produce a block of text to describe what went wrong. Look what happens when we change the test expression:

```
import unittest
import times2
class MultiplicationTestCase(unittest.TestCase):
    def setUp(self):
        self.factor = 2
    def testNumber(self):
        self.assertTrue(times2.times2(5) == 42)
if __name__ == '__main__':
    unittest.main()
```

```
$ python tests.py
```

359

The output of running this code, assuming that you are in the same terminal session and have keyed in the previous functions, will be:

```
F
========================================================================
FAIL: testNumber (__main__.MultiplicationTests)
------------------------------------------------------------------------
Traceback (most recent call last):
  File "tests.py", line 9, in testNumber
    self.assertTrue(times2(5) == 42)
AssertionError: False is not True
------------------------------------------------------------------------

Ran 1 test in 0.001s
FAILED (failures=1)
```

As you can see, it shows exactly which test method generated the failure, with a traceback to help track down the code flow that led to the failure. In addition, the failure itself is shown as an `AssertionError`, with the assertion shown plainly.

In this case, however, the failure message isn't as useful as it could be. All it reports is that `False` is not `True`. That's a correct report, of course, but it doesn't really tell the whole story. In order to better track down what went wrong, it would be useful to know what the function actually returned.

To provide more information about the values involved, we'll need to use a test method that can identify the different values individually. If they're not equal, the test fails just like the standard assertion, but the failure message can now include the two distinct values so you can see how they're different. That can be a valuable tool in determining how and where the code went wrong—which is, after all, the whole point of testing:

- `assertEqual(obj1, obj2, msg=None)`: This checks that both objects that were passed in evaluate as equal, utilizing the comparison features shown in Chapter 5, if applicable.

- `assertNotEqual(obj1, obj2, msg=None)`: This is similar to `assertEqual()`, except that this method will fail if the two objects are equal.

- assertAlmostEqual(obj1, obj2, *, places=7, msg=None): Specifically for numeric values, this method rounds the value to the given number of decimal places before checking for equality. This helps account for rounding errors and other problems due to floating point arithmetic.

- assertNotAlmostEqual(obj1, obj2, *, places=7, msg=None): The inverse of the previous method, this test fails if the two numbers are equal when rounded to the specified number of digits.

With assertEqual() available, we can change testNumber() to produce a more useful message in the event that the assertion fails:

```
import unittest
import times2
class MultiplicationTestCase(unittest.TestCase):
    def setUp(self):
        self.factor = 2
    def testNumber(self):
        self.assertEqual(times2.times2(5), 42)
if __name__ == '__main__':
    unittest.main()
F
======================================================================
FAIL: testNumber (__main__.MultiplicationTests)
----------------------------------------------------------------------
Traceback (most recent call last):
  File "tests.py", line 9, in testNumber
    self.assertEqual(times2(5), 42)
AssertionError: 10 != 42
----------------------------------------------------------------------
Ran 1 test in 0.001s
FAILED (failures=1)
```

Behind the scenes, assertEqual() does a couple of interesting things to be as flexible and powerful as possible. First, by using the == operator, it can compare the two objects using whatever more efficient method the objects themselves may define. Second, the formatting of the output can be configured by supplying a custom comparison method. Several of these customized methods are provided in the unittest module:

- assertSetEqual(set1, set2, msg=None): Because unordered sequences are typically implemented as sets, this method is designed specifically for sets, using the first set's difference() method to determine whether any items are different between the two.

- assertDictEqual(dict1, dict2, msg=None): This method is designed specifically for dictionaries, in order to take their values into account as well as their keys.

- assertListEqual(list1, list2, msg=None): Similar to assertEqual(), this method is targeted specifically at lists.

- assertTupleEqual(tuple1, tuple2, msg=None): Like assertListEqual(), this is a customized equality check, but this time tailored for use with tuples.

- assertSequenceEqual(seq1, seq2, msg=None): If you're not working with a list, tuple, or a subclass of one of them, this method can be used to do the same job on any object that acts as a sequence.

In addition to these methods provided out of the box, you can add your own to the test framework, so that assertEqual() can more effectively work with your own types. By passing a type and a comparison function into the addTypeEqualityFunc() method, you can register it for use with assertEqual() later on.

Using addTypeEqualityFunc() effectively can be tricky, because it's valid for the entire test case class, no matter how many tests there may be inside it. It may be tempting to add the equality function in the setUp() method, but remember that setUp() gets called once for each test method that was found on the TestCase class. If the equality function will be registered for all tests on that class, there's no point registering it before each one.

A better solution would be to add the addTypeEqualityFunc() call to the __init__() method of the test case class. This also has the additional benefit that you can subclass your own test case class to provide a more suitable base for other tests to work with. That process is explained in more detail later in this chapter.

Other Comparisons

Beyond simple equality, `unittest.TestCase` includes a few other methods that can be used to compare two values. Aimed primarily at numbers, these address the question of whether a tested value is less than or greater than what was expected:

- `assertGreater(obj1, obj2, msg=None)`: Similar to the tests for equality, this tests whether the first object is greater than the second. Like equality, this also delegates to methods on the two objects, if applicable.

- `assertGreaterEqual(obj1, obj2, msg=None)`: This works just like `assertGreater()`, except that the test also passes if the two objects compare as equal.

- `assertLess(obj1, obj2, msg=None)`: This test passes if the first object compares as less than the second object.

- `assertLessEqual(obj1, obj2, msg=None)`: Like `assertLess()`, this tests whether the first object is less than the second but also passes if both are equal.

Testing Strings and Other Sequence Content

Sequences present an interesting challenge because they're made up of multiple individual values. Any value in a sequence could determine the success or failure of a given test, so it's necessary to have tools to work with them specifically. First, there are two methods designed for strings, where simple equality may not always be sufficient:

- `assertMultiLineEqual(obj1, obj2, msg=None)`: This is a specialized form of `assertEqual()`, designed for multiline strings. Equality works like any other string, but the default failure message is optimized to show the differences between the values.

- `assertRegexpMatches(text, regexp, msg=None)`: This tests whether the given regular expression matches the text provided.

More generally, tests for sequences need to make sure that certain items are present in the sequence in order to pass. The equality methods shown previously will only work if the entire sequence must be equal. In the event that some items in the sequence are important but the rest can be different, we'll need to use some other methods to verify that:

- `assertIn(obj, seq, msg=None)`: This tests whether the object is present in the given sequence.

- `assertNotIn(obj, seq, msg=None)`: This works like `assertIn()` except that it fails if the object exists as part of the given sequence.

- `assertDictContainsSubset(dict1, dict2, msg=None)`: This method takes the functionality of `assertIn()` and applies it specifically to dictionaries. Like the `assertDictEqual()` method, this specialization allows it to also take the values into account instead of just the keys.

- `assertSameElements(seq1, seq2, msg=None)`: This tests all the items in two sequences and passes only if the items in both sequences are identical. This only tests for the presence of individual items, not their order within each sequence. This will also accept two dictionaries but will treat it as any other sequence, so it will only look at the keys in the dictionary, not their associated values.

Testing Exceptions

So far all of the test methods have taken a positive approach, where the test verifies that a successful outcome really is successful. It's just as important to verify unsuccessful outcomes, however, because they still need to be reliable. Many functions are expected to raise exceptions in certain situations, and unit testing is just as useful in verifying that behavior:

- `assertRaises (exception, callable, *args, **kwargs)`: Rather than checking a specific value, this method tests a callable to see that it raises a particular exception. In addition to the exception type and the callable to test, it also accepts any number of positional and keyword arguments. These extra arguments will be passed to the callable that was supplied, so that multiple flows can be tested.

- assertRaisesRegexp (exception, regex, callable, *args, **kwargs): This method is slightly more specific than assertRaises() because it also accepts a regular expression that must match the exception's string value in order to pass. The expression can be passed in as a string or as a compiled regular expression object.

In our `times2` example, there are many types of values that can't be multiplied by an integer. Those situations can be part of the explicit behavior of the function, as long as they're handled consistently. The typical response would be to raise a `TypeError`, as Python does by default. Using the `assertRaises()` method, we can test for this as well:

```
import unittest
import times2
class MultiplicationTestCase(unittest.TestCase):
    def setUp(self):
        self.factor = 2
    def testNumber(self):
        self.assertEqual(times2.times2(5), 42)
    def testInvalidType(self):
        self.assertRaises(TypeError, times2.times2, {})
```

Some situations are a bit more complicated, which can cause difficulties with testing. One common example is an object that overrides one of the standard operators. You could call the overridden method by name, but it would be more readable to simply use the operator itself. Unfortunately, the normal form of `assertRaises()` requires a callable, rather than just an expression.

To address this, both of these methods can act as context managers using a `with` block. In this form you don't supply a callable or arguments, but rather just pass in the exception type and, if using `assertRaisesRegexp()`, a regular expression. Then, in the body of the `with` block, you can add the code that must raise the given exception. This can also be more readable than the standard version, even for situations that wouldn't otherwise require it:

```
import unittest
import times2
class MultiplicationTestCase(unittest.TestCase):
    def setUp(self):
        self.factor = 2
    def testNumber(self):
        self.assertEqual(times2.times2(5), 42)
    def testInvalidType(self):
        with self.assertRaises(TypeError):
            times2.times2({})
```

COMPATIBILITY: PRIOR TO 3.1/2.7

The assertRaises() method was around before Python 2.5, so it will be available in most Python versions in use today. The regular expression variant, however, was added in Python 3.1 and backported to Python 2.7. The same functionality could be simulated using a try/except combination to get access to the error message directly, where its string value can be verified using a regular expression.

Even though the with statement and context managers were both introduced in Python 2.5, assertRaises() didn't support the context management protocol until version 3.1. Because the assertRaisesRegexp() method didn't exist until that version either, there was no support for context managers in earlier versions. To achieve the same effect without context managers, you'll need to create a new callable—often a lambda function—to pass into the test method.

Testing Identity

The last group contains methods for testing the identity of objects. Rather than just checking to see if their values are equivalent, these methods check to see if two objects are in fact the same. One common scenario for this test is when your code caches values for use later. By testing for identity, you can verify that a value returned from cache is the same value that was placed in the cache to begin with, rather than simply an equivalent copy:

- `assertIs(ob1, obj2, msg=None)`: This method checks to see if the two arguments both refer to the same object. The test is performed using the identity of the objects, so objects that might compare as equal will still fail if they're not actually the same object.

- `assertIsNot(obj1, obj2, msg=None)`: This inversion of `assertIs()` will only pass if the two arguments refer to two different objects. Even if they would otherwise compare as equal, this test requires them to have different identities.

- `assertIsNone(obj, msg=None)`: This is a simple shortcut for a common case of `assertIs()`, where an object is compared to the built-in None object.

- `assertIsNotNone(obj, msg=None)`: The inversion of `assertIsNone()` will pass only if the object provided is not the built-in None object.

Tearing Down

Just as `setUp()` gets called before each individual test is carried out, the `TestCase` object also calls a `tearDown()` method to clean up any initialized values after testing is carried out. This is used quite often in tests that need to create and store information outside of Python during testing. Examples of such information are database rows and temporary files. Once the tests are complete that information is no longer necessary, so it makes good sense to clean up after they've completed.

Typically, a set of tests that works with files will have to create temporary files along the way, to verify that they get accessed and modified properly. These files can be created in `setUp()` and deleted in `tearDown()`, ensuring that each test has a fresh copy when it runs. The same can be done with databases or other data structures.

Note   The key value of `setUp()` and `tearDown()` is that they can prepare a clean environment for each individual test. If you need to set up an environment for all the tests to share or revert some changes after all tests have completed, you'll need to do so before or after starting the testing process.

Providing a Custom Test Class

Because the unittest module is designed as a class to be overridden, you can write your own class on top of it for your tests to use instead. This is a different process than writing tests because you're providing more tools for your tests to use. You can override any of the existing methods that are available on TestCase itself or add any others that are useful to your code.

The most common way to extend the usefulness of TestCase is to add new methods to test different functionality than the original class was designed for. A file-handling framework might include extra methods for testing the size of a given file or perhaps some details about its contents. A framework for retrieving Web content could include methods to check HTTP status codes or look for individual tags in HTML documents. The possibilities are endless.

Changing Test Behavior

Another powerful technique available when creating a testing class is the ability to change how the tests themselves are performed. The most obvious way to do this is to override the existing assertion methods, which can change how those tests are performed. There are a few other ways to alter the standard behavior, without overriding the assertion methods.

These additional overrides can be managed in the __init__() method of your custom class because, unlike setUp(), the __init__() method will only be called once per TestCase object. That makes it good for those customizations that need to affect all tests but won't be affected by any of the tests as they run. One such example, mentioned previously in this chapter, is the ability to add custom equality comparison methods, which are registered with the addTypeEqualityFunc() method.

Another modification you can make to the test class is to define what type of exception is used to identify failures. Normally, all test failures raise an AssertionError behind the scenes—the same exception used when an assert statement fails. If you need to change that for any reason, such as to better integrate with a higher-level testing framework, you can assign a new exception type to the failureException class attribute.

As a side effect of using the failureException attribute to generate failures, you can raise it explicitly using self.failureException to generate a test failure. This is essentially the same as simply calling self.fail(), but it can be more readable in some cases to raise an exception rather than call a method.

Exciting Python Extensions: Pillow

The Pillow library offers Python programmers great power when dealing with images.

The Pillow (or PIL) Python Imaging Library offers Python programmers great power when dealing with images. The main site, https://python-pillow.org, offers a great amount of information about what the library offers, including the three main functions of image archiving, display, and processing. Of course there is much more that the PIL library offers.

How to Install Pillow (PIL)

From a command prompt with administrative privileges, type:
pip3 install pillow **(Enter)**

Now that you have it installed (if pip3 reported a successful install), let's try a few of the features.

Image Display: Determine File Size, Type, and Display It

Using a JPG image of your choice, try the following:

```
#PIL example 1
from __future__ import print_function
from PIL import Image
my_image = Image.open("sleepy_sab.jpg")
#this image:  http://www.jbbrowning.com/user/pages/02.about/sleepy_sab.JPG
#show data about the image
print(my_image.format, ' Image format')
print(my_image.size, ' Image size')
print(my_image.mode, 'Color mode e.g. RGB, etc.')
#Display the image with the default image application
my_image.show()
```

It is important to note that PIL will automatically open most standard image types without any prompting via code.

Image Processing: Crop a Portion of an Image

In this example, we will use the previous jpg image (so if you use a different one the settings will need to be adjusted) and display the original, and then crop a bit and display the new image. This crop function expects a tuple with four coordinate points, 0,0 being the upper left:

```
#PIL example 2
from __future__ import print_function
from PIL import Image
my_image = Image.open("sleepy_sab.jpg")
#Display the image with the default image application
my_image.show()
#Crop a portion of the image from the upper left to
#about halfway and display
#(3456, 2304) is the image size
#0,0 is upper left.  Crop wants a tuple so there are (())
region = my_image.crop((0,0,2000,2000))
region.show()
```

Image Processing: Changing Image Orientation

You can rotate images as well two different ways (both work the same). In the next example we will rotate the image 90 degrees:

```
#PIL example 3
from __future__ import print_function
from PIL import Image
my_image = Image.open("sleepy_sab.jpg")
#Rotate the image 90 degrees
turny=my_image.transpose(Image.ROTATE_90)
turny.show()
```

Image Processing: Filters

There are a number of filters, such as blur and enhance, built in to PIL. Additionally, there are other filters for color transformations, pixel lookups, and so on. The main PIL web site has updates for the current version. To see how handy they are, examine the following example, which embosses the image:

```
#PIL example 4
from PIL import Image
from PIL import ImageFilter
my_image = Image.open("sleepy_sab.jpg")
#Emboss the image
emmy=my_image.filter(ImageFilter.EMBOSS)
emmy.show()
```

If you used the suggested image, poor Sabastian looks like a piece of metal artwork! Are there more things you can do with PIL? Yes! Expand on what you have learned and try your hand with some of the other filters and processing tools.

Taking It With You

The tools described in this chapter are just the basis of a functional test suite. As you write an application, you'll need to fill in the gaps with the important facets of how your code should work. Always remember, however, that tests aren't just for you. By making sure that new code doesn't break existing code, you can provide a much better guarantee for your users once you distribute your code to the public. The next chapter will show how you can get your code to the masses.

CHAPTER 10

Distribution

Once you have a working application, the next step is to decide how and where to distribute it. You might be writing it for yourself, but most likely you will have a wider audience and have a set schedule for releasing it. There are a number of decisions to be made and tasks to be performed before you can do that, however. This process consists primarily of packaging and distribution, but it begins with licensing.

Licensing

Before releasing any code to the public, you must decide on a license that will govern its use. A license will allow you to convey to your users how you intend your code to be used, how you expect others to use it, what you ask from them in return, and what rights you expect them to confer on users of their own code after integrating with yours. These are complex questions that can't be answered in a universal way for every project. Instead, you'll need to consider a number of issues.

Your own philosophy plays a key role, as it affects many other decisions. Some people intend to earn a living from their code, which could mean the source code won't be released at all. Instead, your work could be offered as a service that customers can pay to use. By contrast, you may be interested in helping people learn to do things better, faster, easier, or more reliably. Perhaps the most common license is the GPL.

GNU General Public License

When people think of open source, the GNU General Public License (GPL)[1] is often the first thing to come to mind. As one of the vanguards of the free software movement, its primary goal is to preserve a certain group of freedoms to the users of software. The GPL

---

[1]See GNU Operating System, "GNU General Public License," http://propython.com/gpl.

373

© J. Burton Browning and Marty Alchin 2019
J. B. Browning and M. Alchin, *Pro Python 3*, https://doi.org/10.1007/978-1-4842-4385-5_10

requires that if you distribute your program to others, you must also make the source code of that program available to them. That way they're free to make modifications to your code as they see fit, in order to better support their own needs.

Furthermore, the promise of the GPL is that any users who do alter your code can only distribute their modifications under the GPL or a license that ensures at least the same freedoms. This way users of the software can be confident that if it doesn't work to their satisfaction, they have a way to make it better no matter how far removed it may be from the original author.

Because the GPL places requirements on any modifications made to the original code and code that links to it, it's sometimes referred to as "viral." That's not necessarily an insult; it simply refers to the fact that the GPL forces the same license on anything that uses it. In other words, it spreads through software in much the same way as a traditional virus. This isn't unique to the GPL, but it's the feature many in the business world think of first when they think of the GPL and open source in general.

Because the goal of the GPL is to preserve freedoms for computer users, it can be seen as restricting the freedom of programmers. The freedom of a programmer to distribute an application without divulging the source code restricts the freedom of a user to modify that code. Of those two opposing forces, the GPL is designed to preserve the user's freedoms by placing a number of restrictions on the behavior of programmers.

THE GPL AND PYTHON

The GPL was written primarily for statically compiled languages, such as C and C++, so it often speaks in terms of code in "object form" that may be "statically linked" to other code. In other words, when you create a C++ executable, the compiler inserts the code from the libraries you reference to make a stand-alone program. These terms are central to its vocabulary, but aren't as clearly understood when applied to dynamic languages such as Python. Many Python applications use the GPL because of its overall philosophy, but its terms have yet to be tested in court in the context of a Python application.

It may seem like such details wouldn't really matter because Python code is generally distributed as source code anyway. The term *generally* here has exceptions, such as if you used py2exe to make a Windows-compiled Python application. After all, compiled Python bytecode isn't compatible with all the various systems in which the code might be used.

> But because the GPL also applies to any other applications that use the code, these details become important if, for example, a statically compiled application uses GPL Python code internally for some features. It has yet to be seen whether such use would trigger the GPL's requirements on the distribution of that new application's source code.

Because these restrictions must also be passed on to any other application that includes GPL code, the available licenses that can work with it are limited. Any other license you might consider must include at least the same restrictions as the GPL, although additional restrictions can be added if necessary. One example of this is the AGPL.

Affero General Public License

With the proliferation of the Internet, it's now quite common for users to interact with software without ever obtaining a copy of that software directly. Because the GPL relies on distribution of code to trigger the requirement to also distribute source code, online services such as web sites and mail systems are exempt from that requirement. Some have argued that those exemptions violate the spirit of the GPL by exploiting a loophole in its provisions.

To close that loophole, the Affero General Public License (AGPL) was created. This license contains all the restrictions of the GPL as well as the added feature that any user interacting with the software, even by way of a network, will trigger the distribution clause. That way, web sites that incorporate AGPL code must divulge the source code for any modifications they've made and any additional software that shares common internal data structures with it. Although a bit slow to be adopted by the masses, certainly approval by the Open Source Initiative (OSI) gives this license important support.

Note   Even though the terminology and philosophy of the AGPL are very similar to the GPL, its applicability to Python is a bit more clear. Because just interacting with the software triggers the terms of the license, it doesn't matter as much whether the code is compiled from a static language such as C or built from a dynamic language such as Python. This also has yet to be tested in court for Python cases, however.

Because the AGPL is more restrictive than the GPL itself, it's possible for a project that uses AGPL to incorporate code that was originally licensed with the standard GPL. All of the protections of the GPL remain intact, while some extra ones are added. There's also a variant of the GPL that incorporates fewer restrictions, called the LGPL.

GNU Lesser General Public License

Because the GPL states that statically linking one piece of code to another triggers its terms, many small utility libraries were used less often than they might otherwise have been. These libraries typically don't constitute an entire application on their own, but because their usefulness requires tight integration with the host application, many developers avoided them in order to avoid their own applications being also bound to the GPL.

The GNU Lesser General Public License (LGPL) was created to handle these cases by removing the static linking clause. Thus, a library released under the LGPL could be freely used in a host application without requiring the host be bound by the LGPL or any other specific license. Even proprietary, commercial applications with no intention of releasing any source code can incorporate code licensed with the LGPL.

All of the other terms remain intact, however, so any modifications to the LGPL code must be distributed as source code if the code itself is distributed in any way. For this reason, many LGPL libraries have extremely flexible interfaces that allow their host applications as many options as possible without having to modify the code directly.

Essentially, the LGPL leans more toward using the notion of open source to foster a more open programming community than to protect the rights of the software's eventual audience. Further down that road is one of the most liberal open source licenses available: BSD.

Berkeley Software Distribution License

The Berkeley Software Distribution (BSD) license provides a way to release code with the intent of fostering as much adoption as possible. It does this by placing relatively few limitations on the use, modification, and distribution of the code by other parties. In fact, the entire text of the license consists of just a few bullet points and a disclaimer. Referring to BSD as a single license is a misnomer, however, as there are actually a few variations. In its original form, the license consisted of four points:

- Distributing the source code to the program requires that the code retain the original copyright, the text of the license, and its disclaimer.

- Distributing the code as a compiled binary program requires the copyright, license text, and disclaimer be included somewhere in the documentation or other materials provided with the distributed code.

- Any advertising used to promote the final product must attribute the BSD-licensed code as being included in the product.

- Neither the name of the organization that developed the software nor the names of any of its contributors may be used to specifically endorse the product without explicit consent beyond the license itself.

Notice that this contains no requirement that the source code be distributed at all, even when distributing compiled code. Instead, it only requires that the appropriate attribution is retained at all times and that it remains clear that there are two separate parties involved. This allows BSD-licensed code to be included in proprietary, commercial products with no need to release the source code behind it, making it fairly attractive to large corporations.

The advertising clause caused some headaches with organizations trying to use BSD-licensed code, however. The primary problem is that as the code itself changed hands and was maintained by different organizations, each organization that had a hand in its development must be mentioned by name in any advertising materials. In some cases that could be dozens of different organizations, accounting for a significant portion of advertising space, especially when software often contains quite a few other disclaimers for other reasons.

To address those concerns, another version of the BSD license was created without the advertising clause. This license is called the New BSD license, and it includes all the other requirements of the original. The removal of the advertising clause meant that changes in management of the BSD-licensed code had very little impact on organizations using it, which broadened its appeal considerably.

One further reduction of the BSD license is called the Simplified BSD license. In this variation even the nonendorsement clause is removed, leaving only the requirements that the text of the license and its disclaimer be included. In order to still avoid untrue endorsement, the disclaimer in this version includes an extra sentence that clearly states that the views of both groups are independent of each other.

Other Licenses

The options listed here are some of the more commonly chosen, but there are many more available. The OSI maintains a list of open source licenses[2] that have been examined and approved as preserving the ideals of open source. In addition, the Free Software Foundation maintains its own list of licenses[3] that have been approved as preserving the ideals of free software.

Note   The difference between free software and open source is primarily philosophical, but does have some real-world implications. In a nutshell, free software preserves the freedom of users of that software, whereas open source focuses on the software development model. Not all licenses are approved for both uses, so you may need to decide which is more important to you.

Once you have a license in place, you can start the process of packaging and distributing your code to others who can make use of it.

Packaging

It's not very easy to distribute a bunch of files individually, so you'll first have to bundle them up. This process is called packaging, but it shouldn't be confused with the standard Python notion of a package. Traditionally, a package is simply a directory with an __ init__.py file in it, which can then be used as a namespace for any modules contained in that directory.

For the purposes of distribution, a package also includes documentation, tests, a license, and installation instructions. These are arranged in such a way that the individual parts can be easily extracted and installed into appropriate locations. Typically, the structure looks something like this:

---

[2]See Open Source Initiative, "Licenses by Name," http://propython.com/osi-licenses.
[3]See GNU Operating System, "Various Licenses and Comments about Them," http://propython.com/fsf-licenses.

```
AppName/
    LICENSE.txt
    README.txt
    MANIFEST.in
    setup.py
    app_name/
        __init__.py
        ...
    docs/
        ...
    tests/
        __init__.py
        ...
```

As you can see, the actual Python code package is a subdirectory of the overall application package, and it sits as a peer alongside its documentation and tests. The documentation contained in the docs directory can contain any form of documentation you prefer, but is usually filled with plain text files formatted using reStructuredText, as described in Chapter 8. The tests directory contains tests such as those described in Chapter 9. The LICENSE.txt file contains a copy of your chosen license and README.txt provides an introduction to your application, its purpose, and its features.

The more interesting features of this overall package are setup.py and MANIFEST.in, which aren't otherwise part of the application's code.

setup.py

Inside your package, setup.py is the script that will actually install your code into an appropriate location on a user's system. In order to be as portable as possible, this script relies on the distutils package provided in the standard distribution. That package contains a setup() function that uses a declarative approach to make the process easier to work with and more generic.

Located within distutils.core, the setup() function accepts a wide array of keyword arguments, each of which describes a particular feature of the package. Some pertain to the package as a whole, whereas others list individual contents that are included in the package. Three of these arguments are required for any package to be distributed using standard tools:

- `name`: This string contains the public name of the package as it will be displayed to those who are looking for it. Naming a package can be a complex and difficult task, but as it's highly subjective, it's well beyond the scope of this book.

- `version`: This is a string containing the dot-separated version number of the application. It's common for first releases to use a version of `'0.1'` and increase from there. The first number is typically a major version indicating a promise of compatibility. The second is a minor version number, representing a collection of bug fixes or significant new features that don't break compatibility. The third is typically reserved for security releases that introduce no new functionality or other bug fixes.

- `url`: This string references the main web site where users can learn more about the application, find more documentation, request support, file bug reports, or do other tasks. It typically serves as a central hub for information and activity surrounding the code.

In addition to these three required elements, there are several optional arguments that can provide further detail about the application:

- `author`: The name of the author(s) of the application.

- `author_email`: An email address where the author can be reached directly.

- `maintainer`: If the original author is no longer maintaining the application, this field contains the name of the person now responsible for it.

- `maintainer_email`: An email address where the maintainer can be reached directly.

- `description`: This string provides a brief description of the purpose of the program. Think of it as a one-line description that could be shown in a list alongside others.

- `long_description`: As its name implies, this is a longer description of the application. Rather than being used in lists, this one is typically shown when a user requests more detail about the specific application. Because this is all specified in Python code, many distributions simply read the contents of `README.txt` into this argument.

Beyond this metadata, the `setup()` function is responsible for maintaining a list of all the files necessary to distribute the application, including all Python modules, documentation, tests, and licenses. Like the other information, these details are supplied using additional keyword arguments. All paths listed here are relative to the main package directory where `setup.py` itself is located:

- `license`: This is the name of a file that contains the full text of the license under which the program is distributed. Typically that file is called `LICENSE.txt`, but by explicitly passing it in as an argument, it can be named whatever you prefer.

- `packages`: This argument accepts a list of package names where the actual code is located. Unlike license, these values are Python import paths, using periods to separate individual packages along the path.

- `package_dir`: If your Python packages aren't in the same directory as `setup.py`, this argument provides a way to tell `setup()` where to find them. Its value is a dictionary that maps a package name to its location in the filesystem. One special key you can use is an empty string, which will use the associated value as a root directory to look for any packages that don't have an explicit path specified.

- `package_data`: If your package relies on data files that aren't written in Python directly, those files will only get installed if referenced in this argument. It accepts a dictionary that maps package names to their contents, but unlike `package_dir`, the values in this dictionary are lists, with each value in the list being a path specification to the files that should be included. These paths may include asterisks to indicate broad patterns to match against, similar to what you can query on the command line.

There are other options for more complex configurations, but these should cover most of the bases. For more information, consult the `distutils` documentation.[4] Once you have the pieces in place, you'll have a `setup.py` that looks something like this:

```
from distutils.core import setup

setup(name='MyApp',
      version='0.1',
      author='Marty Alchin',
      author_email='marty@propython.com',
      url='http://propython.com/',
      packages=['my_app', 'my_app.utils'],
)
```

MANIFEST.in

In addition to `setup.py` specifying what files should be installed on a user's system, a package distribution also includes a number of files that are useful to the user without being installed directly. These files, such as documentation, should be available to users with the package but don't have any code value, so they shouldn't be installed in an executable location. The `MANIFEST.in` file controls how these files should be added to the package.

`MANIFEST.in` is a plain text file, populated with a series of commands that tell `distutils` what files to include in the package. The filename patterns used in these commands follows the same conventions as the command line, allowing asterisks to serve as a wildcard for a broad range of filenames. For example, a simple `MANIFEST.in` might include any text files in the package's `docs` directory:

```
include docs/*.txt
```

This simple instruction will tell `distutils` to find all the text files in the docs directory and include them in the final package. Additional patterns could be included by separating the patterns with a space. There are a few different commands available, each of which has an include and exclude version available:

---

[4]See Distributing Python Modules, "2. Writing the Setup Script," `http://propython.com/distutils-setup`.

- `include`: The most obvious option, this command will look for all files that match any of the given patterns and include them in the package. They'll be placed in the package at the same location as they were found in the original directory structure.

- `exclude`: The opposite of `include`, this will tell `distutils` to ignore any files that match any of the patterns given here. This provides a way to avoid including some files, without having to explicitly list every included file in an `include` command. A common example would `exclude TODO.txt` in a package that specifically includes all text files.

- `recursive-include`: This command requires a directory as its first argument, prior to any filename patterns. It then looks inside that directory and any of its subdirectories for any files that match the given patterns.

- `recursive-exclude`: Like `recursive-include`, this command takes a directory first, followed by filename patterns. Any files that are found by this command are not included in the package, even if they're found by one of the inclusion commands.

- `global-include`: This command finds all the paths in the project, regardless of where they may be within the path structure. By looking inside directories, it works much like `recursive-include`, but because it looks through all directories, it doesn't need to take any argument other than the filename patterns to look for.

- `global-exclude`: Like `global-include`, this finds matching files anywhere in the source project, but the files found are excluded from the final package.

- `graft`: Rather than looking for matching files, this command accepts a set of directories that are simply included in the package in their entirety.

- `prune`: Like `graft`, this command takes a set of directories, but it excludes them from the package completely, even if there were matching files inside.

With both `setup.py` and `MANIFEST.in` in place, `distutils` provides an easy way to bundle up the package and prepare it for distribution.

The sdist Command

To finally create the distributable package, your new `setup.py` is actually executable directly from a command line. Because this script is also used to install the package later, you must specify what command you'd like it to carry out. Users who obtain the package later will use the `install` command, but to package up a source distribution, the command is `sdist`:

```
$ python setup.py sdist
running sdist
...
```

This command processes the declarations made in `setup.py` as well as the instructions from `MANIFEST.in` to create a single archive file that contains all of the files you've specified for distribution. The type of archive file you get by default depends on the system you're running, but `sdist` provides a few options that you can specify explicitly. Simply pass in a comma-separated list of formats to the `--format` option to generate specific types:

- `zip`: The default on Windows machines, this format creates a zip file.

- `gztar`: The default on Unix machines, including Mac OS, this creates a gzipped tarball. To also create this archive on a Windows system, you'll need an implementation of `tar` installed, such as the one available through Cygwin.[5]

- `bztar`: This command uses the alternative bzip compression on the archive tarball. This also requires an implementation of `tar` installed.

- `ztar`: This uses the simpler `compress` algorithm to compress the tarball. As with the others, an implementation of `tar` is required to use this option.

- `tar`: Rather than using compression, this option simply bundles up a tarball if an implementation of the `tar` utility is available.

---

[5]See Cygwin, `http://propython.com/cygwin`.

When you run the `sdist` command, archive files for each of the formats you specified will be created and placed inside a new `dist` directory within your project. The names of each archive will simply use the `name` and `version` you supplied in `setup.py`, separated by a hyphen. The example provided earlier would result in files such as `MyApp-0.1.zip`.

Let's try all of the preceding steps in one example. Follow along with each step to create your zip package:

1. Create a folder you can easily access via a command prompt such as c:\test.

2. In the folder, create the following two files named setup.py and MyApp.py:

```
#setup.py
from distutils.core import setup
setup(name='MyApp',
      version='0.1',
      author='Alchin and Browning',
      author_email='authors@propython.com',
      url='http://www.propython.com/',
)
# MyApp.py
print("Hello Burton and Marty!")
gone=input("Enter to close: ")
```

3. Shell out to a command prompt, change into the test directory, and execute the command:

   python setup.py sdist (Enter)

4. Press Enter. (If it does not start Python, you will need to check your search path and ensure that your system can find Python.)

This will create a **dist** directory in the **test** folder with the zip file for your package.

Of course that was a very simple overview, but you have the flexibility to add a manifest file, change compression options, and so on.

Distribution

Once you have these files in place, you'll need a way to distribute them to the public. One option is to simply host your own web site and serve up the files from there. That's typically the best way to market your code to a wide audience because you have an opportunity to put the documentation online in a more readable way, show examples of it in use, offer testimonials from people who are already using it, and anything else you can come up with.

The only problem with simply hosting it yourself is that it becomes fairly difficult to find using automated tools. Many packages will rely on the presences of other applications, so it's often useful to be able to install them directly from inside a script, without having to navigate to a web site and find the right link to download. Ideally, they would be able to translate a unique package name into a way to download that package and install it without assistance.

This is where the Python Package Index (PyPI)[6] comes into play. The secret code name of PyPI is "cheeseshop," which is an allusion to the Monty Python Cheese shop skit where John Cleese tries to purchase cheese from the shop Michael Palin is running . . . which has none available.

PyPI is an online collection of Python packages that all follow a standardized structure, so they can be discovered more easily. Each has a unique name that can be used to locate it, and the index keeps track of which version is the latest and references the URL to that package. All you need to do is add your package to the index and it will be much easier for your users to work with.

Uploading to PyPI for the first time requires registration on the site. A PyPI account will allow you to manage your application details later and upload new versions and updates. Once you have an account, you can run `python setup.py register` to set up a page for your application at PyPI. This is an interactive script that will offer you three options for registering your account:

- Use an existing PyPI account. If you've created an account on the PyPI web site already, you can specify your username and password here.

- Register a new PyPI account. If you'd rather create an account at the command line, you can enter your details here and have the account created during registration.

---

[6]See Python Package Index (PyPl), `http://propython.com/pypi`.

- Generate a new PyPI account. If you'd like to take a simpler approach, this option will take the username you're already using in your operating system, generate a password automatically, and register an account for that combination.

Once you choose your option, the register script will offer to save your account information locally, so you won't have to go through that step every time. With an account in place, the script will register the application with PyPI, using the information in setup.py. In particular, the name and long_description fields will combine to form a simple web page, with other details shown in a list.

With a page in place to hold the application, the last step is to upload the code itself using the upload command. This must be done as part of a distribution build, even if you had previously built a distribution. That way, you can specify exactly what type of distributions you'd like to send to PyPI. For example, you can upload packages for both Windows and non-Windows users in a single step:

```
$ python setup.py sdist --format=zip,gztar upload
```

The distribution files are named according to the name of the application and its version number at the time the distribution was created. The entry in PyPI also contains a reference to the version number, so you can't upload the same distribution type of the same version more than once. If you try, you'll get an error from setup.py indicating that you'll need to create a new version number in order to upload a changed distribution.

Exciting Python Extensions: Secrets Module

The Secrets module offers Python programmers some handy random number and password generating tools. Its main feature though is the cryptographically strong nature of the random number algorithm.

The secrets module, introduced in Python 3.6, has many functions available in it. One is random number generation. And while this has been covered with some other libraries, it is still interesting to examine.

Your computer operating system will factor in on the exact nature of the random numbers generated, but generally for cryptographic work, this random library will do a better job than the other random number generators available in Python. Such cryptographic uses would include: passwords, authentication, and tokens. Read on to see how handy this module is.

Random Numbers

There are quite a few random token and random number generation options. To see how they work, consider that the next example will pick a random number between 0 and 100.

```
#Secrets example 1
from secrets import *
x=1
while (x <= 10):
    print(randbelow(100))
    x+=1
```

In the preceding example we selected 10 random values from 1 to 100. Not exciting, but a better cryptographic representation of random values. Next we will consider random password generation.

Password Generation

In this next example, we will use both the string library and the secrets library to generate a password with ASCII letter, digits, punctuation, and uppercase letters:

```
#Generate six digit passwd with letters, digits, punct, and upper
import string
from secrets import *
chars = string.ascii_letters + string.digits + string.punctuation + string.ascii_uppercase
password = ''.join(choice(chars) for i in range(6))
print (password)
```

If you needed a token for cryptographic work, there are options including *urlsafe*. Consider the following example:

```
#Generate a token value which is URL-safe
from secrets import *
value = token_urlsafe(10)
print('token is: ',value)
```

Here we are using *choice*, but with this library you might try the following:

```
#Generate a secrets random choice
from secrets import *
value = choice(['one', 'two', 'three'])
print (value)
```

Lastly, if you wanted to enter values and select a random set from them, try the following:

```
#Generate a random choice based on only certain values
from secrets import *
foo=input('Enter 10 random values to choose from:  ')
wow=".join([choice(foo) for i in range(3)])
print('These are three exciting choices at random:>   ',wow)
```

There's nothing here to save the world from a zombie apocalypse, but these examples are still very interesting uses of the Python *secrets* module.

Taking It With You

As you can see, the process of packaging and distributing a Python application using PyPI is actually fairly straightforward. Beyond PyPI, it's usually a good idea to put together a dedicated project web site, where you can better promote and support your code. Always remember that distribution isn't the last step. Your users will expect a certain amount of support and interaction as they use your code and hope to improve it, so it's best to find a medium that supports those goals for you and your users.

Applications of all different sizes, audiences, and goals are fair game for distribution. It doesn't matter if you're writing a small utility to help automate common tasks or an entire framework to power a set of features for other users' code. The next chapter will show you how to build such a framework from start to finish, building on many of the techniques shown throughout this book.

CHAPTER 11

Sheets: A CSV Framework

Of course, the most important thing in programming is the program. Tools, techniques, philosophy, and advice don't offer much at all if they're never applied to solve a real-world problem. Sometimes that problem is very specific, but other times it's merely a specific example of a more general problem. These general problems are typically the subject of libraries and frameworks, which can provide the base for a more specific application.

This puts frameworks in an interesting position, because they're focused more on serving the needs of developers rather than ordinary users. The goal is to provide a foundation and a set of tools to aid someone else in the development of a more specific application. Supporting a wider array of uses requires more advanced techniques than would ordinarily be used to solve the problem directly.

In order to be useful to other developers, however, the ideal goal is to provide a sort of translation service so that the advanced techniques used by the framework allow other developers to use simpler techniques to perform those more advanced tasks. In this respect framework design is very similar to other forms of design, but rather than focusing primarily on a visual user interface, the focus is on the application's programming interface, the API.

It's important to look at frameworks like this, because if you're writing a framework your audience is looking for a tool to save them time and energy, so that they can focus on their unique needs. The framework should provide a set of features in a way that encourages integration with other types of applications, so it's necessary to think in terms of how those other applications should work.

© J. Burton Browning and Marty Alchin 2019
J. B. Browning and M. Alchin, *Pro Python 3*, https://doi.org/10.1007/978-1-4842-4385-5_11

There are countless examples of frameworks in use already, serving a wide variety of needs. They all address a general class of problem, such as Django[1] for Web development, SQLAlchemy[2] for database interaction, and Twisted[3] for working with network protocols. These each take different approaches with the style and form of the interfaces they expose to developers, highlighting the various ways a framework can operate.

This chapter will show a framework that uses a declarative syntax similar to the ones used in Django and Elixir. The choice of this approach is based largely on style, and even though there are other approaches you could use, investigating one in detail will highlight many of the decisions that must be made when writing a framework. You'll see all the techniques shown in this book combine to form a single, cohesive whole, exposing a public API that provides a number of useful features.

The particular problem that this chapter will address is the need to work with files that store information as rows of comma-separated values, more commonly referred to as CSV files. These are available for tasks like separating values on a line, separating lines themselves, and encoding individual values within each line, which is how it becomes a very complex topic.

Python already does a lot to help with CSV files by providing a `csv` module.[4] Rather than attempting to duplicate its functionality, we can use `csv` to do most of the heavy lifting behind the scenes. What we're going to do instead is build a layer on top of `csv` to make it easier to work with and integrate with other applications. Essentially, we're just providing a new API on top of an existing one, in the hopes that we can make it a bit friendlier.

Building a Declarative Framework

There are several steps involved in building a framework using a declarative syntax similar to that of Django or Elixir, but the process itself really isn't all that difficult. Making decisions along the way, however, is where things get tricky. In this chapter we will outline the various steps required to build such a framework, as well as examples of many of the decisions you'll have to make. Each will have to be made specifically for your own project, however.

---

[1]See Django, `http://propython.com/django`.
[2]See "The Python SQL Toolkit and Object Relational Mapper," `http://propython.com/sqlalchemy`.
[3]See Twisted Matrix Labs, `http://propython.com/twisted`.
[4]See "CSV File Reading and Writing," `http://propython.com/csv-module`.

But you won't be all on your own. Each decision point along the way will outline the pros and cons of various options so that you can be confident about making an informed choice. Making the right decisions at the outset will help to ensure that your framework will withstand future upgrades, as well as criticisms from those who may not agree with you. Just make sure you have valid, real-world reasoning behind your decisions and you'll be fine.

Rather than leaving you with nothing but theory, this chapter will step through the creation of a framework that's simple enough to introduce the essential concepts, without having to dwell too long on matters specific to its purpose. It also needs to be a good example of when a declarative framework should be used, which first requires us to understand what it is we're really looking at. The word *step* is an important term for you to understand as the examples that follow will be added to, and why they are scripts.

Introducing Declarative Programming

At its core, a declarative framework is a helper to make declarative programming easier—or in some cases, possible. Of course, that definition is useless without defining what makes it declarative, but thankfully very little introduction is necessary. After all, you've already seen declarative programming in action and have probably been using it for quite some time, perhaps without even realizing it.

Declarative programming is the practice of telling a program what you want (declaring), rather than telling it what to do (instructing). This distinction is really more about the programmer than the program, in that there are often no special syntax, parsing, or processing rules and no single way to define what does and doesn't qualify. It's most often defined as the opposite of imperative programming, where the programmer is expected to outline every step the computer needs to perform.

With this in mind, it's easy to note that higher-level interpreted languages, such as Python, are much better suited for declarative programming than their lower-level cousins, such as C. In fact, many forms of it are built right in. Rather than having to declare a memory location, specify its type, and then store a value in memory at that location, you can simply assign a variable and Python does the rest. What follows makes a string variable named foo with "bar" stored in it:

```
>>> foo = 'bar'
```

That's just one form of declarative programming, using one syntax. When we talk about declarative frameworks in Python, however, it usually refers to using a class declaration to configure the framework, rather than a long and complicated set of configuration directives. Whether or not that's the right approach for your needs requires a bit more discussion of the pros and cons.

To Build or Not to Build?

Declarative frameworks have been a rising trend in the Python world in the past few years, but it's important to understand that they are not always the best approach to a given problem. Like anything else, deciding whether to use a declarative framework requires understanding what it really is, what it does, and what it means for your needs.

Declarative frameworks do a great job of wrapping a lot of complex behavior into a simple class declaration. This can be a great time-saver, but it can also seem a lot like magic, something that the Python community is constantly battling against. Whether this is good or bad depends entirely on how closely your API matches what users will expect from a class declaration and how well you document the areas where those expectations may fail.

By having a class as the primary method of conveying your intentions to the framework, it's reasonable to expect that instances will have meaning. Most often, an instance refers to a specific set of data that conforms to a format defined by the class declaration. If your application acts on just a single set of well-defined data, there's little use in having individual instances.

Declarative classes are designed to create many different configurations using the same framework, each designed for a particular configuration of data. If you only have one data format to work with—even if you've got loads of data—it just doesn't make sense to write a framework built for configurability. Just write a solution for your type of data and use it.

In other cases, you may not be able to describe the structure of a data set in advance but instead have to adjust the structure based on the data provided. In these cases there's little value in offering a class declaration, since no single declaration would suffice for the needs of the data you're working with.

A primary value of objects is the ability to perform actions on their contents by way of instance methods. Because a declarative framework results in customized classes that produce individual instances, it stands to reason that these instances should be able to perform useful tasks that would be more difficult without the framework's assistance. This not only increases their usefulness, but it also helps ensure that the resulting instances match with users' expectations.

To review, a declarative framework is a valuable approach if you have:

- Many potential configurations

- Each configuration known in advance

- Many instances of any given configuration

- Actions that can be performed on a given instance

The CSV framework described in this chapter needs to deal with a vast array of possible configurations of columns and structure, with many example files of each type. Actions such as loading and saving data are common, whereas others are unique to specific configurations.

Once completed, this framework will allow applications to specify CSV configurations as classes such as the following, and interact with them using methods automatically attached to the class.

To make sure you have the proper library, go to `https://pypi.python.org/pypi/Sheets/` and download the Sheets ZIP file. Unzip it and put all folders and files in your Python 3.x Lib directory (or use pip to install it):

```
import sheets

class EmployeeSheet(sheets.Row):
    first_name = sheets.StringColumn()
    last_name = sheets.StringColumn()
    hire_date = sheets.DateColumn()
    salary = sheets.FloatColumn()
```

So let's get started.

Building the Framework

There are three primary components of any declarative framework, though one of them may come in different forms, or possibly not at all:

- *A base class*: Because declarative frameworks are all about declaring classes, having a common base class to inherit from gives the frame a place to hook in and process declarations as they're encountered by Python. A metaclass attached to this base class provides the necessary machinery to inspect the declaration at runtime and make the appropriate adjustments. The base class is also responsible for representing instances of whatever structure your framework encapsulates, often with various methods attached to simply common procedures.

- *Various field types*: Inside the class declaration are a number of attributes, typically called fields. For some applications it may make more sense to call them something more specific, but for this discussion, fields will suffice. These fields are used to manage individual data attributes in the structures represented by your framework, and often come in different flavors, each tailored to a different general type of data such as strings, numbers, and dates. Another important aspect of fields is that they must be able to know the order in which they get instantiated, so the ordering specified in the declaration is the same ordering used later on.

- *An options container*: Not strictly a necessary component, most frameworks have use for some type of class-wide options, which shouldn't be specified on every individual field, as that wouldn't be very DRY. Because subclassing doesn't provide any options except the choice of base classes, some other structure must be used to manage these options. How these options are declared and processed can vary greatly from one framework to another; there's no syntactic or semantic standard whatsoever. As a matter of convenience, this container often also manages the fields attached to the class.

As a syntactic aid, most declarative frameworks also make sure that all three of these components can be imported from one single location. This allows end-user code to have a much simpler import block, while also containing all the necessary components on a single, identifiable namespace. The name of this namespace should be something meaningful, so it's easy to read in end-user code. The name of the framework itself is often an ideal choice, but it's important to be descriptive, so make sure it all makes sense when reading it over.

Although deciding what to call the framework can be deferred to later in the process, it helps to have a name in mind early on, if only to name the package that will contain the modules described in the following sections. Using a placeholder like csv would work fine for now, but because Python has its own csv module—which we'll be relying on as well—reusing this name would cause a great many problems. Because CSV files are commonly used to exchange data among spreadsheet applications, we'll call our little framework sheets.

It would seem that our journey should start with the base class, but really any of the three components can be a reasonable place to start. It often depends on which piece requires the most thought, does the most work, or needs to be tested first. For this discussion we'll start with the options container, as it can be created without relying on the implementation details of the other components. This avoids leaving too many vague references to functionality that hasn't been described yet.

Managing Options

The primary purpose of an options component is to store and manage options for a given class declaration. These options are not specific to any one field but rather apply to the entire class, or are used as default values that individual fields can optionally override. For now, we'll set aside the question of how these options will be declared and simply focus on the container itself and its associated needs.

On the surface, options are simply a map of names to values, so we could use a simple dictionary. After all, Python has a fantastic dictionary implementation and simple is most certainly better than complex. However, writing our own class affords us a few extra features that will be very handy.

For starters, we can validate the options that are defined for a given class. They can be validated based on their individual values, their combination with other options, their appropriateness for the given execution environment, and whether or not they're known options at all. With a dictionary, we're stuck simply allowing any type of value for any option, even if it makes no sense.

Mistakes in options would then only be known when code that relies on them chokes because they're incorrect or missing, and those types of errors typically aren't very descriptive. Validating on a custom object means we can provide much more useful messages to users who try to use incorrect or invalid options.

Using a custom class also means we add our own custom methods to perform tasks that, although useful, are either repetitive or don't really belong anywhere else. A validation method can verify that all the included options are appropriate, displaying useful messages if not. Remember also that the options container often manages fields, so there are some methods that can be added for that purpose; these are described later in this section.

In fact, by combining those two features, the options class can even validate field declarations in the context of provided options. Try doing that with an ordinary dictionary.

Because it may end up encapsulating quite a bit of functionality, we'll set up a new module for our options container, unambiguously named options.py. Like most classes, the bulk of the work will be done in the __init__() method. For our purposes, this will accept all known options, store them away as attributes, and set up some other attributes that will be used by other methods later on. Validation is generally only useful when actively defining options, so that belongs in its own method so as not to bog down this one.

And so we come to the next decision in your framework: what options should you accept? Different frameworks will obviously have different requirements, and it's important to lay them out as completely as you can at the outset. Don't worry, you can always add more; it's better to get them in place earlier rather than later.

One useful rule of thumb is that options should always have defaults. Asking your users to not only write a class and provide fields but also provide options every time will get frustrating, especially if the required option often has the same value. In general, if something is truly required and doesn't have some reasonable default, it should be supplied as an argument to the methods that require it, rather than defined as an option on the class.

We're building a framework to interface with CSV files, so there are a number of options available. Perhaps the most obvious is the character encoding of the file, but Python already converts file content to Unicode when the file is opened in text mode. The open() function accepts an encoding argument that allows all the same encodings available with a string's encode() method. It defaults to UTF-8, which should suffice for most common needs.

Note   The encoding used when reading the file seems like a perfect candidate for an option, so you can override the default UTF-8 behavior. Unfortunately, the standard CSV interface requires that the file be already open when it's passed in, so if our framework follows the same interface, we have no control over the encoding. The only way to control it would be to change the interface to accept a filename rather than an open file object.

One common variation in CSV files is whether they contain a header row, containing titles for the various columns. Because we'll be defining columns as fields later on in the framework, we don't really need that header row, so we can skip it. But only if we know it's there. A simple Boolean, defaulting to False for the more common case, will do the trick nicely:

```
class Options:
    """

    A container for options that control how a CSV file should be handled when
    converting it to a set of objects.
    has_header_row
        A Boolean indicating whether the file has a row containing header
        values. If True, that row will be skipped when looking for data.
        Defaults to False.
    """

    def __init__(self, has_header_row=False):
        self.has_header_row = has_header_row
```

There we have a simple, but useful, options container. At this point the only benefit it has over a dictionary is that it automatically prohibits any options other than the ones we've specified. We'll come back and add a more rigorous validation method later.

If you're familiar with Python's csv module, you may already know that it contains a variety of options as part of its support for different dialects. Because sheets will actually defer to that module for much of its functionality, it makes sense to support all of the same options, in addition to our own. In fact, it even makes sense to rename our Options class Dialect instead, to better reflect the vocabulary already in use.

Rather than listing all of the options supported by csv separately, however, let's take a bit more forward-thinking approach. We're relying on code outside our control, and it's a bit of a maintenance hassle to try to keep up with any changes that code might introduce in the future. In particular, we can support any existing options as well as any future options, by simply passing any additional options straight to csv itself.

In order to accept options without naming them, we turn to Python's support for extra keyword arguments using the double-asterisk syntax. These extra options can be stored away as a dictionary, which will be passed into the csv functions later on. Accepting them as a group of keyword arguments rather than a single dictionary helps unify all of the options, which will be important once we actually parse options out of the class declaration:

```
class Dialect:
    """

    A container for dialect options that control how a CSV file should be
    handled when converting it to a set of objects.

    has_header_row
        A Boolean indicating whether the file has a row containing header
        values. If True, that row will be skipped when looking for data.
        Defaults to False.

    For a list of additional options that can be passed in, see documentation
    for the dialects and formatting parameters of Python's csv module at
    http://docs.python.org/library/csv.html#dialects-and-formatting-parameters
    """
```

```
def __init__(self, has_header_row=False, **kwargs):
    self.has_header_row = has_header_row
    self.csv_dialect = kwargs
```

This class will grow some more features later on, but that's enough to get things started. We'll come back to it a few more times before we're done, but for now, let's move on to what may well be the meatiest part of our little framework: fields.

Defining Fields

Fields are generally just containers for specific pieces of data. Because it's such a generic term, different disciplines may use something more specific to refer to the same concept. In databases, they're called columns. In forms, they're often called inputs. When executing a function or a program, they're called arguments. To maintain some perspective beyond this one framework, this chapter will refer to all such data containers as fields, even though for sheets itself, the term "column" will make more sense when naming the individual classes.

The first thing to define is a base field class, which will describe what it means to be a field. Without any details of any particular data type, this base class manages how fields fit in with the rest of the system, what API they'll have, and how subclasses are expected to behave. Because our framework is calling them columns, we'll start a new module called columns.py and get to work.

Fields are Python objects that are instantiated as part of the class declaration and assigned as attributes of the class. Therefore, the __init__() method is the first entry point into field functionality and the only point where the field can be configured as part of the declaration. Arguments to __init__() may vary depending on a field's type, but there are often at least a few arguments that are applicable to all fields, and can thus be processed by the base class.

First, each field can have a title. This allows for more readable and understandable code but also provides a way for other tools to automatically document the fields with more useful information than just the field's attribute name. Planning for validation wouldn't hurt, so we'll also add a way to indicate whether the field is required:

```
class Column:
    """

    An individual column within a CSV file. This serves as a base for attributes
    and methods that are common to all types of columns. Subclasses of Column
    will define behavior for more specific data types.
    """

    def __init__(self, title=None, required=True):
        self.title = title
        self.required = required
```

Notice that the title is optional. If no title is provided, a simple one can be gleaned from the attribute name the field is assigned to. Unfortunately, the field doesn't know what that name is yet, so we'll have to come back for that functionality later. We also assume that most fields will be required, so that's the default, to be overridden on a per-field basis.

Tip   Required fields may not immediately seem to have much value for a CSV framework, since the data comes from files rather than directly from users, but they can be useful. For some things like sheets, it can eventually validate incoming files or the data that's about to be saved to an outgoing file. It's generally a good feature to include at the outset for any framework, to support features that can be added later.

You may already have other arguments in mind for your framework's fields. If so, feel free to add them in now, following the same basic pattern. Don't worry about planning for everything at the outset, though; there will be plenty of opportunity to add more later on. Next on the agenda is to get the fields properly connected to their associated classes.

Attaching a Field to a Class

We need to set up the hook for getting additional data from the class the field is assigned to, including the field's name. This new `attach_to_class()` method is—as its name suggests—responsible for attaching the field to the class where it was assigned. Even though Python automatically adds the attributes to the class where they're assigned, that assignment doesn't convey anything to the attribute, so we'll have to do so in the metaclass.

First, we need to decide what information the attribute needs to know about how it was assigned. After preparing for a title in the previous section, it's clear that the attribute will need to know what name it was given when assigned. By obtaining that name directly in code, we can avoid the trouble of having to write the name out separately as an argument to the attribute instantiation.

The long-term flexibility of the framework will also depend on providing as much information as possible to attributes, so that they can easily provide advanced functionality by introspecting the classes they're attached to. Unfortunately, the name alone doesn't say anything about the class where the attribute now resides, so we'll have to provide that in the metaclass as well.

Finally, the options that were defined earlier, such as `encoding`, will have some bearing on the attribute's behavior. Rather than expecting the attribute to have to retrieve those options based on the class that was passed in, it's easier to simply accept the options as another argument. This leaves us with an `attach_to_class()` that looks something like this:

```
class Column:
    """
    An individual column within a CSV file. This serves as a base for attributes
    and methods that are common to all types of columns. Subclasses of Column
    will define behavior for more specific data types.
    """

    def __init__(self, title=None, required=True):
        self.title = title
        self.required = required
```

```
    def attach_to_class(self, cls, name, options):
        self.cls = cls
        self.name = name
        self.options = options
```

This alone will allow other methods of the attribute object to access a wealth of information, such as the name of the class, what other attributes and methods were declared on it, what module it was defined in and more. The first task we'll need to perform with that information is somewhat more mundane, however, as we still need to deal with the title. If no title was specified when the attribute was created, this method can use the name to define one:

```
class Column:
    """
    An individual column within a CSV file. This serves as a base for attributes
    and methods that are common to all types of columns. Subclasses of Column
    will define behavior for more specific data types.
    """

    def __init__(self, title=None, required=True):
        self.title = title
        self.required = required
    def attach_to_class(self, cls, name, options):
        self.cls = cls
        self.name = name
        self.options = options
        if self.title is None:
            # Check for None so that an empty string will skip this behavior
            self.title = name.replace('_', ' ')
```

This addition takes an attribute name with underscores and converts it to a title using multiple words. We could impose other conventions, but this is simple enough to work with, accurate for most situations, and fits in with common naming conventions. This simple approach will cover most use cases without being difficult to understand or maintain.

As the comment indicates, the `if` test for this new feature goes against standard idioms by explicitly checking for `None` rather than simply letting an unspecified title evaluate to `False`. Doing things the "right" way here would remove the ability to specify an empty string as a title, which can explicitly indicate that no title is necessary.

Checking for `None` allows empty strings to still retain that string as the title, rather than having it replaced by the attribute name. One example of the usefulness of an empty title would be as a way to indicate that the column doesn't need to be presented in a display of the file's data. It's also a good example of where comments can be crucial to understanding the intent of a piece of code.

Tip   Even though this `attach_to_class()` method doesn't use the options that were provided, it's generally a good idea to include it in the protocol. The next section will show that the options will be available as an attribute of the class, but it's a bit more clear to pass it in as its own argument. If your framework needs to apply these class-level options to individual fields, it'll be easier to accept it as an argument than to extract it form the class.

Adding a Metaclass

With the `attach_to_class()` method in place, we must now move on to the other side of the equation. After all, `attach_to_class()` can only receive information; the metaclass is responsible for providing that information. Until now, we haven't even started looking at the metaclass for this framework, so we need to start with the basics.

All metaclasses start out the same, by subclassing `type`. In this case, we'll also add an `__init__()` method because all we need is to process the contents of the class definition after Python has finished with them. First up, the metaclass needs to identify any options that were defined in the class and create a new `Dialect` object to hold them. There are a few ways to go about this.

The most obvious option would be to simply define options as class-level attributes. That would make defining the individual classes easy later on, but it would impose some problems that may not be as obvious. For one, it would clutter up the main class namespace. If you tried to create a class to process CSV files containing information about coded documents, you might reasonably have a column named `encoding`. Because we also have a class option named `encoding`, we'd have to name our column something else in order to avoid one of them overwriting the other and causing problems.

On a more practical note, it's easier to pick out options if they're contained in their own namespace. By being able to easily identify which attributes are options, we can pass them all in as arguments to `Dialect` and immediately know if any were missing or if invalid names were specified. So the task now is to determine how to provide a new namespace for options, while still declaring them as part of the main class.

The simplest solution is to use an inner class. Alongside any other attributes and methods, we can add a new class, named `Dialect`, to contain the various option assignments. This way, we can let Python create and manage the extra namespace for us, so that all we have to do is look for the name `Dialect` in the attribute list and pull it out.

Tip   Even though the inner `Dialect` class inhabits the main namespace alongside other attributes and methods, there's much less chance of a clash because it's only one name instead of several. Furthermore, we use a name that starts with a capital letter, which is discouraged for attribute and method names, so that there's even less chance of collision. Because Python names are case-sensitive, you're free to define an attribute called `dialect` (note the small "d") on the class without fear of bumping into this `Dialect` class.

To extract this new `Dialect` class, we'll turn to the first implementation of a metaclass in this framework. Because this will help form the base class for future inheritance, we'll put the code into a new module, named `base.py`:

```python
from sheets import options

class RowMeta(type):
    def __init__(cls, name, bases, attrs):
        if 'Dialect' in attrs:
            # Filter out Python's own additions to the namespace
            items = attrs['Dialect'].__dict__.items()
            items = dict((k, v) for (k, v) in items if not k.startswith('__'))
        else:
            # No dialect options were explicitly defined
            items = {}
        dialect = options.Dialect(**items)
```

Now that the options have been pulled out of the class definition and have populated a `Dialect` object, we'll need to do something with that new object. We know from the definition of `attach_to_class()` in the previous section that it gets passed into that method for each field attribute that was defined, but what else?

In the spirit of retaining as much information as possible for later, we'll keep it assigned to the class itself. But because the capitalized name doesn't work as well as an attribute name, it's best to rename it to something more suitable. Because it also forms a private interface to the inner workings of the framework, we can prefix the new name with an underscore to further prevent any accidental name clashes:

```
from sheets import options

class RowMeta(type):
    def __init__(cls, name, bases, attrs):
        if 'Dialect' in attrs:
            # Filter out Python's own additions to the namespace
            items = attrs.pop('Dialect').__dict__.items()
            items = {k: v for k, v in items if not k.startswith('__')}
        else:
            # No dialect options were explicitly defined
            items = {}
        cls._dialect = options.Dialect(**items)
```

This simple change removes it from the class namespace where it was given the original name and instead inserts it under a new name, `_dialect`. Both names avoid clashes with common attribute names, but this change makes it use a more standard private attribute name. Previously, it used the standard style for naming a class because that's how it's defined.

With that, we finally have all the pieces in places to continue working with the field attributes. The first task is to locate them in the class definition and call `attach_to_class()` on any that are found. This is easily accomplished with a simple loop through the attributes:

```
from sheets import options

class RowMeta(type):
    def __init__(cls, name, bases, attrs):
        if 'Dialect' in attrs:
            # Filter out Python's own additions to the namespace
            items = attrs.pop('Dialect').__dict__.items()
            items = {k: v for k, v in items if not k.startswith('__')}
        else:
            # No dialect options were explicitly defined
            items = {}
        cls._dialect = options.Dialect(**items)

        for key, attr in attrs.items():
            if hasattr(attr, 'attach_to_class'):
                attr.attach_to_class(cls, key, cls._dialect)
```

This simple metaclass contains a loop that just checks each attribute to see if it has an attach_to_class() method. If it does, the method is called, passing in the class object and the name of the attribute. This way all the columns can get the information they need very early on in the process.

DUCK TYPING

This metaclass uses hasattr() to check for the existence of an attach_to_class() method, rather than simply checking to see if the attribute is an instance of Column. All instances of Column should indeed have the necessary method, but by using hasattr() instead, we open it up for any type of object. You could add attach_to_class() to other types of attributes, descriptors, and even methods and gain quick and easy access to more advanced functionality. The metaclass only checks for precisely what it needs, leaving the rest open for flexibility, which is a primary benefit of duck typing. The name is from the concept of the application of the well-known *duck test*, which states "If it waddles like a duck and quacks like a duck, then it must be a duck," to determine if an object should be used.

Now all that's necessary to fill out the rest of base.py is to include a true base class that individual CSV definitions can subclass. Because each subclass is a single row in a spreadsheet, we can name the base class Row to indicate its purpose. All it needs to do at the moment is include RowMeta as its metaclass, and it'll automatically get the necessary behavior:

```
#in base.py
class Row(metaclass=RowMeta):
    pass
```

Bringing It Together

Technically, all the pieces are now in place to demonstrate at least the basics of a working system, but there's still one important piece to take care of. Currently we have three different modules, each with some of the parts that need to be exposed in a public API. Ideally, all of the important bits should be available from one central import instead of three or potentially even more.

If you haven't already, create an __init__.py module in the same directory as the other scripts mentioned so far. That file can be empty and still have the ability to import all the packages individually, but with a little effort, it can be put to better use. Because this is the file imported when simply importing the package name directly, we can use that as a trigger to pull in the useful bits from all the other files:

Open up __init__.py and put this code in it:

```
from sheets.base import *
from sheets.options import *
from sheets.columns import *
```

> **Note**   Ordinarily, using an asterisk to import everything is a bad idea because it can make it more difficult to identify what came from where. Because this module is only importing code and not doing anything with it, that problem doesn't really apply. As long as the package is imported on its own, such as `import sheets`, there won't be any confusion as to where the objects come from. And because we don't have to mention any of the objects by name, this will hold for anything we may add to those modules as well.

Now we have enough working parts to show that the framework can function, at least at a very basic level. If we create an `example.py` one directory up from the framework code itself, so that `sheets` is on the PYTHONPATH, we can now create a class that does some very simple work to show that it's starting to come together:

```python
import sheets

class Example(sheets.Row):
    title = sheets.Column()
    description = sheets.Column()

if __name__ == '__main__':
    print(Example._dialect)
    print(Example.title)
```

All this really does so far is allow us to name the columns, however. In order to line them up with data in CSV files, we need to know the order in which the fields were defined in the class.

Ordering Fields

As it stands, the fields are all available as attributes of the class itself. This allows you to get some information about individual fields, but only if you know the name of the field. Without a name, you'd have to inspect all the attributes on the class and check which of them are instances of `Column` or its subclasses. Even if you do that, however, you still don't know the order in which they were defined, so it's impossible to line them up with data from a CSV file.

In order to address both of those issues we need to set up a list of columns, where each of the columns can be stored in the order in which it was defined. But first we need to be able to identify that order at runtime, without the benefit of being able to ask the developer. There are at least three different ways to do this, each with its own benefits.

DeclarativeMeta.__prepare__()

Chapter 4 showed that metaclasses can control the behavior of the class namespace while Python is processing the block of code that makes up the class definition. By including a __prepare__() method on the declarative metaclass—in this case, RowMeta—we can provide an ordered dictionary, which can then keep the order of attribute assignments itself. It's as simple as importing an ordered dictionary implementation and returning it from a custom __prepare__() method:

```python
from collections import OrderedDict

from sheets import options

class RowMeta(type):
    def __init__(cls, name, bases, attrs):
        if 'Dialect' in attrs:
            # Filter out Python's own additions to the namespace
            items = attrs.pop('Dialect').__dict__.items()
            items = {k: v for k, v in items if not k.startswith('__')}
        else:
            # No dialect options were explicitly defined
            items = {}

        cls._dialect = options.Dialect(**items)
        for key, attr in attrs.items():
            if hasattr(attr, 'attach_to_class'):
                attr.attach_to_class(cls, key, cls._dialect)

    @classmethod
    def __prepare__(self, name, bases):
        return OrderedDict()
```

411

That only gets us part of the way, however. Now the namespace dictionary contains all the class attributes, and it knows the order in which they were defined, but it doesn't address the issue of having a simple list of just the CSV columns. The namespace dictionary will also hold all the methods and other miscellaneous attributes that were defined, so we'll still need to grab the columns out of it and put them into another list.

One obvious way to do that would be to look at each attribute in the dictionary and check to see whether it's a column or not. That's the same process mentioned earlier in this section, but the difference now is that you can hide the complexity inside the metaclass.

Because __init__() runs after the entire body has been processed, its `attrs` argument will be an ordered dictionary containing all the attributes. All that's left is to loop over them and pull out any columns that were found. Again, in the spirit of duck typing, we'll use the presence of `attach_to_class()` to determine which attributes are columns. In fact, we can use the existing loop and just inject the new code into the inner `if` block.

In order to use it in the real world it will need to be placed somewhere more useful, such as the `Dialect` object stored in the `_dialect` attribute of the class. Rather than simply assigning a list externally, it makes more sense to have `Dialect` manage that itself by giving it an `add_column()` method that we can call from the metaclass instead:

```python
class Dialect:
    """
    A container for dialect options that control how a CSV file should be
    handled when converting it to a set of objects.

    has_header_row
        A Boolean indicating whether the file has a row containing header
        values. If True, that row will be skipped when looking for data.
        Defaults to False.

    For a list of additional options that can be passed in, see documentation
    for the dialects and formatting parameters of Python's csv module at
    http://docs.python.org/library/csv.html#dialects-and-formatting-parameters
    """

    def __init__(self, has_header_row=False, **kwargs):
```

```
    self.has_header_row = has_header_row
    self.csv_dialect = kwargs
    self.columns = []

def add_column(self, column):
    self.columns.append(column)
```

Now that `Dialect` knows how to keep a record of fields, it's only a small matter
to change `RowMeta` to add the columns to the dialect as they're found. Because the
namespace is already sorted according to when the attributes were assigned, we can
be sure that they'll be attached to the class in the right order. Thus, we can simply add a
quick call to the dialect's `add_column()` in the column's `attach_to_class()` method:

```
class Column:
    """

    An individual column within a CSV file. This serves as a base for attributes
    and methods that are common to all types of columns. Subclasses of Column
    will define behavior for more specific data types.
    """
    def __init__(self, title=None, required=True):
        self.title = title
        self.required = required

    def attach_to_class(self, cls, name, dialect):
        self.cls = cls
        self.name = name
        self.dialect = dialect
        if self.title is None:
            # Check for None so that an empty string will skip this behavior
            self.title = name.replace('_', ' ')
        dialect.add_column(self)
```

Note   This example also changes the name of the `options` attribute to `dialect`
instead, to be consistent with the rest of the framework.

413

Now our code has an easy way to get at the columns that were provided to the class, in their original order. There's one fairly significant flaw with it, however: the __prepare__() technique is only available in Python starting with version 3.0. Because there was no equivalent functionality before then, any older versions will need to use a completely different approach to the problem.

We can make use of a basic principle of Python's class processing: the body of a class is executed as a block of code. That means that each of the column attributes are instantiated in the order they were written in the class definition. The Column class already has a block of code that runs when the attribute is instantiated, which can be extended a bit to keep track of each instantiation.

Column.__init__()

The most obvious choice is where we already have code: the __init__() method. It gets called for each Column object as it is instantiated, so it makes a convenient place to keep track of the order those objects are encountered. The actual process is fairly simple. All it takes is a counter that can be maintained in one place regardless of which column is being processed, and a small bit of code to increment that counter every time a new column is found:

```python
class Column:
    """
    An individual column within a CSV file. This serves as a base for attributes
    and methods that are common to all types of columns. Subclasses of Column
    will define behavior for more specific data types.
    """
    # This will be updated for each column that's instantiated.
    counter = 0
    def __init__(self, title=None, required=True):
        self.title = title
        self.required = required
        self.counter = Column.counter
        Column.counter += 1
```

```
def attach_to_class(self, cls, name, dialect):
    self.cls = cls
    self.name = name
    self.dialect = dialect
    if self.title is None:
        # Check for None so that an empty string will skip this behavior
        self.title = name.replace('_', ' ')
    dialect.add_column(self)
```

This code handles part of the problem. Now, each column has a `counter` attribute that indicates its position among the rest.

SIMPLE IS BETTER THAN COMPLEX

Actually, that counter will be maintained across *all* columns, regardless of which class they're assigned to. Even though that's technically a bit of overkill, it doesn't actually hurt anything. Each group of columns will still be ordered appropriately among its peers, so they can be sorted properly without a problem. More important, resetting the counter for each class would significantly complicate the code.

First, we'd need a separate counter for each class that can have columns attached to it. Columns don't know about which class they're assigned to until `attach_to_class()` is called, so we'd have to put some code in there to determine when a new class is being processed. But because that takes place after the counter was already incremented in `__init__()`, it would need to reset the counter while assigning it to a new location for the new class.

It's definitely possible to keep a separate counter for each individual class, but doing so doesn't really add anything to the process. Because the simpler form is just as functional for most cases, the added complexity just isn't worth it. If you have a long-running process that creates Row subclasses dynamically on a regular basis, it's possible the counter will overflow and cause problems. In such a case, you'll need to take these additional steps to make sure everything continues to work properly.

The next step is to use that counter to force the ordering of the columns as they're stored on the Dialect object. In the __prepare__() approach the namespace handled the ordering on its own, so there wasn't anything else to do. Here we need to sort the list of fields explicitly, using the counter attribute to determine the order.

We can't do it right away in __init__() because that gets a dictionary of all the attributes, not just the columns. It doesn't know which attributes are columns until they're processed using their attach_to_class() methods. Sorting the list after processing all the columns with attach_to_class() instead would provide a complete list of just columns in the correct order. Here's what you'll need to add to the RowMeta class:

```
from sheets import options

class RowMeta(type):
    def __init__(cls, name, bases, attrs):
        if 'Dialect' in attrs:
            # Filter out Python's own additions to the namespace
            items = attrs.pop('Dialect').__dict__.items()
            items = {k: v for k, v in items if not k.startswith('__')}
        else:
            # No dialect options were explicitly defined
            items = {}
        cls._dialect = options.Dialect(**items)
        for key, attr in attrs.items():
            if hasattr(attr, 'attach_to_class'):
                attr.attach_to_class(cls, key, cls._dialect)
        # Sort the columns according to their order of instantiation
        cls._dialect.columns.sort(key=lambda column: column.counter)
```

This function call may look a little more complicated than it really is. It's just invoking a standard sort() operation but with a function that will be called to determine what value to use when sorting items. We could add a method to Column that just returns the counter and use that, but because it's only used here, a lambda function will do the same job inline.

SIMPLE IS BETTER THAN COMPLEX

Another option is to actually sort the list while processing `attach_to_class()`. The default `attach_to_class()` implementation shown previously already calls `add_column()` on the provided `Dialect` object, so that's a good place to do the job. Unfortunately, doing so requires a few extra steps. It doesn't make sense to try to sort the whole list every time a new column is added, but we can use the `bisect` module in the standard library to keep the order more efficiently.

The bisect module provides an `insort()` method, which inserts a new item into an existing sequence while preserving a useful order to those items. Unlike a standard `sort()`, however, this function doesn't accept a key argument but instead relies on comparing two items using the `<` operator. If one item compares as less than another, it gets placed further ahead in the sequence. That makes sense, but without the use of an explicit key, we'd need to implement an `__lt__()` method on the `Column` class to support `insort()`.

Sorting after the fact only requires one additional line of code, while trying to sort throughout would introduce another import and another method on the `Column` class. The only thing we'd gain by going that route is the ability to see the order of all the columns that have been processed so far, but because new columns may be placed anywhere within that order, it's not really that useful until all the columns have been processed. Therefore, it's best to keep things simple and just sort the list once afterward.

Most of the code that was added in this approach is necessary whenever `__prepare__()` isn't available, regardless of any other preferences. The only area where we really have any room to use a different approach is where the counter value is updated. There are a few different ways to go about managing that value.

So far we've used the `__init__()` method of the `Column` class because that's always called during instantiation and it already had a basic implementation anyway. The trouble is that many `__init__()` methods are only used to save argument values as attributes on the object, so programmers have come to expect similar behavior. Aside from managing the counter, our own `__init__()` method matches that expectation perfectly.

So if a programmer wants to write a new column that doesn't use any of the same arguments as the base `Column` class, it's easy to write an `__init__()` method that simply doesn't call `super()`. Without using `super()` to fire the original `__init__()` method, that new column won't be ordered properly. Its counter attribute will always be the same as whatever was processed right before it, so sort() won't be able to reliably determine where it belongs.

You could argue that the problem here is with the programmers' assumption that __init__() doesn't do anything of value, but that's not a very productive approach to the problem. There are still a couple of ways that we can try to make things easier for users of the frameworks that can help avoid problems if someone neglects to use super().

Column.__new__()

Thinking about instantiation without __init__(), the next clear choice is __new__(), which is called earlier in the process. Using __new__() provides a chance to do the same work without competing with __init__(), so they can be independent of each other. The initialization of the object can still take place in __init__(), leaving __new__() to manage the counter value:

```python
class Column:
    """
    An individual column within a CSV file. This serves as a base for attributes
    and methods that are common to all types of columns. Subclasses of Column
    will define behavior for more specific data types.
    """
    # This will be updated for each column that's instantiated.
    counter = 0
    def __new__(cls, *args, **kwargs):
        # Keep track of the order each column is instantiated
        obj = super(Column, cls).__new__(cls, *args, **kwargs)
        obj.counter = Column.counter
        Column.counter += 1
        return obj

    def __init__(self, title=None, required=True):
        self.title = title
        self.required = required
```

```
def attach_to_class(self, cls, name, dialect):
    self.cls = cls
    self.name = name
    self.dialect = dialect
    if self.title is None:
        # Check for None so that an empty string will skip this behavior
        self.title = name.replace('_', ' ')
dialect.add_column(self)
```

The code in __new__() grows a bit from what was used in __init__() previously because __new__() is responsible for creating and returning the new object. Therefore, we need to create the object explicitly before assigning the counter to it. Then, the method needs to explicitly return the new object in order for it to be accessible by anything else.

Using __new__() instead of __init__() is merely a way to reduce the odds of colliding with a custom implementation. It may be less likely, but it's still possible for a subclass to provide __new__() on its own, and doing so without using super() would still cause problems. There's still one other option that separates the counting behavior even further.

CounterMeta.__call__()

It is important to understand that there is also another method that gets called when instantiating a class. Technically the class object itself is being called as a function, which means that there's a __call__() method somewhere that would be called. Because __call__() is only executed as an instance method, but instantiation takes place when calling a class, we need to look at the class as an instance of something else: a *metaclass*.

That means that we can create a metaclass to support the counter functionality entirely outside the Column class. A simple CounterMeta class with a __call__() method can keep track of the counter on its own, and Column can then use that as its metaclass. The body of this method looks essentially just like __new__() because it's called as pretty much the same part of the process. It needs to create the object by using super() and return it explicitly:

```
class CounterMeta(type):
    """
    A simple metaclass that keeps track of the order that each instance
    of a given class was instantiated.
    """

    counter = 0

    def __call__(cls, *args, **kwargs):
        obj = super(CounterMeta, cls).__call__(*args, **kwargs)
        obj.counter = CounterMeta.counter
        CounterMeta.counter += 1
        return obj
```

Now that all of this functionality is isolated to a metaclass, the Column class gets a bit simpler. It can get rid of all the counter-handling code, including the entire __new__() method. All it needs now to maintain the counting behavior is to use CounterMeta as its metaclass:

```
class Column(metaclass=CounterMeta):
    """
    An individual column within a CSV file. This serves as a base for attributes
    and methods that are common to all types of columns. Subclasses of Column
    will define behavior for more specific data types.
    """

    def __init__(self, title=None, required=True):
        self.title = title
        self.required = required

    def attach_to_class(self, cls, name, dialect):
        self.cls = cls
        self.name = name
        self.dialect = dialect
```

```
    if self.title is None:
        # Check for None so that an empty string will skip this behavior
        self.title = name.replace('_', ' ')
dialect.add_column(self)
```

In fact, this `CounterMeta` is now capable of providing this counting behavior for any class that needs it. By simply applying the metaclass, every instance of the given class will have a `counter` attribute attached to it. Then you can use that counter to sort the instances according to when they were instantiated, just like the columns in the `sheets` framework.

Choosing an Option

Of the options presented here, it's not always easy to determine which to choose. With each layer of added flexibility comes added complexity, and it's always best to keep things as simple as possible. When working in a Python 3.x environment, `__prepare__()` is definitely the way to go. It doesn't require any additional classes to support it; it doesn't need to sort the list of columns after the fact; and it works without touching the `Column` class at all.

The options for earlier 2.x versions of Python are more subjective. Which one you choose depends largely on how much you expect of your target audience and how much complexity you're willing to allow into your code. The simpler solutions require more vigilance on the part of your users, so you'll need to decide what's most important.

Because this book is designed for use with Python 3.x, the remaining examples of the code will use `__prepare__()`. Of course, the ability to order a set of fields is only useful once you have a collection of fields to work with.

Building a Field Library

In most declarative frameworks, `sheets` included, a primary function of fields is to convert data between native Python objects and some other data format. In our case, the other format is a string contained in the CSV file, so we need a way to convert between those strings and the objects the fields represent. Before we get into the details of specific field types, we need to set up a couple methods for managing data conversion.

The first method, to_python(), takes a string from the file and converts that string into a native Python value. This step is performed for each column, every time a row is read in from the file, to ensure that you can work with the correct type of value in Python. Because that behavior will be different for various types, delegating to a method like to_python() allows you to change this specific behavior on individual classes without having to do so all on one Column class.

The second method is to_string(), which works as an inverse to to_python() and will be called when saving a CSV file with values assigned in Python. Because the csv module works with strings by default, this method is used to provide any special formatting required by a particular CSV format. Delegating to this method means that each column can have its own options to suit the data that belongs in that field.

Even though each type of data behaves differently, the base Column class can support a simple use case by default. The csv module only works with files that are opened in text mode, so Python's own file access manages the conversion to Unicode while reading data. That means the value that comes from csv is already a string and can be used easily:

```
class Column:
    """

    An individual column within a CSV file. This serves as a base for attributes
    and methods that are common to all types of columns. Subclasses of Column
    will define behavior for more specific data types.
    """
    def __init__(self, title=None, required=True):
        self.title = title
        self.required = required

    def attach_to_class(self, cls, name, dialect):
        self.cls = cls
        self.name = name
        self.dialect = dialect
        if self.title is None:
            # Check for None so that an empty string will skip this behavior
            self.title = name.replace('_', ' ')
        dialect.add_column(self)
```

```
def to_python(self, value):
    """
    Convert the given string to a native Python object.
    """
    return value
def to_string(self, value):
    """
    Convert the given Python object to a string.
    """
    return value
```

Now we can start implementing them for individual data types.

StringField

The most obvious field to start with is a string, because it can encompass any number of more specific forms of data. Titles, names, places, descriptions, and comments are just some examples of the more specific values you might find in these fields, but from a technical standpoint they all work the same way. The sheets framework doesn't have to care what form of strings you'll be dealing with, only that they are in fact all strings.

The csv module provides strings on its own, so this class doesn't really have to do much. In fact, to_python() and to_string() don't need any custom implementation at all because they only need to return what they're given. The most important thing that's offered by a StringColumn is actually the name itself.

By having an attribute that's named according to the type of data it interacts with, the attribute becomes somewhat self-documenting. Rather than just using a generic Column to describe how strings are passed back and forth, you can use a StringColumn to be clear about how it works:

```
class StringColumn(Column):
    """
    A column that contains data formatted as generic strings.
    """
    pass
```

In fact, you could even call the base class `StringColumn` instead of just `Column`, because it does the job on its own. Unfortunately that would cause its own confusion when subclassing it, by requiring something like an `IntegerColumn` to subclass `StringColumn`. To keep things clearer, the base class will remain `Column` and each subclass will add only the necessary features on top of it, even though there's nothing useful to add beyond the name.

IntegerColumn

The next field type to add manages integers. Numbers are used quite a bit in spreadsheets, storing everything from ages to sales figures to inventory counts. Much of the time, those numbers will be plain integers that can be converted easily using the built-in `int()` function:

```
class IntegerColumn(Column):
    """
    A column that contains data in the form of numeric integers.
    """

    def to_python(self, value):
        return int(value)
```

`IntegerColumn` doesn't actually need to implement a `to_string()` method because the `csv` module automatically calls `str()` on whatever value is given to it. Because that's all we'd do in a `to_string()` method anyway, we can just leave it out and let the framework handle that task. As you'll see with other columns, `to_string()` is most useful when the column can specify a more explicit format to use. Simply writing out a number doesn't require that much flexibility.

FloatColumn

Many numbers in spreadsheets have finer granularity than integers, requiring additional information to convey the value beyond the decimal point. Floating point numbers are a decent way to handle those values, and supporting them as a column is just as easy as it was with `IntegerColumn`. We can simply replace all the instances of `int` with `float` and be done:

```
class FloatColumn(Column):
    """
    A column that contains data in the form of floating point numbers.
    """
    def to_python(self, value):
        return float(value)
```

Of course, floating point numbers have their share of problems when it comes to viewing them or adding them together in many cases. This is caused by a lack of defined precision in the decimal point: it floats around according to how well a given value can be represented in code. To be more explicit and avoid things like rounding errors, we turn to `DecimalColumn`.

DecimalColumn

Like `FloatColumn`, this can work with numbers beyond just the integers. Instead of working with floating point numbers, however, `DecimalColumn` will rely on the functionality of the `decimal` module provided with Python. Decimal values preserve as much detail in the original number as possible, which helps prevent rounding errors. This makes decimals much more suitable for use with monetary spreadsheets.

In Python, decimals are provided using the `decimal` module, which provides a `Decimal` class to manage individual numbers. Therefore, `DecimalColumn` needs to convert numbers from text in CSV files to `Decimal` objects in Python and back again. Like floats, `Decimal` already converts to strings well enough on its own, so the only conversion `DecimalColumn` really needs to do is from strings to `Decimal` when reading values. Because Decimal is designed to work with strings, it's just as easy as the other columns shown so far:

```
import decimal

class DecimalColumn(Column):
    """
```

425

A column that contains data in the form of decimal values,
represented in Python by decimal.Decimal.
"""

```
def to_python(self, value):
    return decimal.Decimal(value)
```

There's one difference about this method from those in the other classes, however. Each of the others has the added side effect of raising a ValueError if the value can't be properly converted, which we can use later to support validation. Decimal does validate during instantiation, but it raises an exception from the decimal module, InvalidOperation. In order to match the behavior of the others, we'll need to catch that and reraise it as a ValueError:

```
import decimal

class DecimalColumn(Column):
    """
    A column that contains data in the form of decimal values,
    represented in Python by decimal.Decimal.
    """
    def to_python(self, value):
        try:
            return decimal.Decimal(value)
        except decimal.InvalidOperation as e:
            raise ValueError(str(e))
```

Even though DecimalColumn supports a more specialized data type, the code behind it is still fairly simple. Supporting dates, by contrast, requires some added complexity.

DateColumn

Dates are also extremely common in spreadsheet documents, storing everything from employee paydays and holidays to meeting agendas and attendance. Like decimal values, dates require the use of a separate class to provide a native Python data type, but there's one significant difference: dates don't have a universally accepted string representation. There are some standards that are fairly well established, but there are still plenty of variations, from the placement of the date components to the punctuation used to separate them.

In order to support the necessary flexibility, a new `DateColumn` would need to accept a format string during instantiation, which can be used to parse values from the file as well as construct strings to store in the file. Python dates already use a flexible format string syntax,[5] so there's no need to invent a new one just for `sheets`. In order to specify the format during instantiation, however, we'll need to override `__init__()`:

```
class DateColumn(Column):
    """

    A column that contains data in the form of dates,
    represented in Python by datetime.date.
    format
        A strptime()-style format string.
        See http://docs.python.org/library/datetime.html for details
    """
    def __init__(self, *args, format='%Y-%m-%d', **kwargs):
        super(DateColumn, self).__init__(*args, **kwargs)
        self.format = format
```

Notice that the format object has a default value, which makes it optional. It's usually best to provide defaults like this for field attributes so that users can get up and running quickly. The default value used here was chosen because it is fairly common and it places the values in order from the least specific to the most specific—from year to day, respectively. That helps reduce the ambiguity we might otherwise encounter across cultures that format dates differently. Because the goal is to work with existing data, however, it's always possible for a specific `Row` class to override this behavior with whatever format is used by a given file.

---

[5]See "strftime( ) and strptime ( ) Behavior," http://propython.com/datetime-formatting.

Now that the format is available on the DateColumn object, the next step, as it was for the others, is to make a to_python() method. Python's datetime object accepts each component of the date as a separate argument, but because to_python() only gets a string, we'll need another way to do it. The alternative comes in the form of a datetime class method called strptime().

The strptime() method accepts a string value as its first argument and a format string as its second. The value is then parsed according to the format string and a datetime object is returned. We don't actually need a full datetime, however, so we can also use that object's date() method to return just the date portion of the value as a date object:

```
import datetime

class DateColumn(Column):
    """
    A column that contains data in the form of dates,
    represented in Python by datetime.date.
    format
        A strptime()-style format string.
        See http://docs.python.org/library/datetime.html for details
    """
    def __init__(self, *args, format='%Y-%m-%d', **kwargs):
        super(DateColumn, self).__init__(*args, **kwargs)
        self.format = format

    def to_python(self, value):
        """
        Parse a string value according to self.format
        and return only the date portion.
        """
        return datetime.datetime.strptime(value, self.format).date()
```

Note   datetime is the name of the module as well as the name of the class, so that's why it's written twice.

There's a subtle problem with to_python() as it's written here, however. All the other column types so far can accept both a string and a native object as values in to_python(), but strptime() will fail with a TypeError if you pass in a date object instead of a string. In order to construct a row in Python and save it in a file, we'll need to be able to accept a datetime object here, which will be converted to a string later, when saving.

Because to_python() is supposed to return a native object, this is a very simple task. All it takes is checking whether the value passed in is already a date object. If it is, to_python() can simply return that without doing any more work. Otherwise, it can continue on with the conversion:

```
class DateColumn(Column):
    """
    A column that contains data in the form of dates,
    represented in Python by datetime.date.
    format
        A strptime()-style format string.
        See http://docs.python.org/library/datetime.html for details
    """
    def __init__(self, *args, format='%Y-%m-%d', **kwargs):
        super(DateColumn, self).__init__(*args, **kwargs)
        self.format = format

    def to_python(self, value):
        """
        Parse a string value according to self.format
        and return only the date portion.
        """
        if isinstance(value, datetime.date):
            return value
        return datetime.datetime.strptime(value, self.format).date()
```

Writing the to_python() method was actually the most troublesome part of the DateColumn class. Converting an existing date value to a string is even simpler because there's an instance method, strftime(), available to do the job. It just accepts a format and returns a string containing the formatted value:

```python
import datetime

class DateColumn(Column):
    """
    A column that contains data in the form of dates,
    represented in Python by datetime.date.
    format
        A strptime()-style format string.
        See http://docs.python.org/library/datetime.html for details
    """
    def __init__(self, *args, format='%Y-%m-%d', **kwargs):
        super(DateColumn, self).__init__(*args, **kwargs)
        self.format = format
    def to_python(self, value):
        """
        Parse a string value according to self.format
        and return only the date portion.
        """
        if isinstance(value, datetime.date):
            return value
        return datetime.datetime.strptime(value, self.format).date()
    def to_string(self, value):
        """
        Format a date according to self.format and return that as a string.
        """
        return value.strftime(self.format)
```

Tip   A useful way to remember the difference between the two method names is that p stands for "parse" and f stands for "format."

We could go on adding more and more fields, but the ones shown here cover the basic forms of data found in most CSV files, as well as most of the techniques necessary to build your own field attributes in a declarative framework. Next, we'll need to set up the CSV functionality in order to bring these data types to life.

Getting Back to CSV

So far this chapter has been fairly generic, showing tools and techniques that can be applied to any variety of declarative class frameworks. In order to put them to real-world use, we need to get back to the problem of parsing CSV files. Much of the work done in this section will also be applicable to other frameworks, but will be presented in a way specific to CSV.

The first thing to do is take a look at how Python's own csv module works. There's no sense completely reinventing the wheel. It's important to understand the existing interface so that we can match it as closely as possible. The csv module's functionality is provided in two basic object types: readers and writers.

Readers and writers are configured in similar ways. They both accept a file argument, an optional dialect, and any number of keyword arguments that specify individual dialect parameters to override the main dialect. The main difference between readers and writers is that readers require a file to be opened for read access and writers require write access.

For readers, the file argument is typically a file object but may in fact be any iterable object that yields a single string for each iteration. Because the csv module also handles more complex newline usage, such as newlines encoded within a value, you should always open the file with the argument newline=" to make sure Python's own newline handling doesn't get in the way. In the next example, make sure that you have the example.csv file in the directory you are running this from:

```
>>> import csv
>>> reader = csv.reader(open('example.csv', newline="))
```

Once instantiated for use with a particular file and dialect, a CSV reader object has an extremely simple interface: it's an iterable object. Iterating over a reader will yield each row in the CSV file as a data structure that's usable outside the `csv` module. The standard `csv.reader` yields a list of values for each row, because the only thing it knows about is the position of each value in the row.

A more advanced options is `csv.DictReader`, which also accepts a sequence of column names during instantiation, so that each row can be produced as a dictionary. Our framework goes even further, yielding an object with each value from the file converted to a native Python data type and made available as an attribute.

Writer objects, by contrast, are slightly more complex. Because simple iteration only allows reading values, rather than writing them, writers rely on a couple of methods to do the necessary work. The first, `writerow()`, writes out a single row to the file, as its name suggests. Its companion, `writerows()`, accepts a sequence of rows, which will be written to the file in the order they're found in the sequence.

Exactly what constitutes a row will differ based on what type of writer is used. As with readers, the `csv` module provides some different options. The standard `csv.writer` accepts a simple sequence of values for each row, placing each value on the row in the position it's found in the list. The more complex `DictWriter` accepts a dictionary, which uses the sequence of column names passed in during instantiation to determine where in the row each value should be written.

The interface for working with our framework should look as much as possibly like the interfaces to these standard readers and writers. A `sheets` reader should be an iterable object that yields instances of the custom class where all the column attributes were defined. Likewise, the writer should accept instances of that same class. In both cases, the order of the column attributes in the class definition will be used to determine where the values go.

One key factor of both the reader and the writer, however, is the notion of a row object. So far, we don't have any such object for the sheets framework, so we need to create one. As a class-based framework, `sheets` is already well equipped to build an object that can represent a row. The columns and dialect are already defined on a class, so the ideal way to create an object would be to simply instantiate that class with a set of values. This will bring in aspects of the dialect and column classes described in earlier sections in order to produce a usable object.

The obvious place to implement this behavior is __init__(), but from there things get a little tricky. The first question is how to accept the values that will populate the attributes. Because we don't yet know anything about the layout of any particular Row subclass, we'll have to accept all arguments and deal with the requirements in the __init__() method itself.

Checking Arguments

As with any function, arguments to __init__() can be passed positionally or by keyword, but that decision has particular impact here because the object can be instantiated in one of two ways. When instantiating from a CSV file, as the next section will show, it's easiest to pass the values in positionally. When building an instance manually, however, it's highly convenient to be able to pass values in by keyword as well. Therefore, it's best to accept all positional and keyword arguments and manage them internally.

Two cases of invalid arguments are clear at the outset: too many positional arguments and keyword arguments that don't match any column names. Each of these cases requires a separate bit of code to support it, but they're both fairly easy to work with. For the positional case, we can simply check the number of arguments against the number of columns:

```
class Row(metaclass=RowMeta):
    def __init__(self, *args, **kwargs):
        # First, make sure the arguments make sense
        if len(args) > len(self._dialect.columns):
            msg = "__init__() takes at most %d arguments (%d given)"
            raise TypeError(msg % (len(self._dialect.columns), len(args)))
```

That takes care of the case where too many positional arguments are passed in, using the same error message Python would issue when the arguments are defined explicitly. The next step is to make sure that all of the provided keyword arguments match up with existing column names. This is easy to test by cycling through the keyword argument names and checking to see if each is also present in the list of column names.

Because the dialect only stores a list of columns, and not the list of column names, it's easiest to make a new list of column names here before testing them. Additional code to be added to __init__() later will also make use of this new list, so it's best to create it now:

```
class Row(metaclass=RowMeta):
    def __init__(self, *args, **kwargs):
        # First, make sure the arguments make sense
        column_names = [column.name for column in self._dialect.columns]
        if len(args) > len(column_names):
            msg = "__init__() takes at most %d arguments (%d given)"
            raise TypeError(msg % (len(column_names), len(args)))
        for name in kwargs:
            if name not in column_names:
                msg = "__init__() got an unexpected keyword argument '%s'"
                raise TypeError(msg % name)
```

That takes care of the obvious cases, but there's still one situation not yet covered: keyword arguments that target columns that also have positional arguments. To address this concern, we'll look at the behavior of Python itself. When confronted with an argument passed positionally and by keyword, Python raises a TypeError, rather than be forced to decide which of the two values to use:

```
>>> def example(x):
...     return x
...
>>> example(1)
1
>>> example(x=1)
1
```

```
>>> example(1, x=1)
Traceback (most recent call last):
  ...
TypeError: example() got multiple values for keyword argument 'x'
```

Providing that same behavior of our own __init__() is a bit more complex than the previous examples, but it's still fairly straightforward. We just need to look at each of the positional arguments and check whether there's a keyword argument matching the corresponding column name.

A useful shortcut for situations like this is to use a slice on the column name array to get only as many names as there are positional arguments. This way, we don't have to look through more names than necessary, and it eliminates the separate step of having to look up the column name by index inside the loop:

```
class Row(metaclass=RowMeta):
    def __init__(self, *args, **kwargs):
        # First, make sure the arguments make sense
        column_names = [column.name for column in self._dialect.columns]

        if len(args) > len(column_names):
            msg = "__init__() takes at most %d arguments (%d given)"
            raise TypeError(msg % (len(column_names), len(args)))

        for name in kwargs:
            if name not in column_names:
                msg = "__init__() got an unexpected keyword argument '%s'"
                raise TypeError(msg % name)

        for name in column_names[:len(args)]:
            if name in kwargs:
                msg = "__init__() got multiple values for keyword argument '%s'"
                raise TypeError(msg % name)
```

With all the argument checking out of the way, __init__() can continue on with certainty that no invalid arguments were provided. From here, we can use those arguments to populate the values on the object itself.

Populating Values

There are actually two steps involved in populating the values on the object. The first is due to __init__() accepting both positional and keyword arguments. By offering both options, we now have arguments in two separate locations: args and kwargs. In order to set the values in one pass, we'll need to combine them into a single structure.

Ideally, that structure would be a dictionary because it combines the names and values, so we'll need to move positional arguments into the dictionary already provided by kwargs. For that, we'll need an index for each of the values passed in positionally and a reference to the corresponding column name, so the value can be assigned to the right name.

The last check from the previous section already provides that loop, so we can reuse that block to assign the value to kwargs. The only change we need to make to the loop is to use enumerate() to get the index of each column as well as its name. That index can then be used to get the value from args:

```
class Row(metaclass=RowMeta):
    def __init__(self, *args, **kwargs):
        # First, make sure the arguments make sense
        column_names = [column.name for column in self._dialect.columns]
        if len(args) > len(column_names):
            msg = "__init__() takes at most %d arguments (%d given)"
            raise TypeError(msg % (len(column_names), len(args)))
        for name in kwargs:
            if name not in column_names:
                msg = "__init__() got an unexpected keyword argument '%s'"
                raise TypeError(msg % name)
        for i, name in enumerate(column_names[:len(args)]):
            if name in kwargs:
                msg = "__init__() got multiple values for keyword argument '%s'"
                raise TypeError(msg % name)
            kwargs[name] = args[i]
```

Now, kwargs has all the values passed into the constructor, each mapped to the appropriate column name. Next, we'll need to convert those values to the appropriate Python values before assigning them to the object. To do that we'll need the actual column objects, rather than just the list of names we've been working with so far.

There's still one minor issue to consider. Looping through the columns gets us all the columns that were defined for the class, but kwargs only contains the values that were passed into the object. We'll need to decide what to do for columns that don't have a value available. When pulling in data from a CSV file, this won't usually be a problem because every row in the file should have an entry for each column. But when populating an object in Python, to be saved in a file later, it's often useful to assign the attributes after instantiating the object.

Therefore, the most flexible approach here is to simply assign None to any of the columns that don't have a value. Checking for required fields can be performed as a separate step later, when we get to validating fields for other things as well. For now, assigning None will work just fine:

```python
class Row(metaclass=RowMeta):
    def __init__(self, *args, **kwargs):
        # First, make sure the arguments make sense
        column_names = [column.name for column in self._dialect.columns]
        if len(args) > len(column_names):
            msg = "__init__() takes at most %d arguments (%d given)"
            raise TypeError(msg % (len(column_names), len(args)))
        for name in kwargs:
            if name not in column_names:
                msg = "__init__() got an unexpected keyword argument '%s'"
                raise TypeError(msg % name)
        for i, name in enumerate(column_names[:len(args)]):
            if name in kwargs:
                msg = "__init__() got multiple values for keyword argument '%s'"
                raise TypeError(msg % name)
            kwargs[name] = args[i]
```

```
# Now populate the actual values on the object
for column in self._dialect.columns:
    try:
        value = column.to_python(kwargs[column.name])
    except KeyError:
        # No value was provided
        value = None
    setattr(self, column.name, value)
```

With this functionality finally in place, you can see the Row class in action on its own. It's now capable of managing a set of columns, accepting values as inputs, converting them to Python objects while loading, and assigning those values to the appropriate attributes:

```
>>> import sheets
>>> class Author(sheets.Row):
...     name = sheets.StringColumn()
...     birthdate = sheets.DateColumn()
...     age = sheets.IntegerColumn()
...
>>> ex = Author('Marty Alchin', birthdate='1981-12-17', age='28')
>>> ex.name
'Marty Alchin'
>>> ex.birthdate
datetime.date(1981, 12, 17)
>>> ex.age
28
```

Now we can finally implement the code to actually interact with CSV files.

The Reader

Using the `csv` module directly, you obtain a reader by instantiating a class and passing in a file and the necessary configuration options. The sheets framework allows each custom Row class to specify all the columns and dialect parameters directly on the class, so that now contains everything we need. The direct analogy with `csv` would be to pass a file and a Row class into a function that then returns a reader object capable of reading the file.

The trouble with that approach is that it requires any code that wants to use the reader to import the `sheets` module in order to get the function that creates the reader object. Instead, we can get by with just the Row class itself by providing a class method that can do the necessary work. Then, the only argument that method needs to accept is the file to read. To match the existing `csv` naming conventions, we'll call this new method `reader()`.

In order to work like the standard readers, our own `reader()` will need to return an iterable object that yields a row for each iteration. That's a simple requirement to fulfill, and it can be done without even involving any new objects. Remember that generator functions actually return an iterable object when they're first called. The body of a generator is then executed on each iteration of a loop, which makes an ideal way to support a CSV reader.

In order to get the values from a CSV file, `reader()` can rely on the existing `csv` module's own reader functionality. The standard `csv.reader` returns a list for each row in the file, regardless of what the actual values mean or what their names should be. Because a row class can already process arguments that are stored in sequences such as lists, it's very simple to bind the two together:

```
import csv

class Row(metaclass=RowMeta):
    def __init__(self, *args, **kwargs):
        # First, make sure the arguments make sense
        column_names = [column.name for column in self._dialect.columns]
        if len(args) > len(column_names):
            msg = "__init__() takes at most %d arguments (%d given)"
            raise TypeError(msg % (len(column_names), len(args)))
```

```
    for name in kwargs:
        if name not in column_names:
            msg = "__init__() got an unexpected keyword argument '%s'"
            raise TypeError(msg % name)

    for i, name in enumerate(column_names[:len(args)]):
        if name in kwargs:
            msg = "__init__() got multiple values for keyword argument '%s'"
            raise TypeError(msg % name)
        kwargs[name] = args[i]

    # Now populate the actual values on the object
    for column in self._dialect.columns:
        try:
            value = column.to_python(kwargs[column.name])
        except KeyError:
            # No value was provided
            value = None
        setattr(self, column.name, value)

@classmethod
def reader(cls, file):
    for values in csv.reader(file):
        yield cls(*values)
```

This neglects one important aspect of reading from CSV files, however. There are enough variations in how values are stored within a file that you may need to specify some options to control how the file is processed. Earlier, the Dialect class provided a way to specify those options on the Row class, so now we need to pass some of those options along in the call to csv.reader(). In particular, these are the options stored in the dialect's csv_dialect attribute:

```
@classmethod
def reader(cls, file):
    for values in csv.reader(file, **cls._dialect.csv_dialect):
        yield cls(*values)
```

That covers the options that the csv module already knows about, but remember that our own Dialect class allows for another option to indicate whether the file has a header row. In order to support that feature in the reader, we'll need to add some extra code that skips the first row if the dialect indicates that row would be a header:

```
@classmethod
    def reader(cls, file):
        csv_reader = csv.reader(file, **cls._dialect.csv_dialect)

        # Skip the first row if it's a header
        if cls._dialect.has_header_row:
            csv_reader.__next__()

        for values in csv_reader:
            yield cls(*values)
```

Because all the reader needs to provide is an iterable that yields a row for each object, this method now does everything it needs to. It's not very forward-thinking, however. Because we're building a framework that may need to be improved later, it's always a good idea to at least consider future expansion.

Rather than relying solely on a generator function, a more flexible approach would be to create a new iterable class that will do the same job. As we'll see in the next section, the writer will need a separate class as well, so building this new iterable will create a pair of classes that will be easier to understand. First, the reader() method gets a whole lot simpler:

```
    @classmethod
    def reader(cls, file):
            return Reader(cls, file)
```

That delegates all the real work to a new Reader class, which must implement __iter__() and __next__() in order to function as an iterator. There are a few things that need to be stored away in __init__() first, however, including the row class that can create each instance and a csv.reader object to actually read the file:

441

```
class Reader:
    def __init__(self, row_cls, file):
        self.row_cls = row_cls
        self.csv_reader = csv.reader(file, **row_cls._dialect.csv_dialect)
```

The __iter__() method is easy to support because the Reader itself will be the iterator. Therefore, all that's necessary is to return self:

```
class Reader:
    def __init__(self, row_cls, file):
        self.row_cls = row_cls
        self.csv_reader = csv.reader(file, **row_cls._dialect.csv_dialect)

    def __iter__(self):
        return self
```

Because __next__() will be called for each iteration, its logic can be a bit simpler for the obvious task of returning individual row objects. All it needs to do is call __next__() on the csv.reader's iterator, passing the values into the row class that was stored in __init__():

```
class Reader:
    def __init__(self, row_cls, file):
        self.row_cls = row_cls
        self.csv_reader = csv.reader(file, **row_cls._dialect.csv_dialect)

    def __iter__(self):
        return self

    def __next__(self):
        return self.row_cls(*self.csv_reader.__next__())
```

You'll remember from Chapter 5 that when manually building an iterator, you have to be careful to raise a StopIteration exception in order to avoid an infinite loop. In this case, we don't have to do that directly because the csv.reader will do that on its own. Once it runs out of records, our own __next__() method just needs to let StopIteration go by without being caught.

The last feature to implement is the header row, which gets slightly more complex. In the generator function shown earlier, it's easy to just deal with the header row before getting into the real loop. As a manual iterator, we have to manage it separately because __next__() will get called from the beginning for each record.

To do so, we'll need to keep a Boolean attribute that indicates whether we still need to skip the header row. At the beginning, that attribute will be the same as the dialect's has_header_row attribute, but once the header row has been skipped, that attribute needs to be reset so that __next__() can yield a valid record every other time:

```
class Reader:
    def __init__(self, row_cls, file):
        self.row_cls = row_cls
        self.csv_reader = csv.reader(file, **row_cls._dialect.csv_dialect)
        self.skip_header_row = row_cls._dialect.has_header_row
    def __iter__(self):
        return self
    def __next__(self):
        # Skip the first row if it's a header
        if self.skip_header_row:
            self.csv_reader.__next__()
            self.skip_header_row = False
        return self.row_cls(*self.csv_reader.__next__())
```

You can test it by supplying a simple CSV file and reading it in. Consider a file containing a rough table of contents, with a column for the chapter number and another for the chapter title. Here's how you could write a Row to represent that file and parse the contents:

```
>>> import sheets
>>> class Content(sheets.Row):
...     chapter = sheets.IntegerColumn()
...     title = sheets.StringColumn()
...
>>> file = open('contents.csv', newline="")
>>> for entry in Content.reader(file):
...     print('%s: %s' % (entry.chapter, entry.title))
...
1: Principles and Philosophy
2: Advanced Basics
3: Functions
4: Classes
5: Protocols
6: Object Management
7: Strings
8: Documentation
9: Testing
10: Distribution
11: Sheets: A CSV Framework
```

This completes the transition from rows in a CSV file to individual Python objects. Because each of the rows in an instance of the Content class, you can also define whatever other methods you like and have those available when processing entries from the file. For the other side of the framework, we need a writer to move those objects back into a CSV file.

The Writer

Unlike the reader, the interface for a CSV writer requires some instance methods, so the implementation is a bit more complex. A generator method won't cut it this time around, so we'll need to add a new class to the mix in order to manage the file writing behavior. We can still rely on the csv module's own behavior to do most of the heavy lifting, so this new class only has to manage the additional features of the sheets framework.

The first part of the interface is simple. To mirror the availability of the reader, the writer should be accessible from a method on the Row subclass. This method will also take a file object, but this time it must return a new object rather than doing anything with that file right away. That makes the implementation of this writer() method simple on its own:

```
@classmethod
    def writer(cls, file):
        return Writer(file, cls._dialect)
```

Note   The SheetWriter can't get by with just the file, because it's separate from Row and wouldn't otherwise have access to any of the dialect options.

This obviously doesn't do anything useful yet, however, so the main task is to create and fill out the SheetWriter class. There are two necessary methods to satisfy the writer interface, writerow() and writerows(). The former is responsible for taking a single object and writing out a row to the file, while the latter accepts a sequence of objects, writing them each out as a separate row in the file.

Before starting on either of those methods, Writer needs some basic initialization. The first obvious information it will need access to is the list of columns for the class. Beyond that, it'll also need the CSV options, but those are only necessary to create a writer using the csv module itself, just like the reader did. Finally, it needs access to the one option that csv doesn't know about its own, has_header_row:

```
class Writer:
    def __init__(self, file, dialect):
        self.columns = dialect.columns
        self._writer = csv.writer(file, dialect.csv_dialect)
        self.needs_header_row = dialect.has_header_row
```

445

Before moving on to the all-important `writerow()` method, notice the header row option is actually named `needs_header_row` when assigned to the class. This allows `writerow()` to use that attribute as a flag to indicate whether the header row still needs to be written. If no row is needed in the first place, it starts as `False`, but if it comes in as `True`, it can be flipped to `False` once the header has actually be written to the file.

To write the header row itself, we can also defer to the `csv.writer` instead that will be used later to write the value rows. The `csv` module doesn't care what the overall structure of the file is, so we can pass in a row of header values and it'll be processed the same way as all the other rows. Those header values come from the `title` attribute of each column on the class, but we can use the string's `title()` method to make them a bit friendlier:

```python
class Writer:
    def __init__(self, file, dialect):
        self.columns = dialect.columns
        self._writer = csv.writer(file, dialect.csv_dialect)
        self.needs_header_row = dialect.has_header_row

    def writerow(self, row):
        if self.needs_header_row:
            values = [column.title.title() for column in self.columns]
            self._writer.writerow(values)
            self.needs_header_row = False
```

With the header out of the way, `writerow()` can move on to write the actual row that was passed into the method. The code to support the header already lays out most of what needs to be done. The only difference is that rather than getting the title of each column, the list comprehension needs to get the corresponding value from the row object that was passed in:

```python
class Writer:
    def __init__(self, file, dialect):
        self.columns = dialect.columns
```

```
        self._writer = csv.writer(file, dialect.csv_dialect)
        self.needs_header_row = dialect.has_header_row

    def writerow(self, row):
        if self.needs_header_row:
            values = [column.title.title() for column in self.columns]
            self._writer.writerow(values)
            self.needs_header_row = False
        values = [getattr(row, column.name) for column in self.columns]
        self._writer.writerow(values)
```

Finally, the writer also needs a writerows() method that can take a sequence of objects and write them out as individual rows. The hard work is already done, so all writerows() needs to do is call writerow() for each object that was passed into the sequence:

```
class Writer:
    def __init__(self, file, dialect):
        self.columns = dialect.columns
        self._writer = csv.writer(file, dialect.csv_dialect)
        self.needs_header_row = dialect.has_header_row

    def writerow(self, row):
        if self.needs_header_row:
            values = [column.title.title() for column in self.columns]
            self._writer.writerow(values)
            self.needs_header_row = False
        values = [getattr(row, column.name) for column in self.columns]
        self._writer.writerow(values)

    def writerows(self, rows):
        for row in rows:
            self.writerow(row)
```

With a CSV reader and writer, the sheets framework is complete. You can add more column classes to support additional data types or add more dialect options based on more specific needs you may have, but the framework on the whole is intact. You can verify the full functionality by reading an existing file and writing it back out to a new file. As long as all the dialect parameters match the file's structure, the contents of the two files will be identical:

```
>>> import sheets
>>> class Content(sheets.Row):
...     chapter = sheets.IntegerColumn()
...     title = sheets.StringColumn()
...
>>> input = open('contents.csv', newline=")
>>> reader = Content.reader(input)
>>> output = open('compare.csv', 'w', newline=")
>>> writer = Content.writer(output)
>>> writer.writerows(reader)
>>> input.close()
>>> output.close()
>>> open('contents.csv').read() == open('compare.csv').read()
True
```

Taking It With You

In this chapter you've seen how to plan, build, and customize a framework using many of the tools Python makes available. What was a complicated task that would have had to be repeated multiple times has been reduced to a reusable and extendable tool. This is just one example of how the techniques in this book can combine for such a complex task, however. The rest is up to you.

Index

A

add() method, 60
add_column() method, 412
addTypeEqualityFunc() method, 362, 368
Affero General Public License (AGPL), 375
American Standard Code for Information Interchange (ASCII), 312–313
annotation_processor(), 134
append() method, 60
Arithmetic operations, 228, 229
ASCII, *see* American Standard Code for Information Interchange (ASCII)
attach_to_class() method, 403

B

Backward compatibility, 25–26
Berkeley Software Distribution (BSD) license, 376
Bitwise operations, 234–236
__bool__() method, 227
Bound methods, 205–206
break statement, 43
Built-in function type, 83
Built-in id() function, 270
Built-in type() function, 149
Byte string
    chr() and ord(), 306
    standard strings, 305
    struct module, 307

C

Cache, 29
Callables, 259
__call__() method, 419
chain() function, 56
Classes
    attributes
        descriptors, 201
        functions, 198
        "get" and "set" functions, 198, 202, 204
        properties, 198
    creation
        code block, 186–187
        individual plugin, 195
        metaclasses, 190, 196
        namespace controlling, 196
        plugin framework, 192
        plugin mount class and plugin subclass, 194
        runtime, 188
    inheritance
        contact class, 163–164
        "get" and "set" functions, 162
        introspection, 184
        MRO (*see* Method resolution order (MRO))
        multiple inheritance, 165
        Person and Company classes, 164
        Python class, 162

R

S